The fact that independent minds like you are being rebuked equally by official America and official Russia is significant and also to a degree amusing.

Albert Einstein to Linus Pauling (1952)

The entire world owes you a great debt of gratitude for your commitments and efforts on behalf of our children and grandchildren. Your outstanding accomplishments in the fields of science, medicine, and peace will make life for future generations better, safer, and more progressive.

Former President Jimmy Carter to Linus Pauling

As I read my *New York Times* or listen to PBS, I wonder: Who owns the missiles now in Siberia? Do all Mideast countries have the bomb? They say the Bikini atoll is still so hot that the Marshall Islanders cannot go home. There are frightening stories—of nuclear accidents around the world, of unexplained rising death rates from leukemia. . . . And each day I hear the news I think: Linus Pauling said it 30 years ago. Now we all agree with him. There is no argument left. . . . So I say: He was a prophet, with honor in his time.

Frank Catchpool, M.D.

A great man is always missed, but his beliefs and ideals live on. [Let us] be comforted in the memory of this magnificent man, and his immense love for humanity.

Oscar Arias, former President of Costa Rica, Recipient of Nobel Peace Prize, 1987

Linus Pauling made immense contributions to humanity during his long and rich life, expanding the frontiers of science. His tireless activism for the cause of peace helped force international leaders to reassess their priorities, ultimately making our world a safer place. . . . Because of Linus Pauling's talents and commitment the world is brighter for generations to come.

President William J. Clinton

LINUS PAULING ON PEACE

A Scientist Speaks Out
on Humanism and World Survival

WRITINGS AND TALKS BY
Linus Pauling

SELECTED AND EDITED BY
Barbara Marinacci
and
Ramesh Krishnamurthy

INTRODUCTION BY
Linus Pauling, Jr., M.D.

Rising Star Press
Los Altos, California

Rising Star Press
Los Altos, California

Library of Congress Catalog Card Number: 98-86622

Interior design and copyediting by Joanne Shwed, Backspace Ink
Cover design by Rudy Marinacci
Front cover photograph of Linus Pauling by Dan Escobar

Publisher's Cataloging-in-Publication
(Provided by Quality Books, Inc.)

    Pauling, Linus, 1901-1994
       Linus Pauling on peace : a scientist speaks out on
humanism and world survival / writings and talks by Linus
Pauling ; selected and edited by Barbara Marinacci and
Ramesh Krishnamurthy ; introduction by Linus Pauling, Jr.
-- 1st ed.
       p. cm.
       Includes bibliographical references and index.
       Preassigned LCCN: 98-86622
       ISBN: 0-933670-03-6
       1. Peace. 2. Pauling, Linus, 1901-1994. 3. Pauling, Ava
Helen. I. Marinacci, Barbara. II. Krishnamurthy,
Ramesh. III. Title.

JX5560.P38 1998   372.1'72
                   QBI98-954

Printed in Canada

To the memory of Ava Helen Miller Pauling,
without whose influence
there would have been no *Linus Pauling on Peace*

Contents

Introduction 7
by Linus Pauling, Jr., M.D.

Editors' Foreword 11
by Barbara Marinacci and Ramesh Krishnamurthy

PRELUDE: A Scientist's World 19
(from new introduction to *No More War!*—25th Anniversary Edition, 1983)

PART I: EDUCATION AND SCIENCE IN A DEMOCRACY 23

An Education in Social Responsibility 24
(from OAC "Senior Class Oration," MS 1922)

What Is Democracy? 28
(from "Science and Democracy," MS 1940)

Imperiled Democracy: World War II 31
(from "Union Now" talk, MS1940)

The Scientists Behind Technology 33
(from "Science in the Modern World," 1951)

Teaching Science in Our Schools 39
(from "The Significance of Chemistry to Man in the Modern World," 1951)

The Statistical Basis of Democracy 43
(from "The Significance of Chemistry to Man in the Modern World," 1951)

Science Knowledge Is Essential to Culture 45
(from "Technology and Democracy," MS 1955)

PART II: WAR, PEACE, AND DISSENT 49

The End of War? 51
(from "Atomic Energy and World Government," MS 1945)

Can We Live in Peace with Russia? 55
(from "Will the United States Accept Its Greatest Responsibility?"
MS 1947)

A Model for Activist Commitment 57
(from "Thomas Addis 1881-1949," coauthored with Kevin V. Lemley, 1994)

A Question of Loyalty 62
(from Linus Pauling's testimony to California Senate Investigating
Committee on Education, 1950/1951)

Passport Pending 66
(from interview with Griffin Fariello in *Red Scare*, published in 1995)

Punishing Another Dissenter 68
(from "A Disgraceful Act," a 1954 defense of Oppenheimer)

Don't Believe Your Elders! 70
(from "Advice to Students," 1954/1955)

The Russell-Einstein Manifesto of 1955 72
(from "The Social Responsibilities of Scientists and Science," 1966)

The Scientists Protest 77
(from interview with Robert Richter, transcript, 1977)

Defending the Right to Petition 80
(from testimony at Senate Internal Security subcommittee hearings on the
origin of the test-ban appeal, 1960)

INTERLUDE: A Partnership in Life . . . and Peace Work:
Ava Helen and Linus Pauling 85
(photos and excerpts from interviews, published and unpublished)

PART III: IN THE NUCLEAR AGE 101

Meet the Atom Bombs 102
(from "Atomic Energy and World Government," MS 1945)

Here Come the Superbombs 105
(from "The Ultimate Decision," 1950)

Megaton Madness 108
(from "The World Problem and the Hydrogen Bomb," 1954)

A Slow Death from the Sky: Fallout 111
(from interview with Robert Richter, transcript, 1977)

The Fallout Debate 115
(from "Every Test Kills," 1958)

Can't We Halt the Arms Race? 121
(from Chapter 9, *No More War!*, 1958)

Stop the Spread of Nuclear Weapons! 124
(from the Oslo Statement, 1961)

No Havens from Fallout 128
(from "Why I Am Opposed to Fallout Shelters," 1961)

The Importance of a Test-Ban Treaty 132
(from "Science and the Future of Humanity," 1963/4)

The Now-Proven Hazards of High-Energy Radiation 140
(from addendum to Chapter 6, *No More War!*—25th Anniversary Edition,
1983)

PART IV: PEACE THROUGH HUMANISM 147

I Believe in the Power of the Human Spirit 149
(from Chapter 9, *No More War!*, 1958)

Transition to Peace 151
(from Chapter 10, *No More War!*, 1958)

The Need for Peace *Now* 152
(from "Research for Peace," MS 1959)

Albert Schweitzer, Physician and Humanitarian 156
(coauthored with John F. Catchpool, M.D. / MS 1965)

Developing a Moral Philosophy 163
(from notes, marginalia c. 1960)

Minimizing Suffering 165
(from "Humanism and Peace," 1961)

Squabbling Among Peacemakers 168
(from Pauling-Ikeda dialogue, published in 1992)

Nobel's Great Reward for Peace Action 170
(from the Nobel Peace Prize Lecture, 1963)

The Future Reign of World Law 173
(from the Nobel Peace Prize Lecture, 1963)

PART V: THE SCIENTIST IN SOCIETY 181

Morality Among Nations 183
(from "World Morality and World Peace," 1964)

Three Modern Revolutions 187
(from "World Morality and World Peace," 1964)

The Combat Between Two Economic Systems 190
(from Introduction to *The Futile Crusade*, 1964)

The Right to a Good Life 193
(from "The Nature of the Problem," *Pacem in Terris (I)* Conference, 1965)

Facts vs. Words 198
(from "The Social Responsibilities of Scientists and Science," 1966)

A Scientist Looks at India's Problems 200
(from *Science and World Peace* [Azad Lectures], 1967)

The Immoral War in Vietnam 208
(from *Foreign Policies and Disarmament* [Chettyar Lecture], 1967)

I Am Sick of This War! 212
(a protest speech on Vietnam War, MS 1970)

Health Considerations for the World 216
(from "The Possibilities for Social Progress," 1970)

PART VI: FUTURE PROPHECIES 221

Now Is the Time for Change 222
(from "Reverence for Life," MS 1975)

Goals Ahead for the U.S. 225
(Senate bicentennial testimony, MS 1976)

A Dark Vision 232
(from "What Can We Expect for Chemistry in the Next 100 Years?", 1976)

The Goal Is Still Peace 234
(from "The Path to World Peace," 1983)

Organizing the Peace Efforts 238
(from addendum to Chapter 10, *No More War!*—25th Anniversary Edition, 1983)

Looking Ahead 241
(from "Chemistry and the World of Tomorrow," 1984)

Saving the Planet 243
(from "The Cavtat Declaration," 1988)

This Extraordinary Age 245
(from "Prospects for Global Environmental Protection and World Peace As We Approach the 21st Century," 1990)

And Still the Wars Go On 247
(from "Reflections on the Persian Gulf 'War,'" 1991)

Research on the Science of Peace 252
(from Chapter 10, *No More War!*, 1958)

New Nuclear Nations 257
(from *Science and World Peace* [Azad Lectures], 1967)

POSTLUDE: Make Your Voice and Vote Count! 263
(from "The Duties of a Graduate," Cook College/Rutgers University, 1983)

Acknowledgments 267

Permissions 269

Notes on Sources 271

Linus Pauling and Peace: A Timeline 279

Index 287

About the Editors 295

LINUS PAULING, Sculpture by Erna Weill

Introduction

As the 20th century draws to a close and we enter a new millennium, people should consider the words and actions of an extraordinary scientist who had a far-reaching and crucial influence on society in our era: Linus Pauling.

This man, my father, wanted an anthology to be published of his words relevant to his peace efforts. I am pleased that editors Barbara Marinacci and Ramesh Krishnamurthy have gathered together here a selection of a number of his written and spoken statements to represent the long humanitarian career of this unique man of science.

My father was a truly remarkable human being. He was endowed with prodigious intelligence, memory, energy and ambition. His phenomenal ability to absorb information and correlate previously unassociated material enabled him to rewrite the science of chemistry, to initiate a completely new science (molecular biology), and to advocate peace as a rational and necessary alternative to the horror of modern war.

To me, remarkable as were those traits, his most admirable characteristic was courage, the courage to venture onto uncharted seas in science and also the courage to campaign for his beliefs, often in the face of oppression and calumny from the government of the country he loved, disapproval and avoidance from his colleagues, and insult from the news media.

The need for containment of radiation and the avoidance of nuclear war is taken for granted nowadays. It was not always so, as this book makes clear. From the mid 1940s to at least the mid '60s the American public had been led to believe the official statements that nuclear war might be necessary and even justifiable, and that fallout risks from the testing of weapons were worth taking because of an improved ability to defend the nation from communist assault. In that period, conformity ruled. Organizations and individuals like my father who promoted world peace were treated as subversives.

Now, half a century later, public and governmental opinion is very different. The change came from conveying correct information to the world's people and awakening their awareness of peril. The coming of the nuclear age forced humankind at last to seek peaceful means of resolving conflicts among nations. Radioactive fallout and the proliferation of nuclear weapons were in fact unacceptable to health, safety, and sanity. My father devoted a large portion of his life to this urgent educational campaign—through hundreds of speeches, articles, debates, and interviews. His personal impact on public opinion is incalculable.

My own life was inevitably influenced by him in many ways. Being the son of a man of such extraordinary talent has presented a continuous challenge, especially since I carry the same name. I was fortunate to have been associated, whether at close hand or from a distance, with events in his politically active life. For instance, at the age of 15 and 16, I was occasionally asked to sit behind the desk at the Pasadena office of Union Now, an organization which advocated alliance of the democracies against fascist nations, a concept rejected by the isolationist public majority and many fearful politicians of the United States of America at that time. Then, early in 1942, after the nation entered World War II, my Japanese-American schoolmates suddenly disappeared, herded with their families into the stables of the nearby Santa Anita racetrack prior to relocation to concentration camps further inland. My parents outspokenly condemned this abrogation of civil rights. I absorbed this attitude, a condition that did not endear me to those in control of my fate after I was drafted into the army.

Sometime during my adolescence I realized that I was not the kind of person my father was. Although reasonably bright, I could never even come close to following in his extraordinarily brilliant footsteps. I therefore set off on my own course, to live a life different from his. In the late '40s and well into the '50s I dealt with my own professional work: medical school, internship, and residency, finally setting up my own practice of medicine as a psychiatrist. The situation allowed me to observe objectively my father's activities and accomplishments.

However, being independent from my father and living at some distance from him did not mean that I was out of contact with him and with his peace-connected work. I watched from afar as my father struggled with the Passport Office. I was there to see him receive the Nobel Prize for Chemistry in Stockholm. I listened to a number of his impassioned and usually extemporaneous speeches making all too clear the inevitable results of nuclear war. In 1957 I distributed copies of his scientists' petition to the United Nations. In 1963 I rejoiced as I heard of the signing of the partial nuclear test-ban treaty. I saw him receive the Nobel Peace Prize in Oslo. With disbelief I read, and sometimes saw enacted on television, the vicious media attacks on him. I listened (and objected) as he proclaimed that, having passed the age of 60, his creative scientific life was over and therefore he would be leaving the California Institute of Technology, the site of his great discoveries. Afterwards I noted his growing disillusionment and frustration with the inactivity of the "think-tank" Center for the Study of Democratic Institutions. Being part of the medical establishment, I initially viewed with suspicion his espousal of vitamin C as a panacea (I later became a disciple). In 1973 I agreed to be a trustee of his new Linus Pauling Institute of Science and Medicine. Having retired in 1990 after 35 years of medical practice and with considerable experience as a board member and officer of nonprofit organizations, I ran the Institute for him at his request. Then, in 1996, I arranged to move LPI into its permanent home at Oregon State University.

Finally, I helped to nurse my father during his last days. As his 93-year-old body weakened, his mental acuity remained intact. So did his sense of humor. He did not have any profound "last words" to convey to posterity because he knew that any such messages were already embodied in his life and work, and in the millions of words that he had written and spoken. Along with his passion for science in its many forms, he had devoted incredible time and energy to persuading our species to travel on a positive future evolutionary path, away from the course leading us and other life on our planet to the brink of extinction. His clarion voice and actions must join with those of many others, now and in the future, to perpetuate this salutary and essential effort.

Linus Pauling, Jr., M.D.

Editors' Foreword

L inus Pauling, who was born in 1901 and died in 1994, lived through almost the entire 20th century. During his life he witnessed extraordinary developments in scientific knowledge and technological advances that have transformed our civilization.

Pauling is the only person ever to receive two unshared Nobel Prizes. Remarkably, they were for two very different areas of accomplishment. His first Nobel award, in chemistry, came in 1954 for his influential ideas about the nature of the bonds formed among atoms and molecules, and for exploring the complex structures of proteins. The second one, the Nobel Peace Prize for 1962, acknowledged the effect of his prominent efforts in galvanizing public opinion to persuade nations to stop testing nuclear weapons above ground. For years he had doggedly disputed assurances by the United States government's chosen experts that radioactive fallout from the tests did not endanger public health. Since it can take years for this damage to appear, a cause-and-effect relationship was difficult to establish.

Today it is widely recognized that Pauling's position was correct, and that those of the "chosen experts" were either incautious or downright deceitful. *Any* amount of high-energy radiation, including that coming from medical X-rays and even the natural environment, carries risks for genetic mutations and cancer.

Pauling's two Nobel Prizes are among dozens of awards and honors he received during his lifetime. Others came posthumously. His scientific work spanned all major domains of the sciences—physics, chemistry, geology (especially crystallography and mineralogy), biology (notably as a founder of molecular biology), and medicine (including immunology, hematology, genetics, and nutrition). In each field he made important contributions. His ambitious, wide-ranging work encompassed more fields than any other scientist of this century. The total number of his accomplishments may exceed those of any other single scientist of any period.

Though always heavily engaged in a multitude of research projects, Pauling somehow found time, or rather made time, to consider ways to improve the human society around him. He became a social scientist, applying the scientific method to the examination of societal problems. In the process he also became an ethicist, devising a system for measuring and judging societal morality on every human scale: individual, community, nation, and the world at large.

A remarkably versatile and productive scientist, Pauling was also a born educator. He became a chemistry teacher during his college years. Later, on the faculty of the California Institute of Technology (Caltech), he was a charismatic lecturer in freshman chemistry, even while earning fame as a groundbreaking theoretical chemist. When he spoke to nonscientists he expanded his topics and talked so his listeners could understand. Sometimes the lecture podium became his political platform or pulpit. He enjoyed being interviewed for print publications, and when television arrived, he was at ease with that medium, too.

Because he was often in the limelight of controversial causes, Linus Pauling probably possessed the best-known name, face, and voice of his generation of American scientists: those born just after the turn of the 19th century, who came of age after the First World War, and served their country (alongside scientists from other nations) in important technological ways during the Second World War.

In the tense postwar period, democratic and largely capitalistic nations were pitted against the communist totalitarian bloc controlled by the Soviet Union, which was later joined by China and by Cuba. As each side sought dominance, or to confine the other's expansion, the Cold War was characterized by espionage and mounting military preparations and threats. Pauling believed that the invention of nuclear weapons now required the achievement of world peace, which could only come about by cooperative coexistence and rational accommodation of other nations' viewpoints. He became notorious as a prominent scientist who often publicly opposed U.S. government policies. He was especially critical of policies allotting a major portion of the national budget to military purposes—particularly the arms race and nuclear-weapons research—rather than to urgent human-service and community-building needs.

He believed the inevitable alternative to world peace was world destruction. Many people admired his outspoken manner and determined courage in the face of scorn and persecution. But many others deplored his placing the goal of international cooperation, world peace, and human rights above the safety and self-interests of nationalism. To his critics Pauling was regarded either as naive, brash, and foolish—a pawn of the communist ideology—or as a deliberate subversive, a traitor to his homeland. But Pauling, who always saw himself as a loyal American, regarded much of the West's anticommunist efforts as a program to undermine the Soviet economy and provide protection or expansion for profit-seeking capitalism to benefit the privileged or rapacious. He believed these efforts were not consistent with American ideals.

Though Pauling liked to believe that he maintained the objective rationality of the scientist, he had an intensely human side that could not be concealed where peace and humanitarian issues were concerned. In fact, this emotionalism, not permitted in the "pure" science that was his livelihood, made his messages particularly influential and appealing to people who shared his concerns. Pauling cared deeply about what happened to humankind and its fragile planet. This self-declared agnostic possessed a depth of spirit that propelled him first into social activism, then into a prophetic role. The simplicity of his vision of achieving peace on Earth was compelling. Yet to some it came across as zealotry, especially when he was driven to frustration by national and world events.

Pauling the peace promoter was, in the best sense of the word, an *agitator*, a special and crucial role in any democracy, though it also caused him to sometimes be regarded as an annoying gadfly. He shook up the status quo by questioning authority, dogma, opinions, and group behaviors that adversely affected others. He spoke directly to audiences about important issues that concerned them—or that he believed *should* concern them. And he wrote articles and published books about the problems faced by human society.

The causes he took up as a dissenter were often volatile—or became so when he raised his banner and began the battle. To stop the tradition of resolving conflicts by threatening war, he supported the idealized concept of the United Nations and a powerful supreme court of world law that would administer justice and assure human rights everywhere. He attacked the military-industrial establishment's costly buildup of nuclear weaponry, with its grotesque capacity for overkill. He decried his nation's ostracism of emergent or reconstructed nations such as the People's Republic of China, Cuba, and Nicaragua, treated as outlaws from the start (as the USSR had been before them) because they now had a communistic, not capitalistic, political and socioeconomic orientation.

Pauling, like other "peaceniks," would point out what he saw as U.S. hypocrisy: at the same time it attacked communist crackdowns on civil liberty, it gave wholehearted support to right-wing dictatorships that refrained from interfering with U.S. economic investments in their lands. He noisily denounced, in turn, the "immorality" of the Vietnam and Persian Gulf wars and the Balkan genocide. He protested the short-sighted and rampant exploitation and degradation of the environment and its finite natural resources. He insisted that populations must be curtailed to avoid an eventual planetary disaster. He challenged governments to improve the nutrition, health care, and education of their lowliest citizens, giving them a chance to share in the general good.

In his later years Linus Pauling became best known for championing vitamin C as a preventive and therapeutic substance—a possible cure-all for many human ills. A number of scientists regarded his inventive concept of "orthomolecular medicine" as a lamentable, one-way excursion into senility, while physicians objected to his brash intrusion into their realm. But his core beliefs derived from research evidence and speculative thinking, and he was by nature an enthusiast. Nutritional medicine, when based on molecular biology, biochemistry, and physiology, is fast becoming respectable. The jury is still out on his last crusade.

It is this remarkable person—scientist, educator, humanitarian, political activist—whom we present here in an overview provided primarily by his own words. Some were spoken or written at the time an issue was being debated. Some came later in a reminiscence. Because of space limitations, our representative selections here of Pauling's writings and talks are seldom presented in their full original texts. Nor are we able to show much of the witty and warmly humorous side of Pauling, which his friends knew and cherished. Audiences often experienced it too, which tempered the intensity of his messages.

It is not our goal to provide a scholarly biography or to explain in depth the motivations for his ideas and actions. This interpretive area has already been covered by several biographers, notably Thomas Hager in *Force of Nature*, and the Goertzels' *Linus Pauling: A Life in Science and Politics*. Many more studies will come. Our focus is to do something biographers cannot do: provide Pauling's words themselves in pithy, provocative chunks.

Linus Pauling has often been ranked with Albert Einstein. These were the two 20th-century scientists named by the British journal *New Scientist* as among the 20 greatest scientists of all time. Einstein, too, was an ardent and vocal peace advocate. But it cannot be said that his scientific knowledge and work as a theoretical physicist were as wide-ranging as Pauling's, or as applicable to everyday life. Nor did he get "down and dirty" in his activism, as Pauling often did. Einstein stayed above all that.

We cannot assume that all readers, especially younger ones, will be familiar with the period in which Pauling gave voice to his diverse political stands. Therefore, we provide introductions to the principal sections (Parts I-VI) of the book as well as commentaries preceding the individual selections. There are over 60 selections altogether.

As a word stylist, Pauling did not aim to be a fine writer or spellbinding orator. The *message* was his focus, and he had little patience for conjuring up verbal niceties. Still, he occasionally created compelling images or summoned up passages with a sonorous archetypal cadence, perhaps with biblical, classical, or Elizabethan roots.

No wonder, then, that once Pauling settled on something that he and an audience liked, he often recycled the words from one article or speech to another. Also, he necessarily repeated statistics and quotations that backed up his arguments (many of which changed over time). And he tended to recount the same stories about past events, with small variations. To make the material more readable, we have restricted or removed such repetitions unless they are important within the context or emotional thrust of the piece. We have also made alterations in the original punctuation, orthography, capitalization, and other minor matters to create a more consistent appearance among pieces that were written or edited in diverse styles. Some long paragraphs were divided to make the text less dense.

Pauling credited his wife, Ava Helen, as a crucial partner in the humanitarian and social-activist side of his thinking and work. We have brought her in to "speak out," too, in the book's "Interlude." This section also provides a selection of photographs of Ava Helen and Linus, their family, and some of their peace activities.

We chose pieces to show the evolution of Pauling's ideas, messages, and actions over time. Many of the previously published selections were essentially ephemeral, appearing only in periodicals. Pauling's book *No More War!* is the most durable form of his peace-advocating, antinuclear writing, although some of his speeches, articles, and interviews have been printed in anthologies or small books. Other selections, from transcriptions, typescripts, and handwritten manuscripts or notes—over a dozen in all—have never been published until now.

Pauling was a prolific writer: his bibliography lists over a thousand publications. From the early 1950s on, a sizable number are on issues relating to peace, nuclear weapons, and societal problems. The Ava Helen and Linus Pauling Papers at Oregon State University comprise several hundred thousand separate documents, published and unpublished, including correspondence and "notes to self." A number are still being unpacked and catalogued. We expect that in future years, scholars of the history of the peace movement and students forming new strategies for world peace will spend time with the Special Collections at the Valley Library at Oregon State University in Corvallis. There are enough relevant materials there to fill a dozen or more large volumes. We have selected some of the best for this book. The much larger body of Pauling's diverse scientific work attests to the value of one individual's contributions to our knowledge of the physical universe.

This book for general readers, then, contains only a small portion of the documents relating to the Paulings' efforts to ensure the survival of humankind in the nuclear age. Linus Pauling still has intensely relevant things to say to the younger generations, those he hoped would live and thrive in the 21st century. In a world continuously transformed by science and technology, there is an urgent need for the clarity of humanism and the charity of humanitarianism—whether from religious belief or moral education. Pauling said that peace could come when all nations and all individuals could agree on and adhere to a rational and coherent system of basic ethical principles. The solutions he proposed again and again—the heart of this book—were simple, forthright, and wise. The complexities and vagaries of human nature and nationalism make them difficult to achieve. But no matter how difficult the struggle, Pauling would never have abandoned the quest for world peace—nor would he want us to. Otherwise, the dark vision this accustomed optimist sometimes had of humanity's future in the next century would almost certainly become real.

"It does not take much to change the world," Linus Pauling said of his own work. He encouraged other people to feel that they, too, could add some new discovery to our wisdom, or solve social problems. We hope that this selection of Pauling's writings and talks will show how this brilliant scientist, with a strong sense of responsibility for the wellbeing of human society, did just that.

Barbara Marinacci
Saratoga, California

Ramesh Krishnamurthy, Project Director
Ava Helen & Linus Pauling Papers
Oregon State University
July 1998

The scientist as peace activist: Pauling at a 1960 peace rally and walk in Los Angeles. (Photo courtesy of Robert Cohen)

Prelude

A Scientist's World

Throughout his career as a renowned scientist, Linus Pauling spoke and wrote often about the responsibility, indeed the duty, that professional practitioners of the sciences have toward society. They should take an active role, not just as all citizens should, by voting their opinions and selecting their representatives and leaders, but as the special educators to others not as well informed about science.

Pauling repeatedly reminded us that science shaped the modern world, increasingly affecting both the course of human civilization and our individual lives. To function properly in the modern era, everyone should acqure a basic understanding of science. Everyone should also be trained to use that primary tool of inductive reasoning and objective problem-solving: the scientific method.

This passage—written in 1983 for the 25th Anniversary Edition of Pauling's book *No More War!*—has a timeless message.

M an has the intelligence to understand the universe, to appreciate the astounding complexity of the universe—the subatomic particles, the electrons, protons, and neutrons; the elements and their compounds, the self-replicating molecules of DNA, the minerals, the mountains and oceans, the single-cell organisms, plants and animals, the human brain, the planets and the sun, the nebulae and black holes, the expanding universe from the time of the big bang.

Now man's intelligence has provided him with the power to destroy himself, to bring an end to civilization, an end to the human race. I believe that our intelligence, our common sense, is good enough to prevent this ultimate insanity.

People who practice or study politics may find Linus Pauling's views of societal and world problems single-minded and his proposed solutions to them simplistic. However, his courageous commitment to the great goal of permanent world peace does not deserve to be rejected as unrealistic and therefore unachievable.

As a scientist Linus Pauling had an uncanny ability to consider a mass of facts and discordant theories and out of them construct a viable whole, converting confusion and conflict into a fundamental guiding principle that others could apply in solving practical problems. Confronting a baffling scientific problem, he would discard invalid findings, find flaws in other people's logic, seek new information, challenge skeptics, and use creative intuition to produce a meaningful conceptual structure. Often scientists marveled at the sheer simplicity of his vision.

In the larger world, people as concerned as he was about the fate of humankind and of Earth itself admired his vision and his words. He could see and cut through manipulation, excuses for inaction, duplicity, strutting, illogic, disguised greed, and power mania—traits all too prevalent among government leaders and bureaucrats.

Pauling was not always right in his opinions or courteous in delivering them, but his intent was always righteous.

Perhaps we do not solve many of our problems because we focus on the overwhelming assortment of details that may be interconnected and defy easy solution. Fearful of adding to past mistakes or of getting punished for words of protest, we may feel paralyzed and do nothing, or permit others to make the decisions and do things that we ourselves would not have done. As situations in society and in the natural environment become more convoluted and perilous, workable solutions continually evade us.

But Pauling, like some moral philosophers, ethicists, and theologians, reduced the issues of decision-making and improving human behavior—which for him encompassed the behavior of nations toward each other—to a single governing precept. He thought, perhaps naively, that if we could finally manage to apply this simple operating principle to all human affairs, we humans just might continue to dwell upon this planet, and permit other creatures to thrive here, too.

There was, he said, a science of morality. Or, anyway, there should be.

Linus as a young boy in chaps in Condon, Oregon, 1906. Pauling spent most of his early childhood in eastern Oregon, a ranching and agricultural area that still had cowboys and Indians. (Photo courtesy of Linda Pauling-Kamb)

Part I

Education and Science in a Democracy

Linus Pauling subscribed to the principles of the American form of democracy. To him this meant respecting the will of the majority in choosing representatives and leaders, making or altering laws, and other public matters that affected their lives. Ideally, everyone should be informed about important issues before voting. They should also be able to think effectively about them before expressing their opinions in other ways guaranteed by the first amendment in the U.S. Constitution's Bill of Rights—notably the freedoms of belief, speech, press, assembly, and petition. The surest way to guarantee a well-functioning democracy would be to establish and maintain an excellent education system, enabling everyone to learn essential skills.

Democracy, as Pauling saw it, would assure citizens' basic freedoms, dispense justice, and honor human and civil rights. Democracy would benefit from free enterprise, but on a modest, manageable scale. In his thinking, democracy was scarcely synonymous with capitalism, an economic system he viewed as flawed and unfair because it permitted unprincipled individuals or ruthless corporations to unduly influence political decisions and exploit people. Capitalism created or preserved wide disparities in income and opportunity within the population.

Nor, in Pauling's view, could democracy be found within the sphere of an autocratic ruler or totalitarian nation-state—even if the initial power came from the people themselves, as with Hitler and Nazism in Germany or Stalin and the Communist Party in the Soviet Union.

23

When a new or established democracy came under attack from without or within, Pauling was likely to respond, as he did before and during World War II. He based many of his later criticisms of U.S. military and economic actions on his belief that they trampled on the human and political rights of other nations' citizens.

Pauling thought democracy and education were inextricably linked. So, too, were democracy and science. It followed, then, that to him an education in basic science was important to the citizens of a democracy.

Pauling prided himself on being a product of American public schools. He took a keen interest in educational issues and spoke at conferences of science educators. Not surprisingly, he insisted that science should always be part of the school curriculum, from early education through college, even for students not intending to take up some branch of science as a career. He urged scientists themselves to take more interest in educating the public about science.

This first section of the book presents edited selections from Linus Pauling's talks and writing about democracy, education, and science—particularly education in science relating to the health and preservation of a democratic society.

AN EDUCATION IN SOCIAL RESPONSIBILITY

"Education, true education . . . is preparation both for a life of appreciation of the world and for a life of service to the world."

People who think of Linus Pauling as a dissident, as someone who habitually challenged "the establishment" in government, politics, the news media, medicine, and even science itself, might be interested in viewing him at an earlier stage in his development: the end of his undergraduate college years. Pauling's graduation speech displays that positive nation-building zeal, the pragmatic, enterprising spirit which still characterized the American democratic culture to the rest of the world, as it pushed for continued "mastery and control of the forces of nature." Pauling always considered that the nation's West epitomized this spirit. It was with pride that he told people he was born and educated in Oregon.

In October of 1917, at age 16, Pauling arrived on the campus of Oregon Agricultural College (OAC, now Oregon State University) in Corvallis. He was admitted into the freshman class though he hadn't earned a high school diploma, having missed taking a required second-semester course in American history. In his desire to get on with an education in science, Pauling decided to leave Portland. His father had died when he was 10, and his widowed mother, burdened with supporting herself and Pauling's two younger sisters, could not provide financial help. For five years he earned his way through the state's land-grant college, beginning with an assortment of manual-labor jobs. He ended up teaching chemistry classes at OAC, starting between his sophomore and junior years, when he had to drop out to earn money to help support his family as well as himself.

Low-tuition public colleges and universities such as OAC were started by a Congressional act in 1857. They opened the doors of academe throughout the country to young Americans like Pauling who otherwise could not afford higher learning. Throughout his life Pauling expressed gratitude for this opportunity—as in the following excerpt from the heartfelt speech he prepared for his graduating class's commencement ceremony.

To provide a well-rounded education, OAC's science curriculum had been balanced by liberal-arts courses. Already fascinated with chemistry and practical-minded, Pauling had first aimed to become a chemical engineer after getting his bachelor's degree. It would have been a highly practical profession, since demand for industrial chemists had greatly increased, particularly after World War I. But fate and Pauling's brilliance as a theorist in structural chemistry decreed otherwise. By the time of his graduation in June of 1922, Pauling had decided to enter a doctoral program at the California Institute of Technology (Caltech) in Pasadena, California—a recently established academic and research institution that trained both undergraduate and graduate students for professional careers in science and engineering.

Pauling had studied elocution in college, taking part in oratorical contests and debates. Here, in the classical manner, he recited statements made by authorities of the past to bolster his own assertions. In his later career he would frequently quote "authorities" with whom he agreed or disagreed in both scientific and political matters, to underscore his arguments. In the age-old but now archaic legacy of language usage, Pauling often used the generic term "man" to mean humans, and "men" (or masculine-singular pronouns) to cover both genders. Yet OAC had many female students, and in the year following this speech he married one of them—Ava Helen Miller. A strong-minded idealist, she would exercise great influence on the side of Pauling's character that honored societal commitment, particularly regarding humanitarian and peace concerns. (See "Interlude," pages 85-99.)

In many ways young Pauling's sober discourse conforms to the standard valedictorian's oration. However, it provides an interesting early indication of his future political activism in such matters as peace and public health. In retrospect, his earnest words go beyond conventional rhetoric—for unlike most college graduates then and now, he was destined to amply fulfill this early pledge of service to society. Pauling showed an intent to repay his debt to OAC by serving the larger society beyond it, thereby reflecting credit on the state college that had nurtured his great ambition: to probe the basic structures of matter. In much the same way, 25 years later he would vow to work for world peace. And themes introduced here in 1922 often resounded in commencement addresses he gave to young graduates in later years. (See "Postlude," pages 263-266.)

The college days of the Class of '22 are nearly over. For four years we have worked and played, planned and executed. When we recall the lessons we have learned, the contests we have fought, the pleasures we have experienced, we feel pangs of regret and sorrow at leaving the college which has been such a potent factor in our lives; but when we look into the future, when we consider what remains to be done, we realize that we have just finished gathering together our tools, and that our work is waiting for us. . . .

It is to OAC that we are indebted for our preparation for life. To make ourselves happier and to serve others better are the two chief purposes of living, and the function of education is to help us in fulfilling these ends. Our lives are to stand as testimonials to the efficacy of the work that our college is doing. Education, true education, such as our own college gives us, is preparation both for a life of appreciation of the world and for a life of service to the world. . . .

The Oregon State Agricultural College is a technical institution. Its graduates are scientifically trained, but they also receive the benefits of a cultural education, the importance of which must not be overlooked. The technical instruction and the cultural courses have their own parts to play in the education of a man or woman. The first duty of a man is to live a full, complete and happy life. This is possible only for one who, in addition to having the technical education requisite for the earning of a living, has achieved by means of his cultural training the ability to appreciate the finer things of life.

And as for the second aim of existence—the bettering of the world, the advancement of civilization along all the avenues open for advancement—this also is dependent on these two types of instruction. Broad, cultural instruction is necessary to point out the path of improvement, and to impress on one the necessity for improvement; and technical education, by giving men the ability to do things, enables them to make the advances which they see should be made.

OAC has contributed in a wonderful way to solving the multitude of problems arising in the state; but the improvements which have been made in the past few years, great as they are, are small compared with those yet to be accomplished. The greatest contribution of our college is its preparation of men to attack these problems. The technical training in agriculture, engineering, mining, commerce, and many other fields is pointing the way to a better world by showing men how to disclose the bounties of nature and to adapt them to man's use. The homes of the future will be brighter and the children of the future will be better because of the knowledge and instruction given the young women at OAC. And every man and woman trained in this college is being benefited and broadened by the study of languages, music, science, and literature.

"Gradually see what kind of work you individually can do; it is the first of all problems for a man to find out what kind of work he is to do in this universe." This was Thomas Carlyle's advice to the students at Edinburgh University, and one of the functions of a college is to assist men and women to follow it. But there is more to the function of a college than that. The college makes it possible for you to find what work you can do, the college gives you the preparation you need for your work, and you owe it to the college to do your work as well as you can. OAC is benefiting the state and the United States inestimably by training men to act, and by showing them the deeds to be done.

The technical institutions of the country are the custodians of the legacy bequeathed to each generation by the preceding one—the legacy of knowledge. May the members of the senior class of every year go into the world inspired with the recognition of the debt they owe to their alma mater, and tense with the resolution to repay that debt by each one accomplishing in the best way his chosen task.

It is not given to every man to be unusually successful, to be extraordinarily talented, or to be exceptionally gifted to render service to the world. We can do no more than we are able, but by doing as much as we are able, by doing our best, we shall be accomplishing our task, and repaying our debt. For our college has given us something which will allow us to do more than we otherwise could; and we must do more than we otherwise would.

Snowden expressed the duties accompanying the gift of education by saying, "The educated man is that much more of a man and should be of that much more use to the world. His eye should be clearer to see human needs and his heart kinder and his hand abler to meet them. His shoulder should be the stronger and the readier to go under the burdens of his fellow men and to help carry the load of the world's need. His presence should be so much wisdom and inspiration and cheer in his own circle and in the community. The wider his education, the stronger and richer his personality, the wider and deeper should be his sympathy and service and sacrifice."

The problems looming up in the development of the state and country are enormous in volume and overwhelming in complexity. Advancement and growth depend upon the discovery and development of the resources of nature, on the mastery and control of the forces of nature, and the investigation and interpretation of the laws of nature. In the course of progress social relations are strained, and industrial, political, and educational problems arise. The country is crying for a solution of all these difficulties, and is hopefully looking to the educated man for it.

This, then, is the way we can repay OAC—by service. Our college is founded on the idea of service, and we, its students, are the representatives of the college. It is upon us that the duty falls of carrying out that basic idea. We are going into the world inspired with the resolution of service, eager to show our love for our college and our appreciation of her work by being of service to our fellow men.

Daniel Webster was challenging us when he said, "Let us develop the resources of our land, call forth its powers, build up its institutions, promote all its great interests, and see whether we also in our day and generation may not perform something worthy to be remembered."

We, the members of the Class of 1922 of the Oregon State Agricultural College, accept the challenge, and pledge ourselves in answer to perform in our day and generation something worthy to be remembered.

WHAT IS DEMOCRACY?

"The alternative [to democracy], of dictatorship, is that of slavery, with the individual subject to the whim of the ruler. This freedom is something worth fighting for, worth going to war for if necessary."

In the late 1930s and into 1940, the Paulings, like many Americans, watched with shocked disbelief as Hitler's Germany began invading its European democratic neighbors. They grew ever more horrified as the Nazi juggernaut toppled nation after nation. It was difficult for the Paulings, who had fond memories of the sociable and intellectually stimulating year and a half, from 1926 to 1927, spent mostly in Germany among scientists. They had returned to Germany for several visits afterward. The triumphant success of the manic firebrand Hitler and his program of extremist ideas were incomprehensible to them. National Socialism scarcely fit their own favored idea of socialism. The rabid anti-Semitism was alarming. What could be done to help the many brilliant Jewish scientists still trapped in Europe? Pauling tried to get visas and employment at Caltech for some researchers desperate to get into the U.S., but he discovered that the Institute had a definite and very small quota for Jews on its payroll. (Later, he greatly regretted not challenging it.)

More and more, Pauling found himself thinking, reading, and talking about the historical parallels between democracy's origin and rise and the development of science. He was also much influenced by British physicist (and Marxist) J. D. Bernal's book, *The Social Function of Science,* published in 1939, and discussed its social-activist messages with his colleagues and students. Though as a lecturer he was expected to present scientific topics at formal gatherings, he sometimes now strayed into political matters—as he did while speaking on "Science and Democracy" at a scientific fraternity event at Caltech in November of 1940. Pauling made it clear that democracy was worth fighting for—as would happen in the U.S., in little more than a year. (See pages 31-33.) He was also already envisaging the political evolution leading toward world government.

I n these days we all have a greater consciousness of social and political subjects, and hence it may be allowed me to talk on the subject expressed in a general way by the title "Science and Democracy."

Democracy in its development has run a parallel course to science. Democracy, that form of government in which the people rules itself, originated in Greece, at the time that science got its start. The science of the Greeks was not perfect—thus Aristotle thought that a body weighing two pounds would fall twice as fast as one weighing one pound; and Lucretius (a Roman, to be sure) said that the molecules of honey and milk are round, whereas those of wormwood are hooked. Similarly the democracy of the Greeks was the rule of only a portion of the people—the others, the slaves, were in fact not considered to be people.

Democracy and science both faltered and lagged in the Middle Ages. Then came the renaissance of science and the revolutions which led to the rebirth of democracy—a better democracy than that of the ancients. This started with the revolutions of 1642 and 1688 in England, which consolidated the parliamentary system; then the American revolution; the French revolutions of 1789, 1830, and 1848; and democracy got a firm and, we hope, lasting start in the world.

Thomas Jefferson, who may be considered the father of American democracy, stated that it was closely linked with science. He wrote in a letter to John Adams that he and his followers had believed "in the improvability of the human mind in science, in ethics, in government, etc.

Those who advocated a reformation of institutions, *pari passu* with the progress of science, maintain that no definite limits could be assigned to progress. The enemies of reform, on the other hand, denied improvement and advocated steady adherence to principles, practices, and institutions of our fathers which they represented as the consummation of wisdom and the acme of excellence beyond which the human mind could never advance."

Thus Jefferson contended that government, like science, could grow and improve through research. This is what democracy has done. There have been continual reforms, leading to a greater and greater voice of the people as a whole in the affairs of state. Thus in the time of Andrew Jackson, who was truly the representative of the people, the old caucus system of electing the president was abolished in favor of the modern one, with the electors pledged to vote for a certain candidate, and now we are talking of election by popular vote.

The alternative, of dictatorship, is that of slavery, with the individual subject to the whim of the ruler. This freedom is something worth fighting for, worth going to war for if necessary.

And now let me talk a bit about science and war, since war and government are linked together. Man has always been a warlike animal, and he has usually been fighting for his freedom of action in one way or another. In the earliest times he fought with his neighbor when their interests clashed. Then when he had learned to form tribes for the common good and protection the tribes fought. In time, with the development of the science of agriculture, there arose towns, which fought with neighboring towns, and then small countries with other small countries. Now where are we, and what can we hope for? We have large countries—a score or more, with a half-dozen of importance. These countries are fighting: the democracies, in which people are free, against the totalitarian states, in which people are the slaves of the rulers. England is fighting not alone for democracy but for existence—yet this is essentially for democracy. We are arming [our nation too]. . . .

[What about] the future? We can extrapolate—with the progress of science the countries of the future will be larger. Ultimately—perhaps in our lifetime—there will be a world government. The great question is this: Will it be a world democracy or a world dictatorship? Either is possible.

The present war will lead to larger countries. Perhaps one will be so large as to dominate the world from now on—then the war would be over. Otherwise the issue will be settled by a later war or wars.

The best hope is that the democracies will win this war and then continue to dominate the world.

IMPERILED DEMOCRACY: WORLD WAR II

"We as individuals do not believe either in fighting with our fists or clubs. But we would fight a thug who attacked us."

Two years before America's entry in the Second World War in December of 1941, the Paulings joined Clarence Streit's Interdemocracy Federal Union (IFU) movement, or "Union Now." It aimed to unite the isolationist U.S. with the British Commonwealth nations around the world. It actively promoted immediate, full-scale military and economic assistance for Great Britain, which finally stood alone in Europe in resisting the totalitarian German ambition to eliminate democracy everywhere and eventually take over the world, sharing portions of it with Axis allies Italy and Japan.

Preceding and during the war, though afflicted in 1941 with a serious kidney disease initially considered fatal (see pages 57-58, 95), Pauling directed and worked on a dozen war-connected research and development projects for the U.S. government. These contributions earned him the National Medal for Merit, awarded by President Truman in 1948.

From the late 1940s on, however, a number of Americans were convinced that Pauling was willing to "sell out" the political independence of the United States, either to the United Nations or, worse, the Soviet Union. This sometimes vehement opinion (held by several Caltech trustees, among others) was based on Pauling's insistence on achieving world peace through rational dialogue with communist nations, and through a system of international law, preferably through the U.N. Pauling's critics had surely never heard or read any of the impassioned public talks he gave in 1940 on behalf of Union Now. Here are the words of a deeply patriotic man who would never settle for anything less than democracy in his own land, despite being accused of undermining the U.S. and favoring the despotism of Josef Stalin's Soviet Union.

The goal of our social development is freedom—freedom of individual action, freedom of speech, religious freedom, and freedom from the fear of unjust and arbitrary oppression and persecution. By centuries of struggle and sacrifice this goal has been in its essentials achieved in the democracies of the world.

Now there is being waged a great war between democracy and totalitarianism, to decide between the free way and the slave way. And this war may well determine, as Hitler says it will, the course of the world for the next thousand years. Through the development of methods of transportation and of technology in general the world has effectively become so small that world rule is to be expected soon. The great decision which will be made before many years—surely during the present century, and possibly within the coming decade—is whether the world will be ruled by totalitarian masters or whether it will be a free democratic state.

We have become accustomed to this freedom, and we had begun to accept it without question, as something that was given us for nothing, something for which we do not need to struggle and fight. But events are showing us that this is not right—that the fight for freedom is not yet over. During the last few years we have seen many of the people of Germany persecuted and robbed of their freedom and their lives, and in recent months it has been the people of peaceful democracies who have been enslaved and killed.

In a democracy, such as ours, there is little danger of loss of freedom from actions within the country. The democratic system is, to be sure, slow and unwieldy and inefficient, but it is safe, in consequence of the fact that the important decisions are made by the people themselves. The one great danger that threatens a democratic country is the danger of attack and overthrow by militant enemies with the lust to conquer and enslave. . . .

This is a war whose outcome involves the decision between freedom and slavery for the people of the world; it is a struggle between democracy and the enemies of democracy. We all recognize that this is our war, and that Britain is fighting our fight—just as did Norway and Holland and Belgium and France until they were overcome. Recognizing this, the president and the great majority of the people favor the policy of the government of advancing all possible material aid to Britain. It would be proper, then, to acknowledge the unity of purposes of the democracies by the formation of the Union. Moreover, it is our belief, as members of IFU, that the future peace and happiness of the world depend on the formation of a democratic world government, and this is the time to form it.

There is another thing that we must consider. This step would mean going to war, and we, as idealists, are by nature pacifists and opposed to war. But we are being forced into war anyway—we are vigorously preparing for war, and who among us believes sincerely that we are not going to have war sooner or later? We as individuals do not believe either in fighting with our fists or clubs. But we would fight a thug who attacked us. And if the thug were to attack a peaceful neighbor of ours, would we not come to his aid rather than wait until he had beaten our neighbor into insensibility and had begun on us? This is the situation of the United States. Should not our country help Britain now to fight off the thug who is attacking her and will most probably attack us when she is polished off? . . .

A further advantage is that the United States would be put at once on a wartime basis of production and preparation. Our preparedness program is moving more and more rapidly—every time a democracy falls before the aggressor it is speeded up a bit—but we are still far from acting as vigorously as the emergency requires, and as vigorously as we are capable of acting. . . . At the present moment the United States is far from favoring the idea of forming the Union and thus getting into the war. But conditions and opinions change very fast in wartime. On April 9th the Nazis invaded Denmark and Norway, and tens of millions of Americans decided in a day that the United States should enter into combat with a ruthless aggressor who could thus strike down these peace-loving nations, who had pursued their peaceful courses for a century. . . .

When we consider that during the last few months half the democracies of the world have been brutally and ruthlessly conquered or surrounded and enslaved by the antidemocratic dictatorial totalitarian forces of evil; that the British democracies are now fighting off the aggressors and may be overpowered and conquered during the coming months, despite the aid which we are giving them; that we in the United States are beginning a desperate attempt to prepare for the war that we see ahead of us—must we not admit that it would be the part of wisdom for us to recognize our unity of purpose with democracy throughout the world, to form at once a Federal Union with the remaining free democracies, and thus to make the united stand which would win for the side of freedom the great Battle for the World of the Future?

THE SCIENTISTS BEHIND TECHNOLOGY

"The atomic power plant and the atomic bomb are now a part of the world. The people of the world must decide what to do about them."

In the years following World War II, Pauling moved increasingly into public speaking. He took time away from his work at Caltech to respond to requests to share what knowledge he had about the hot new topic called atomic energy. He began advocating the need to establish permanent world peace, recognizing that atom bombs had made another major war unthinkable. He actively supported the formation of the United Nations. (See Parts II and III.)

In a talk given in 1947 to a group of nonscientists ("One World—or None at All"), Pauling said:

I am afraid that if a war—an atomic war—were to take place, no one in the world might remain alive. This is the fear which scientists have—the fear that the people will not understand that there must not be another war. Atomic energy and the atomic bomb must be under international control. The nations of the world must give up their sovereignty, and submit to a worldwide authority. . . .

We are faced with a political problem—the greatest political problem which the world has ever had to consider. We must solve this problem and we must not fail—we shall not have a second chance.

Ava Helen and Linus Pauling had become members of the First Unitarian Church of Los Angeles. They admired its free-thinking minister and appreciated the church's intelligent, social-activist members. From time to time Pauling even gave lecture-sermons there, as in his memorable "Science in the Modern World." In this 1951 talk Pauling acquainted listeners with how scientists think and work, even when they produce something like the atomic bomb.

Since technological applications often came from the speculations and explorations of "pure science," Pauling stressed that such originators, operating out of sheer interest and curiosity, were not responsible for immoral uses to which their discoveries and inventions might ultimately be put. However, scientists such as Einstein and Oppenheimer had every right—and probably an obligation as well, though this was widely questioned—to continue warning humankind about the harmful consequences of this latest, most dramatic form of applied science. Pauling's own antinuclear and peace-promoting voice joined theirs, eventually becoming stronger and more long-lasting than most of his generation. He also anticipated the new thermonuclear or H-bomb that would greatly boost the atomic bombs' destructive power.

The ethical implications of applying scientific discoveries for profit or military dominion continue to perplex society today, a half-century later.

I n past ages man's power to kill man has not been great; wars have not been devastating. The great killer of the past centuries was disease—pestilence—which might wipe out half the people of a nation . . . in a period when a great war would kill only one percent. Now—through the advance of science, we have conquered disease—and war has conquered us.

By discovering how to release at will the great stores of energy within the nuclei of atoms, scientists have learned how to make terrifying bombs that can destroy cities, kill hundreds of thousands, perhaps millions of people, in a single detonation.

Moreover, in such a detonation there are released great quantities of radioactive atoms, some of which retain their radioactivity for years. This radioactive material might be used to wipe out all life in one region of the globe. Indeed, a young radioscientist at the University of Chicago has published, in the *Bulletin of the Atomic Scientists*, his analysis of this weapon, and his conclusion that plant and animal life on all the lands on Earth could be destroyed, by use of plutonium, tritium, and cobalt, by the expenditure of the sum of money that we now devote to war each year.

No one, of course, wants to kill all of the people on Earth. But there are some persons who are willing that hundreds of millions of people be killed in an atomic war that will be waged if the efforts toward permanent peace are not successful.

Scientists are often accused of being responsible for the present world situation through having discovered how to make atomic bombs. Physicists are said to have a feeling of guilt, and even Oppenheimer once said that physicists have known sin—he may have meant the sin of devoting themselves to destructive military applications of science rather than to pure science itself.

I deny that scientists have been guilty in making their discoveries. They have, however, failed in some part to do their duty as citizens.

Let me say a word about the nature of scientific research. A pure scientist, such as a professor in a university, is a searcher for knowledge. He is striving to discover something new about the world in which we live. He cannot say that the discovery that he will make will be used only for the benefit of man, and not for his harm—as a weapon of destruction, say. If all men were men of good will, his discovery would be either of little benefit or of great benefit, because its harmful use could be avoided by decision of man himself. It is man himself—all citizens, all people, who have to decide to use man's knowledge, man's power over nature as revealed by the scientist, for the betterment of the world rather than for destruction.

If the scientists alone were to make such a decision, we would be abandoning our democracy for an autocracy of scientists.

There is also to be mentioned that a scientist cannot foresee how his discovery will be used; in fact, he cannot foresee what his discovery will be. A pure scientist is an explorer who is penetrating into the unknown, who hopes, as he pushes through the jungle into the next valley, by carrying out his newly devised experiment or by making his original calculations, that he will come upon something new—a new fact about the world, a fact that no one before him has known. It is the spirit of adventure that makes men scientists—the spirit of overwhelming curiosity, the desire to know more and more about the world, about stars, about atoms, about life.

After the scientists have done their work, engineers, technical workers, and businessmen take over and put the discoveries to use for improving living conditions or for making war.

Einstein was not trying to solve any practical problem when, in 1905, as a young man of 25, working in the Swiss patent office, he made his great discovery of the theory of relativity. He was not even trying to discover the theory of relativity. He was endeavoring to understand the world, to bring the facts of observation and experiment into simple relation with one another. Through the penetrating power of his great intellect, he obtained an insight into the nature of the world that had never been known to man before. This was the theory of relativity. He did not know that he was going to discover it. No one could have ordered him to discover it. Only freedom of intellectual effort permitted its discovery.

Nor did he know that it would lead to the development of the atomic bomb. He discovered as part of the theory of relativity the relation between energy and mass, $E = mc^2$, which tells that when a few pounds of plutonium detonate, with the nuclei of the atoms splitting into half-size nuclei and with decrease in mass of 0.1 percent, the amount of energy liberated is the same as on the detonation of 20,000 tons of TNT—20,000 one-ton blockbusters. He could not foresee that atomic bombs would be made, based on his theory—nor could he have prevented it by suppressing his knowledge, because man's curiosity will not be thwarted, and the discovery would have been made by someone else sooner or later.

The conquest of the atomic nucleus should provide man with hope for the future. Uranium and thorium, the fissionable elements, occur in the Earth's crust in large quantities—as much as the common metal lead, though not so conveniently concentrated into deposits of rich ores. One ton of uranium is equivalent to a million tons of coal or oil, and thus fuel will be available when in a hundred years our oil is used up, and in a thousand years our coal.

Many scientists, in many countries, contributed to this conquest of the nucleus. In 1932 Carl Anderson in Pasadena discovered the positron, and Chadwick in England discovered the neutron; then nuclear fission was discovered by Hahn in Germany, neptunium and plutonium were discovered by workers in Berkeley, and scores of scientists in the United States, England, Germany, and other countries pointed out the possibility of using the nucleus, either as a fuel for power for peacetime use or as a devastating explosive.

The atomic power plant and the atomic bomb are now a part of the world. The people of the world must decide what to do about them.

Although scientists cannot take over the responsibility of making the decision for their fellow citizens, they have a special duty as citizens; namely, to give their fellow citizens the benefit of their special knowledge and understanding. It is the duty of all scientists to point out that the world of today is not the world of yesterday; that a world war now would result in the death not of 20 million people, as did the First World War, nor of 40 million, as did the Second, but of hundreds of millions, perhaps a billion people; and that the loss in property, in great areas rendered uninhabitable, in moral values, would be such that the world might never recover. . . .

The scientific method consists in being completely open-minded—in examining the evidence scrupulously and accepting facts as facts, no matter how surprising, how unexpected, how unpleasant they may be. For nearly three hundred years physics had been firmly based on Newton's laws of motion. Then Einstein pointed out that new experimental results required that small changes be made in the laws whenever moving objects were going very fast. Scientists were rather loath to accept the new idea; but they examined the evidence, carried out new experiments that gave results supporting Einstein, and within a few years they were convinced, and accepted the changed theory.

A scientist is a skeptic. He accepts the "laws of nature" only so long as there is no contradictory fact. . . .

Let us continue our scientific inquiry into the matter of international relations.

First, we have pointed out that an atomic war, if it comes, will be extremely devastating. Even now, in time of peace (with only a small nonatomic war, which has produced only a million or so casualties, and devastated only one small country) we are devoting nearly a quarter of our national income to war, and undergoing a serious inflation. On the other hand, with peace in the world there could be, as a result of the scientific and technological progress that has been made, happiness and prosperity greater than the world has ever known before.

We conclude that there should be peace.

Now we ask what the path is to peace. In science we recognize that a steady state, an equilibrium, is reached when the rate in one direction is equal to the rate in the opposite direction—when there is equality in the two opposing quantities.

I interpret this to mean that there would be peace in the world if people and nations were treated alike. I believe that there would be peace in the world if right and justice, rather than self-interest, were to determine the policy of nations. I believe that the words of Christ should be heeded: "And as ye would that men should do unto you, do ye also to them likewise."

What is the guiding principle of our diplomatic representatives, and of those of other countries? Is it to search for the right and the just path, and to follow it? No—it is to grasp for the minutest bit of national advantage, without regard for justice. We cannot expect these officials to change their ways—it is the people of this country and of other countries who must stand firm, who must say, "We believe in justice, and in right, for people in other countries of the world, as well as in our own, and we place these principles above material self-interest."

This policy, and no other, will save the world from war.

The part that selfishness, greediness, both national and individual, plays in producing war needs to be explored. . . .

Scientists all over the world are striving to prevent war. Last month [1951] a group of 200, under the leadership of Lord Boyd Orr, the President of the National Peace Council, met in London. They said:

> *We are in danger of a third world war and we are determined to do what we can, both as citizens and as scientists to prevent it. . . . It is our duty to appeal to peoples and governments for a negotiated and lasting settlement which will prevent a recourse to the instruments of extermination. It is our duty to provide the public with information both on the destructiveness and misery of modern war and on the benefits that constructive science can bring.*
>
> *We assert the international character of science; it is a worldwide republic of the mind. Scientists form one fraternity, united in a common attempt to understand nature and a common concern for human betterment. It is our duty to strive for the removal of all barriers that restrict or embarrass the free intercourse of scientists throughout the world.*

Now there are barriers to the free intercourse of scientists raised by every large country, including the United States. In this, as in other ways, the national policy is not one that will tend towards peace. It is essential that everyone do his bit to get nations to accept the Golden Rule, toward the time when we have an effective world government.

I am sure that the final step toward a peaceful world, a world permanently without war, will be taken. If we look back at the history of man, we see that there has been steady progress, a steady increase in the size of the groups within which there is peace. First there was prehistoric man, with the peaceful group consisting only of the family, and with every family at war with every other family. Then small villages formed, within which there was law and order; and these villages grew into larger communities, which with the passing centuries have become large countries. Now there remains only the final step to be taken—and we are forced, by the horror of a possible atomic war, to take this final step before civilization destroys itself.

The time has come for the good that is in man to win out over the evil.

TEACHING SCIENCE IN OUR SCHOOLS

"The concepts of chemical change and of atomic structure and other concepts of modern science are no more difficult to understand than the concept that the Earth is round."

By the late 1940s Pauling was a widely known and well-respected chemistry professor, researcher, and author. His *The Nature of the Chemical Bond* (1939) had revolutionized the way many chemists thought and worked, and his first textbook, *General Chemistry* (1947), changed teaching methods in colleges around the world. These were professional accomplishments that in most respects were separate from his other life as a peace advocate. But because he had also become "politicized" by events such as the continuing development of atomic bombs and the building of nuclear arsenals, he felt he had to speak out. Indeed, he seemed to consider it his sacred duty to do so. He also kept reminding other scientists to be more involved in educating others about the science-connected issues of the times, and to become actively engaged in the workings of society and government.

In 1949 Pauling was elected to serve as president of the American Chemical Society, the chief professional association of chemists in research and education. He often used this prominent position to advocate research-furthering actions, such as government support of scientific projects—now possible with the founding of the National Science Foundation. He also invited generous industrial funding of research programs. But to the dismay of some of its 50,000 members, he also asked that ACS support certain extremely controversial public policy measures, notably President Truman's proposed federal program for socialized medicine (an idea that the medical profession and the nation itself are scarcely ready for five decades later).

As a highly visible spokesperson for science, Pauling could be expected to lay out ambitious and well-considered plans to revise the American educational system to enhance science teaching. Pauling appreciated the value of many professions and trades other than science. But he hoped that someday everyone would be trained in the disciplined thinking of science, beginning with kindergarten. He was especially interested in the intellectual nurturance of young people still in the process of becoming citizens in a world that they themselves might shape anew—and better. In his view, how science should be taught to young people was almost as important as having it taught at all.

He hoped that people would begin using the new scientific knowledge and technologies, which had already radically changed human society, to better purposes than they often had been put in the past. He believed that finding effective solutions to problems depended on rational and objective methods and facts—science's realm. Purposeful pursuit of something not yet fully known—or "attack," as he often phrased it, adapting military parlance—employed the scientific method. If several different hypotheses, theories, conclusions, or solutions emerged, seemingly contradictory or in conflict, one would judge their relative merits based on known facts and observations. Scientific thinking also allowed for revising or discarding one's ideas based on new facts or valid findings that had been previously ignored or discounted.

In an insightful 1951 article, "The Significance of Chemistry to Man in the Modern World," Pauling maintained that the healthy, sustained operation of a democracy within modern society might be guaranteed through providing universal education in science. In its conclusion he stated that:

> The sources of happiness in life are not so bountiful that mankind can afford to neglect such an important one. If the ever-present oppressing danger of world war can ultimately be averted, and the world can enter into a continuing period of peace and friendliness, the intellectual activities of the average man may become a source of happiness to him comparable to that provided by his emotions.

The final paragraph of the following excerpt typifies Pauling's frequent reminders of the prevailing fearfulness in the postwar period. This followed the Soviet Union's parallel development of atomic weaponry, and communist incursions and takeovers in Europe and Asia in the late 1940s. It was also in accord with the vow he had made in December 1947 en route to an honorary professorship at Oxford University in England: to devote half his time toward achieving world peace. He also intended to mention this urgent issue in every talk he gave. Some found their way into print, as this one did.

In 1957 the Soviets launched Sputnik, the first artificial space satellite. Only then did the U.S. begin to take more seriously—for competitive and strategic purposes—the need to develop science-teaching programs for schoolchildren. Pauling himself was more concerned about the impact of scientific knowledge in maintaining democracy.

The time has now come for the study of science to be made a part of the curriculum in every grade, at every level. There should be a class in science in the kindergarten, in the first grade, in the second grade, in the third grade, and so on.

Every boy and girl who finishes grammar school should know science, in the same way that he now knows arithmetic, languages, and history. Every boy and girl who finishes high school should know still more about science. Every college student should begin his college work with a sound knowledge of the whole of science—comparable to the knowledge that he now has, at this stage, of mathematics—in order that he might devote his years in college to the more advanced aspects of the subject. Only in this way can we train citizens for life in the modern world. Only in this way can we develop a citizenry able to solve the great social and political problems that confront the world. . . .

In a relatively few schools a small amount of information about the nature of the physical and biological world is presented to the students during the first few years of primary school work. If one classroom period per day were devoted to science throughout the years of primary school instruction, the work might begin with very simple discussions of the physical world, including simple demonstrations. The fields of knowledge covered would be largely descriptive in nature, in all branches of science—physics, chemistry, biology, geology, astronomy, geography, etc.; but in addition there could be, even in the earliest years, instruction in the scientific method and the scientific attitude.

The concepts of chemical change and of atomic structure and other concepts of modern science are no more difficult to understand than the concept that the Earth is round. We teach students in the elementary schools that the Earth is round, even though convincing proof is so difficult that the fact has been generally accepted only during the last few centuries. In the same way the important basic principles of atomic science could now be taught to beginning students, in the elementary schools, with rigorous proof of the truth of the concepts deferred until a later time. . . .

There has been just as great reluctance to introduce extensive teaching of science into the field of adult education as into the field of elementary education. The best methods to be used in giving scientific information and instruction in the scientific method to mature individuals who have only an extremely limited background in science probably still need to be discovered. It is likely that a thorough study of existing alternative methods and a search for new ones would yield very important results.

The argument might be presented that it is hopeless to attempt to give the average citizen an understanding of science, because of the complexity of science at the present time and the enormous rate of increase in scientific knowledge. How can even the foremost scientist keep abreast of the rapidly advancing front of knowledge when millions of new facts are being discovered every year? I believe that this pessimism is not justified, and that, indeed, science as a whole is becoming simpler, rather than more difficult. Many parts of physics have already passed through the stage of greatest complexity—the stage at which the body of knowledge in the field consists of an aggregate of largely disconnected facts. With the recognition of relationships among these facts, great numbers of them can be encompassed within a single principle. An understanding of the field as a whole can then be obtained by the process of understanding the general principles.

It is not necessary for every fact to be learned; instead a few of the facts can be considered, in order to discover their relationship to the general principles, and thereafter other facts that, for practical or accidental reasons, come to the attention of the individual can immediately be correlated by him with the general principles. . . .

One way in which an increased knowledge of the nature of the physical and biological world can be of value to the individual citizen is through the conferring on him of an increased equanimity, an increased confidence in natural law and order. The wellbeing of an individual may be greatly impaired by his fear of the unknown, which may far exceed the fear that he would have of a known danger, which he might prepare to meet in a rational way.

In a world in which human beings have achieved extreme powers of destruction of one another, through the use of an astounding new source of energy, the nonunderstanding individual might well become extremely apprehensive, in such a way as to prevent him from making the correct personal and political decisions, and to cause him to accede without a trace of protest to suggestions or orders from a dictatorial leader.

An incidental advantageous result of scientific education for all people which is of more than negligible significance is the personal satisfaction and pleasure that accompany pure knowledge and understanding. The physical and biological world in which we live is truly astounding and wonderful. No matter what the extent of his general education nor the caliber of his mental abilities, every human being might achieve satisfaction and increased happiness through an increased knowledge and understanding of the world.

THE STATISTICAL BASIS OF DEMOCRACY

"The principle upon which a true democratic system operates is that . . . correct decisions are to be made by the process of averaging the opinions of all of the citizens in the democracy."

Pauling sometimes crowned mathematics as "the queen of the sciences." Scientific research utilizes numbers, numerical relationships, frequencies of occurrence, and many other measurements to develop hypotheses or arrive at valid conclusions about some subject. In his investigations and public debates over controversies such as the health effects of nuclear testing, Pauling usually applied scientific statistical analysis as well as logic. (See Parts III-V.)

Believing implicitly in democracy and self-government, Pauling respected the innate intelligence of ordinary people everywhere. A confirmed egalitarian and free thinker, he allowed for extremes in beliefs and urged people to vote their opinions. But a well-balanced education was essential in acquiring sufficient knowledge to vote intelligently.

He also approved highly of efforts to provide continuing science education to adults in diverse ways. The possibilities for enticing people into acquiring knowledge greatly expanded as the print, film, and electronic media developed in the latter part of the 20th century. Just as he knew that a basic education would make people better citizens, he felt that an education in science would prepare them to understand more about the new technologies and products that were influencing daily life. He also saw it as conferring the advantage of protection from economic exploitation.

Above all, however, Pauling knew the advantages of the scientific method—that careful step-by-step investigation of facts—to define and solve problems of all kinds, whether in science, one's own life, or society.

In this selection, also taken from "The Significance of Chemistry to Man in the Modern World," Pauling extended the rationale for early training in mathematics as well as science. (See "Teaching Science in Our Schools" above.)

The laws of probability have as much significance in nonscientific fields as in scientific fields. We all understand how a life insurance company calculates its premium payments. The statistician for the life insurance company collects information about the number of people dying at various ages—30, 31, 32, 40, 50, 60, 70, 80, 90, 100, even 110 years of age. From all of these data he calculates the average expectancy of life, and thus finds the average number of premiums that will be paid. If he were to say, "It is abnormal for a man to live to be 85 years old, or older: therefore I must discard the data about these abnormal people," he would obtain a wrong value about the average expectancy of life, and the life insurance company would go bankrupt.

Yet, just this foolish procedure is sometimes carried out in the operation of a democratic system of government.

The principle upon which a true democratic system operates is that no single man is wise enough to make the correct decisions about the very complex problems that arise, and that the correct decisions are to be made by the process of averaging the opinions of all of the citizens in the democracy. These opinions will correspond to a probability distribution curve, extending from far on the left to far on the right.

If, now, we say that all of the opinions that extend too far to the right—beyond the point corresponding to the age 85 in the above example, say—are abnormal, and are to be excluded in taking the average, then the average that we obtain will be the wrong one.

An understanding of the laws of probability would accordingly make it evident to the citizen that the operation of the democratic system requires that every one have the right to express his opinion about political questions, no matter what the opinion might be.

It is of the greatest importance to modern man that he understand the modern world. He must have knowledge enough about the world to make the right decisions—and since the modern world is largely scientific in its constitution, the citizen must understand science.

How can the citizen get scientific knowledge? The answer to this question can be drawn from past experience. Hundreds of years ago it was recognized that mathematics is of great value to the individual. Mathematics is a difficult subject: one might be tempted to say that, since it is difficult, the study of it should be put off till the college years. Yet, through experience we have learned that the way to teach mathematics is to start with the teaching of numbers in kindergarten, arithmetic in the first grade and other elementary grades, and to continue steadily, without interruption, through algebra, geometry, trigonometry, calculus. This is the way in which science should be taught.

SCIENCE KNOWLEDGE IS ESSENTIAL TO CULTURE

"It is impossible for the technology of a country to develop satisfactorily if it does not rest upon a sound basis of pure science."

Beginning with his experience at OAC, Pauling maintained that it was essential to get a well-rounded education while preparing for a profession or trade. Nonscientists should undertake a cross-disciplinary education by learning about science; young people aiming for a career in science should study literature and arts, foreign languages, and the social sciences. Both should balance their studies to become well-informed, cultivated persons. In this excerpt from a talk on "Technology and Democracy" to students and faculty at the University of Puerto Rico in 1955, Pauling revealed his annoyance over how narrowly focused and unjustifiably smug some liberal arts professors could be.

His main interest, however, was in showing the close relationship between the teaching and practice of "pure science" at universities, and the technology that fueled industrial and medical progress in democracies—which should be encouraged in developing countries.

One reason for people to be cultured is that a knowledge of the nature of the world in which we live contributes to our happiness. Man finds a special pleasure in the satisfaction of his intellectual curiosity. Science deals with the nature of the world, both the nonliving world and the world of life, and every human being can find pleasure in learning about the extraordinary discoveries that are made every year about the inorganic and the organic world.

Yet, I remember (not as an isolated instance) the time when a colleague of mine, a professor of English, said to me, "I do not know *anything* about science." He was not shamefaced as he said this; he did not hang his head the way that I would if I were forced to say, "I do not know anything about history, literature, art." No, he seemed, for some incomprehensible reason, to be proud. But he was confessing that he is an ignorant man, an uncultured man—a man who knows nothing about the greatest feature of the modern world, who knows nothing about science in this age of science, who because of his ignorance is unable to appreciate the world fully, to be a proper part of the 20th century. He is as much of an anachronism as a Stone Age man would be in Elizabethan times, in the times of Shakespeare—a Stone Age man who refused to learn about the Greeks and Romans, the Egyptians and Chaldees; who proudly said, "I know nothing about philosophy, about history, about

Euclid and his geometry, about Marlowe and Shakespeare and their plays." Why does my English professor friend not feel ashamed? I think because he is not alone in being lacking in culture. In my travels around the world I have found uncultured people of this sort in every country.

Another reason for the study of science is that it is the basis of technology, and that human happiness is increased by technology—by the raising of the standards of living of the people through the development of industry, the more effective utilization of natural resources, and through the alleviation of human suffering by the application of modern medicine.

The question may be asked as to whether it is not technology itself—engineering and medicine—that is important. Does science, pure science, have any significant role to play? . . .

My answer to this question is that in my opinion it is impossible for the technology of a country to develop satisfactorily if it does not rest upon a sound basis of pure science, and that the pure scientists cannot long remain effective in the 20th century when pure science is advancing so rapidly and so many new discoveries are being made, unless the professors and the students are directly involved in scientific research.

It is only through a system of scholarships that advantage can be taken of the reservoir of talent that exists in a country. It often happens that the most brilliant young man or woman is one whose parents cannot afford to send him to the university, and it is the duty of the government, in order that the nation reap the maximum benefit from its human resources, to see that all the talented young people have the benefits of the education that they need to make their greatest contribution to society. It is not enough, however, for medical students to be given scholarships. [Any country] needs in the modern world to have engineers and pure scientists. The most able boys and girls . . . who are especially attracted to pure science and applied science should, I think, also be picked out and given the scholarship support that they need in order to complete their education, and to permit them to make their careers in these fields.

A university in a modern democracy faces many special problems. One of these problems is that of the selection of professors and the supervision of the activities of professors. For some centuries there has existed the principle of academic freedom. I should like to say a word about this principle, to answer the question as to why professors should have any more freedom than other people—than engineers, for example, who are working for some industrial firm. The answer to this questions lies in the nature of the work that a professor does, in his attempts to fulfill his primary obligation, that of discovering something about the world that was never known before.

The reason that a professor must be free to make his own decisions about his research activities is that if the university has done its work well in selecting him, he is the man who knows more about his subject than anybody else in the world—or, at any rate, than anybody else in the world except a few other professors in other universities. No one else is able to decide where the greatest promise for discovery in his field lies. Indeed, in a sense, discoveries often occur when the idea behind the discovery first arises in the mind of a man. No one could have told Albert Einstein to discover the theory of relativity; no one knew that there was the possibility of developing such a theory. When the idea of the theory arose in Einstein's mind, the discovery was made—he had only to work out the equations, to show that the idea was a good one and not a faulty one, and the great job of changing all of man's thinking about the physical universe was done, that day in 1905. . . .

During recent decades we have seen the disgraceful spectacle of the overthrowing of academic freedom and of other hard-won rights of the people by Nazi Germany and other dictatorial governments. I have been greatly disturbed that our own country has been involved in a serious attack on academic freedom and on civil rights for which our fathers fought—as through restriction of the rights of travel.

Pauling's references at the end of this talk to academic and research freedom and the right to travel abroad were not merely statements of his basic principles (under attack for some years, as the Cold War gained momentum). He was obliquely referring to his problems in this period with government officials and Caltech administrators because of his reluctance to abstain from political activism during that increasingly tense period. He noisily decried the government's great investment in military hardware, nuclear weaponry above all. He also protested the mistreatment of a number of persons, including scientists like himself, who were being labeled as "Commies" and fellow-travelers during the venomous McCarthy era.

The next section follows Pauling's postwar political activism, and reveals more of its consequences on his personal life and professional career as a scientist.

Linus Pauling, ROTC cadet at Oregon Agricultural College. He joined in 1917, soon after the U.S. entered World War I, and earned the rank of major by his graduation in 1922. (Photo courtesy of Linda Pauling-Kamb)

Part II

War, Peace, and Dissent

Even as a child, Linus Pauling was fascinated with history. He observed that much of human history consisted of tales of ferocious warfare, conducted with increasingly ingenious strategies and new weapons. It was obvious that many wars took place because of the worst human faults—greed, arrogance, prejudice, lust for power, an undue sense of entitlement. Often wars involved vendettas that dated back to distant times and overrode the better human qualities of reason, forbearance, empathy, patience, and tolerance. "Justice" meant retaliation. A sense of common humanity was missing.

As an adult devoted to promoting world peace, Pauling was not a pure pacifist in the usual sense. He had never refused to take part in a war. When he went to Oregon Agricultural College in the autumn of 1917, the United States had recently entered World War I. A patriotic young man, he enrolled in what became the ROTC (Reserve Officers Training Corps) and eventually attained officer's rank.

He condoned, indeed urged, America's entry into World War II, which he felt was essential to save democracy. Pauling demonstrated his patriotism by working on research projects to help America's war effort, mostly developing explosives, rocket fuel, and medical innovations. He also served on several important government committees, such as the National Defense Research Council (NDRC). He participated in a medical team that investigated the state of U.S. public health delivery. Their recommendations were instrumental in greatly expanding the National Institutes of Health (NIH), now the main source of medical research funding.

Pauling's move into peace activism after World War II was strongly motivated by his belief that atomic weapons had now made major wars ultimately unwinnable. He saw that both sides in such a conflict would suffer immense damage and loss of life. Therefore, great efforts must be made to find ways to avoid war.

Pauling soon discovered that he was vulnerable to attacks on his patriotism because he questioned the ways his nation often dealt with international disputes. He suggested that rational negotiation and a spirit of cooperation might achieve far better results than belligerence and fierce economic, political, and military competition with the Soviet Union—which had now replaced Germany and Japan as the main threat to America's wellbeing.

Ever since the Russian Revolution of 1917, when the Bolsheviks established communism as the forcible operating economic system, the Union of Soviet Socialist Republics had been regarded with disapproval and even fear by most Americans. They worried that free enterprise, a feature of their own revolution-created democracy, might somehow be overthrown by a twisted Marxist vision of a classless society. This was especially worrisome during the Great Depression of the 1930s, brought on by the stock market crash of 1929. Many people who had been gambling with high stakes using paper fortunes suddenly found themselves destitute. And many more people who had trusted banks with their life savings became penniless when the money ran out. Jobs ended as industries failed.

The Depression years were hard on almost everyone. During this time a number of disillusioned Americans investigated the possible benefits of incorporating state socialism or communism into American democracy. Some had even joined the American Communist Party and talked of taking part in a new economic revolution against a wealthy, privileged class that still owned or controlled much of the country's assets. Confidence in the American economic system gradually recovered during President Franklin D. Roosevelt's first two terms. His New Deal introduced some socialistic ideas along with government controls into its emergency programs.

Fortunately for him and his growing family, Linus Pauling had a secure position at Caltech. Raised as a Republican, he had voted for Hoover in 1932, while his wife had backed Roosevelt. However, the experience of the Depression and talks with his wife and other liberals eventually put him in the Democratic Party's camp. In the intense campaign for the California governorship in 1934, he supported candidate Upton Sinclair, nominally a Democrat but a confirmed socialist who proposed a radical plan to End Poverty in California (EPIC). Sinclair lost to the Republican candidate. By the 1936 election Pauling voted for FDR, and in 1940 in a public debate he argued effectively for reelecting the president.

The long-stunned and stunted American economy began booming again when industries and agribusiness geared up for World War II. While the war lasted, Russia was considered a staunch ally in the fight against Nazi Germany despite the abiding struggle between communism and capitalism. But even before the war ended, the old animosities between the United States and the Soviet Union were stirred up, especially on government levels and in conferences deciding the fates of conquered lands. From the mid 1940s on, anyone in the U.S. who spoke in favor of maintaining Soviet-American cooperation and friendship was regarded with distrust and dislike. China soon joined the hostile "other side." Even "peace" became a suspicious word. At first the highest priority was to protect the secret formula for making atomic bombs from Russian espionage. But once the Soviets succeeded in assembling their own nuclear arsenal, helped by secret agents, the U.S. military game plan turned to maintaining superiority in numbers, technology, globe-circling bombers and submarines, missile range, and launching sites.

It was in this climate that Linus Pauling launched his crusade for peace and common sense.

THE END OF WAR?

"No one understands how great is the significance of atomic energy and the atomic bomb to the world so well as do the scientists, and this understanding has forced them into activity."

If World War II had been won with conventional weapons, Linus Pauling probably would have happily turned away from developing munitions and gone back to his work in "pure science." By then his work included the beginnings of what would later become known as molecular biology and molecular medicine.

But the placid ideal of Pauling's future was diverted by a shattering event. In early August of 1945, the United States dropped atomic bombs created by the top-secret Manhattan Project on the Japanese cities of Hiroshima and Nagasaki. The horrendous devastation killed or seriously maimed several hundred thousand people.

The world had never experienced such mighty weapons before. Their use shocked people around the world. One of them was Linus Pauling. As a chemist he well understood atomic structure and nuclear physics. He did not need access to classified information to figure out in theory how such extraordinary explosive substances might be manufactured and implemented. "Scientists recognized immediately in 1945 that it was their duty to help educate their fellow citizens, so that we all can take part in the democratic process, in making decisions, informed decisions," Pauling said later.

Beginning in the mid 1940s, Pauling often gave introductory explanations of the atomic bombs that had been dropped on Japan. His background as a teacher enabled him to gear his lectures or articles to his audience. At first he confined himself to the technicalities of the subject. But he soon saw these public-speaking engagements as an opportunity to discuss the importance of securing world peace so that such terrible weapons would never again be used, or even manufactured. Pauling said of this period:

> Until 1945, I doubted that the world would ever be rid of war and foresaw a third world conflict between the Soviet Union and the United States, or at any rate between communists and capitalists. In 1945, however, I came to think, as did Albert Einstein, that the existence of nuclear weapons had finally made it imperative to abandon war once and for all. As seemed only logical to me, these weapons force us to accept the idea of coexistence and cooperation. Now that the facts about nuclear weapons are relatively well known to the general public, we must realize that the future of the human race depends on our willingness and ability to cooperate and work together to solve global problems without belligerence.

"Atomic Energy and World Government," excerpted here, comes from a typescript that Pauling apparently used as a boilerplate when giving his first talks to lay audiences in 1945. This was shortly after atomic bombs brought the war with Japan to an end, several months after the surrender of Nazi Germany. Since Pauling regarded these technical public lectures as springboards for presenting the need for a world government, in this somber speech he combined two diverse topics: atomic bombs and peace.

The atomic bomb, Pauling said at the start, "is responsible for my being here tonight—just as the atomic bomb may be responsible for our all not being here a few years from now." (The more technical part of this talk is given in Part III, pages 102-104.) By the end of his discourse, however, he managed to sound more optimistic. For in the autumn of 1945, when he gave this lecture, the charter for the United Nations had already been shaped in San Francisco. Pauling's perennial belief in the value of the U.N., along with the need for enforceable world law, greatly disturbed his conservative critics in the U.S. They decried his trust in the principle of international cooperation, which they found naive at best, and subversive at worst.

Pauling never forsook that early hope of finding a sensible way to address this new crisis in civilization, of eliminating the fear that irrational nationalism and terrorism might kill off everybody and everything. In fact, he convinced himself that the creation of nuclear power for weaponry actually forced humankind to give up war entirely. As the following selections indicate, he was scarcely alone in his crusade. Many other scientists and peace advocates held this idealistic belief in nuclear deterrence. Pauling stuck with it despite years of virulent condemnation, which followed him to the end of his days and even posthumously.

Pauling credited his wife, Ava Helen, with initiating his careful study of current events and history. (See "Interlude," pages 89-95.) The scope of his interests was unusually large. To get a sense of where the nation and the world were heading, Pauling closely scrutinized newspapers and newsmagazines. He noted how they reported the news that interested him: military activities and budgets, the presidential administration's positions, and diplomatic crises. But he also read that period's equivalent of today's "alternative" press. Sometimes these were subterranean ragsheets put out by far-left-wing organizations. More often they were credible, intelligent periodicals such as *The Nation* and *I.F. Stone's Weekly,* which reported news and views that were rarely seen in mainstream publications. During the late 1940s and '50s, whenever Pauling wanted to get something of a controversial political nature published, these were usually the only periodicals willing to print them.

L ike most other scientists, I have in the past stuck pretty close to my work and paid little attention to politics and to world affairs, perhaps even less than the average citizen. Most scientists have a deep interest in their work—in the job of discovering the nature of the physical world— and they have little time for or interest in such crude activities as politics and world affairs. Now, however, scientists have made a discovery which truly revolutionizes the world.

No one understands how great is the significance of atomic energy and the atomic bomb to the world so well as do the scientists, and this understanding has forced them into activity, has caused them, individually and in groups such as the Federation of Atomic Scientists, to begin a campaign of talking, of presenting the facts about the atomic bomb, in the hope that everyone, as he begins to understand the possibilities of the future, will be horrified by them, and will pledge himself to take the individual action which is necessary to save the world. . . .

The next war [may] be equal to one hundred like the one we have just gone through. Offensive action will be easy and cheap, but defensive action will be hard and expensive. No good means of defense exists, and it seems inconceivable that an effective one will be found.

Ladies and gentlemen, this is the danger now facing the world. What can be done to avoid it? Scientists discovered the basis of the atomic bomb and the atomic scientists on the bomb project have had a longer time to think about the problem it poses than other people have had. They believe, and I believe, that there is only one way to avoid world disaster— and that is to abolish war, to have effective international control of the atomic bomb, and, as soon as possible, to form a world government to which the nations of the world give up their sovereignty in matters which serve as causes of war.

The Federation of Atomic Scientists has formulated a statement to this end, urging "that the President of the United States immediately invite the governments of Great Britain and the Soviet Union to a conference to prevent a competitive armaments race, to plan international control of mankind's most devastating weapons, and jointly to initiate international machinery to make available to all peoples the peacetime benefits of atomic energy." This statement has been signed by hundreds of workers at Oak Ridge, Hanford, and Los Alamos, and by many hundreds of other scientists in southern California and elsewhere on the Pacific Coast and throughout the nation.

I believe that the only hope for the world is to prevent war, and that war can be prevented only by a sovereign world government to which individuals are directly responsible. Talk about a world government has always been considered visionary—even now there seems to be a feeling, especially among editorial writers, that the practical people of the United States will never consent to this nation's giving up its sovereignty.

But is not the formation of a world government, abolishing war, the practical thing to do? Would it not be more realistic, more practical for the United States and other nations to give up some of their sovereignty, that relating to waging war, to a world government than for these nations to retain all their sovereignty and to be destroyed? Is it not more realistic, more practical to use the gifts of nature, as discovered by science, for the good of all the people of the world, considering them as brothers, than for death and destruction?

I believe that the discovery of atomic power will be recognized as necessitating world unity, and that the goal of a continually peaceful and happy world, which a few years ago was hardly visible in the greatly distant future, will be achieved within our generation.

CAN WE LIVE IN PEACE WITH RUSSIA?

"The United States has the moral responsibility to lead the world to permanent peace."

In 1947 Pauling was still positive about the good uses to which the new nuclear power could be put: efficient, clean energy in limitless supplies, in contrast to the rapidly diminishing fossil fuels. But by the late 1960s he would no longer favor nuclear power plants because of the health and safety risks to workers and the public. By then he also believed that the mineral resources consumed would be far better utilized in advanced future technologies.

In the two years after World War II, Pauling became greatly concerned that the growing conflict between the U.S. and the USSR would accelerate the development and threat of nuclear weapons. He proposed a simple approach to defusing the problem. He based it on his assessment of the psychology of the Russian people and their leaders, who deeply resented the years of invasion, ostracism, and isolation by Western countries. The U.S. had feared worldwide attacks on capitalism after the Russian Revolution, and deplored the iron-fisted regimes of Lenin and Stalin. A temporary truce had taken place between the nations only during the war years, when they were fighting a common foe.

Like many other liberals at the time, Pauling believed that his own powerful country could well afford to behave, and should somehow manage to behave, much more generously toward other nations than it had in the past—especially Russia. If it did so, he felt that the problems between the two rival economic systems would surely diminish. One might speculate how differently history might have played out if U.S. diplomacy had tried to follow this ingenuous suggestion—negotiating in a cooperative, helpful spirit, despite the often dour, manipulative, and aggressive behavior of the Soviet government. But then, few Americans would have been willing to take that chance. It might have ended up proving disastrous to American and other democratic nations' political and economic interests. So the Cold War progressed, with its espionage, alarming standoffs when thermonuclear war seemed imminent, and an exorbitant and irrational arms race. Though the Cold War has ended, the ramifications of this deadly competition, including dangerous nuclear remnants located around the globe, defy easy international solutions.

"Will the United States Accept Its Greatest Responsibility?" is what Linus Pauling asked his audience in 1947. He hoped, of course, that the U.S. would. He was going to be disappointed.

If there is peace in the future, atomic energy will make the world a far better place for man, will raise the standards of living of all people. One ton of a fissionable element, uranium or thorium, can produce as much heat as two and one-half million tons of coal. There is a great amount of these two elements in the Earth's crust—as much as of the common metal lead, enough to supply all the energy needed by man for millions of years. Dr. Szilard and Mr. Lilienthal have estimated that in about 15 years we should have atomic power plants enough to double the power production of the country, supplementing the hydroelectric plants and gradually replacing the steam plants which burn coal.

The many new radioactive isotopes made by nuclear reactions will also contribute greatly to the increased wellbeing of man. These isotopes are already being used in the treatment of disease, and they are rapidly becoming one of the most valuable tools for scientific and medical research.

The world can become a far better world, as a result of this great discovery. But the chance that it will become a better world is small, because the discovery also has led to the atomic bomb.

The United States and Russia are now preparing for a Third World War—an atomic war. Neither the United States nor Russia wants this war, but each is preparing to try to win it if it occurs, even though every nation will be the loser in an atomic war.

Such a war would devastate the world. It would effectively destroy civilization. Atomic bombs of the Nagasaki type, each one of which could destroy a city and kill 100,000 people, are being made in large numbers in the United States. Russia, too, will soon be making atomic bombs. New atomic superbombs may be built, which at one blow could kill every living being in a whole region of the country. There is no defense against atomic bombs.

What can we do, when the world is faced with these alternative prospects? Our only hope is to prevent another war, to enter upon an era of permanent peace.

Another war can be prevented only if some nation takes active leadership toward this end. The United States has the moral responsibility to lead the world to permanent peace. The people of the United States have a moral obligation to the people of the whole world. It is not enough for our nation just to get ready to win another war. Our nation must formulate and carry through a program of permanent world peace, and it must do this at once.

We cannot expect Russia to lead the world to permanent peace. Russia is a very large country, but it is still poor, suffering from the devastation of the last world war. Russia is a young, unsure nation, with an inferiority complex, which causes her diplomats to be recalcitrant, disagreeable, ready to fight for every possible advantage.

The United States is by far the richest nation in the world, by far the most stable, and by far the most powerful. It is clearly our moral duty to accept responsibility for the world as a whole, and by our firm, thoughtful, and determined leadership to eliminate war and ultimately, with the cooperation of all nations, to build a responsible world community.

This will not be an easy task for our government; but the job must be done, and the people of our nation must insist that it be done.

A MODEL FOR ACTIVIST COMMITMENT

"Addis was prepared to learn from, as well as to teach, everyone: 'wives, mothers, and sisters, who, with our patients, are our true colleagues with whom we work and from whom we learn.'"

Thomas Addis, M.D., ranks among the persons who most influenced Pauling in politics and humanitarianism in World War II and the early postwar period. Dr. Addis had virtually saved Pauling's life in 1941, after he was stricken with glomerular nephritis. Pauling spent two weeks as Addis's patient at the Stanford Hospital while the physician did precise clinical evaluations of his condition and determined a course of treatment. This involved eliminating complex meat proteins from the diet. Pauling got to know Addis well over the years, and they often talked and corresponded about politics. He also appreciated his personality and his colorful oddities. (Pauling loved to describe others' idiosyncrasies.)

When Pauling was in his early 90s he worked with Kevin V. Lemley to produce a biographical profile of Addis for publication by the National Academy of Sciences. Statements in this memoir indicate Pauling's deep personal gratitude to Addis, in part for modeling the role of a compassionate physician-scientist who also managed to be a political liberal (even radical) and a social activist—thereby risking professional opprobrium. Pauling would remember Addis when developing his ethical framework of basing commitments and moral decisions on the principle "minimize suffering." Also, Addis's example led Pauling to expect idealism and nonconformity within the medical profession. He was pleased whenever he saw it later, as in organizations such as Physicians for Social Responsibility.

As Pauling indicates in this selection, the overall experience with Addis introduced him to the potential value of science-based nutritional medicine in treating diseases, particularly ones—like his—considered intractable. In his later career, Pauling often feuded with the medical establishment, many of whose members resented his intrusion into their domain with his vitamin-promoting "orthomolecular medicine."

I was Dr. Addis's patient from March 1941 until his death [in 1949]. . . . I was placed on a salt-free diet, which eliminated the edema in four months, and on a rigorous minimum-protein diet, which I followed for 14 years. Addis also had me take supplementary vitamins and minerals, drink much water, and rest in bed to the extent that my professional duties permitted. I am now, 50 years later, in quite good health.

I remember that at one time, about 1942, I was with him in his cubicle, talking about the state of my health. We were interrupted by a phone call, which seemed to be about some political activity. He started to discuss it with me, and then interrupted himself to say, "No—pay no attention. Your job is to get well."

I now realize that Addis's regimen was completely orthomolecular. I received no drugs. My treatment involved only the regulation of the intake of substances normally present in the human body: increased intake of water, vitamins, and minerals and decreased intake of protein and, for a time, salt, combined with some rest in bed.

I dedicated my 1950 book *College Chemistry* to him with these words: "To the memory of Dr. Thomas Addis, who in applying science to medicine kept always uppermost his deep sympathy for mankind."

Tom Addis is remembered by his colleagues as a gentle and charismatic man, of broad learning and interests. He was no "ivory tower scientist." His daughter Jean remembered that his knowledge of poetry and economics and music "reached into his work . . . there was no division to all these things."

William Dock considered that "as a medical scientist he was in a class by himself." His approach to clinical problems was logical and incisive but also extremely practical. Although a consummate researcher, Addis was, according to Ray Wilbur, committed "not [to] research just for research's sake, but to [relieving] human suffering." To Arthur Bloomfield his relations with his patients were marked by "deep friendship and concern."

Despite the efforts of Addis and his colleagues, many patients eventually died of renal disease. This was a part of every "kidney man's" experience, before the advent of dialysis and transplantation. Addis found it very difficult to visit his patients when the end was near. But they would not be satisfied with any of his associates, so in the end he would see them and provide what comfort he could. "It is our job to do our best to keep [the patients] on the firing line to the very last gasp. Since our best endeavor amounts to almost nothing we need not take ourselves too seriously. . . . More and more we cease to play even a minor role in the drama. We retreat to the wings to watch the last act of the tragedy." The respect his patients' families felt for him was such that permission for postmortem examination was usually granted. Many of his wealthier patients and their families contributed financially to his clinic at Stanford.

Addis had eccentricities. Most of his professional correspondence was written by hand, Mrs. Addis typing only the most formal reports. He was rather indifferent toward payment for his services as a doctor, since seeing patients was one of those activities for which he was paid as a university professor. He was also probably the only man in San Francisco to have a charge account on the ferry and cable car lines, because he was so likely to forget his change. The conductors knew that Mrs. Addis would be by periodically to settle accounts. He was as likely to go home wearing his white lab coat as his blue suit coat, and he could announce that he was leaving for New York as casually as though he were just crossing the bay.

Although he rarely, if ever, held formal lectures at the medical school, Addis had a profound influence on many of the students and young physicians working in his clinic. He was instrumental in furthering the careers of several of them. . . .

The renal clinic was run along very democratic lines. All members were involved in virtually all aspects of the experiments, and pre-experiment "conferences" saw to it that everyone understood and viewed the "enterprise as an organic whole." Addis was prepared to learn from, as well as to teach, everyone: "wives, mothers, and sisters, who, with our patients, are our true colleagues with whom we work and from whom we learn." Addis's longtime laboratory assistants, Lee J. Poo and William Lew, would say that they worked "not for but with Dr. Addis." Indeed, both of them appeared often as coauthors on publications with him.

Addis's attitudes toward medicine and science cannot be separated. "[In the beginning] I was all set on measuring things and was trying to be 'scientific.' But anyone who has patients and patience can scarcely help coming at last to see that experiments that don't answer questions about patients are, for the doctor, pretty irrelevant. For the last 10 years or so we have not asked any questions from our rats that did not give us at least a hope of getting answers that referred to our patients." Addis's attitude toward his patients dominated his research work, and the Clinic for Renal Diseases at Stanford University held its sessions right in the laboratory, in the midst of experiments ("we can't separate the rats and the patients").

On clinic days the laboratory was a sight to be remembered. It was humming with activity. Patients sat all about, watching with interest the tests, both those that were routine and those that were part of some special research project, being made in front of their eyes. Then, when Dr. Addis saw one of his patients, the information about his or her condition was up to the minute. No distinction was made between clinic (usually nonpaying) and private patients, and each visitor waited in turn to see Dr. Addis. The normal administrative procedures of the hospital were often bypassed for renal patients in view of the frequency of their visits intended simply to follow the course of the disease. . . .

Although Addis could be found in his laboratory any day of the week during an experiment, life in the barnlike lab retained a pleasant and cultured atmosphere. Addis was a great lover of classical music, and during clinic days some Beethoven or Brahms chamber music might be playing on the phonograph in his office. Traditional tea time was also observed in the renal lab, attended by a variety of colleagues (such as Bloomfield and Dock) as well as laboratory personnel. Topics of discussion during these sessions could be the arts or history . . . although through the course of the 1930s the discussions turned increasingly often to political and social problems, such as the international rise of fascism.

Addis was an advocate of the civil rights of blacks, Jews, and the politically oppressed. In 1941 he interceded to try to get a teaching position for his friend Dr. Alfred Mirsky (because, he wrote to a friend, "It is true that it is hard for Jews to get teaching positions"). His political involvement was well summarized in a memorial address by his Stanford colleague physiology professor Frank W. Weymouth:

Injustice or oppression in the next street or . . . in any spot inhabited by men was a personal affront to Tom Addis and his name, from its early alphabetical place, was conspicuous on lists of sponsors of scores of organizations fighting for democracy and against fascism . . . and [he] worked on more committees than could reasonably have been expected of so busy a man. A picture comes to mind of his spare frame stretched out in a waiting room chair calculating from current experimental data on his slide rule as he waited with a delegation to present a complaint at the City Hall. . . . Tom Addis was happy to have a hand in bringing to the organization of society some of the logic of science and to further that understanding and to promote that democracy which are the only enduring foundations of human dignity.

Addis had great sympathy with the Republican cause in Spain. Josep Trueta, the noted trauma surgeon and occasional kidney physiologist, once wrote to Addis that he hoped to meet him one day "and talk of so many of the subjects of our common interest, like the kidney & Spain." Addis was for 12 years chairman of the San Francisco chapter of the Spanish Refugee Appeal. This organization, with the Joint Anti-Fascist Refugee Committee, was dedicated to helping political refugees from Franco's Spain, in part by supporting the Varsovia Hospital in Toulouse, France. The hospital was opened during the liberation of southern France during World War II and was run solely for the medical care of Spanish refugees from Franco's fascism. After Addis's death, funds raised by his San Francisco chapter helped to build a new diagnostic laboratory pavilion in the hospital. The pavilion, inaugurated on January 1, 1950, was named for Addis.

Addis was a onetime chairman of the San Francisco chapter of Physicians' Forum, a national organization favoring national health insurance. Such activities cost several physician acquaintances of Addis their membership in the medical association. In fact, Addis had been in and out of the American Medical Association throughout his career, resigning (or being expelled) shortly before his death for refusing to make a required $25 contribution to finance an AMA public relations campaign opposing President Truman's plan for national health insurance.

Addis made no secret of his sympathies toward the Soviet Union, at a time when one could be branded a "premature anti-fascist" simply for supporting the Spanish Republicans. Addis came back from a 1935 tour of the Soviet Union enthusiastic about the medical accomplishments of the socialist state (which included experimental human cadaveric kidney transplants as early as 1933). He also supported (at least in discussions at lab tea times) the concept of democratic centralism, which in retrospect played an important role in the development of Stalinism. He seemed to view it as an extension of the same organization of work that operated in his lab. One close colleague described his commitment to the Soviet system as "an act of faith." Left-wing political views and friendships with leftist activists such as Harry Bridges were "generally accepted as part of his eccentricities," according to Leona Bayer, tolerable foibles in such a respected scientist. Even conservative colleagues, such as the neurosurgeon Fred Fender, were among his admirers.

There is little consensus among his 28 former colleagues on how much Addis's political views and public stands may have influenced the decision to take away his lab at Stanford. Addis certainly perceived himself as somewhat of a nuisance to the administration at Stanford. He

expressed surprise as well as pleasure with the Festschrift in his honor
published in the Stanford Medical Bulletin (1948) "because I have spent
35 years . . . systematically insulting them because of what I regard as
their extraordinarily antiquated and dangerously stupid political notions."

A QUESTION OF LOYALTY

"You never know what you will do until the time arrives for you to do it."

There was always much more to Linus Pauling's life and work than his
ardent and visible peace advocacy, though after World War II this concern was never far from his mind or conscience. Readers should always
keep in mind that, in addition to his extensive political activism beginning
in the mid 1940s, Dr. Pauling was always deeply immersed in his own
professional work—as a chemistry professor; as a researcher involved in
many important scientific studies (including some in the new field of
molecular biology); and as chairman of the Division of Chemistry and
Chemical Engineering at the California Institute of Technology.

During the late 1940s and early '50s Pauling increasingly got into difficult straits because of his outspokenness and his inclination to join
associations and sign petitions—not necessarily because he knew much
about them, but because he agreed with their declared principles or
platforms and wanted to encourage them. This was a perilous and para-
noid time for liberals. The Cold War had arrived, and would endure for
four decades. The prewar alarm over the Soviet Union's human rights
violations under Stalin was reactivated by aggressive takeovers of Eastern European countries and the squabble over the status of Berlin. The
specter of world communism loomed. By 1949 Soviets had exploded
their first atomic bombs, and Mao Zedong's Red Army had conquered
China. It was only a question of time before the "Commies" got their own
mega-nuclear hydrogen bombs, probably mostly by stealing America's
secrets.

The "Red Scare" had begun. During this time a large number of
American citizens were blacklisted and otherwise persecuted because
of politically "leftist" beliefs and affiliations. The phenomenon is sometimes called McCarthyism because the best-known accuser and perse-
cutor was Senator Joseph McCarthy of Wisconsin. Another main figure
was California's Richard M. Nixon, who first gained attention on the
House Un-American Activities Committee (HUAC). He was elected to the
Senate in 1950 after an effective Commie-bashing political campaign.

In 1948, President Harry S. Truman responded to the growing concern over the Soviet potential to gain ascendancy over America by issuing Executive Order 9835. It required federal employees to take loyalty

oaths swearing that they were not members of the American Communist Party, which was accused of plotting the violent overthrow of the U.S. government. By 1950 faculty members at state universities were also compelled to sign a similar document. Pressure mounted on those professors at California universities who, out of principle, balked at signing. Most eventually capitulated; some resigned. A few others, facing termination from their positions, appealed for verbal and moral support from Pauling. As a tenured professor at a private academic and research institution, he was not obliged to take an oath. He wrote protest letters and spoke out publicly against the loyalty oath requirement, which he considered demeaning—and pointless, since people who really wished to sabotage the U.S. would have no scruples against simply lying.

Pauling was already snared in the widespread suspicion against independent-minded and "internationalist" activists. The bureaucratic agencies of nation and state, as well as administrators of academic institutions and management in industries and the entertainment business, worried about the possible presence of spies and agent-provocateurs within their own ranks. They did not wish to be even suspected of harboring any, which would reflect badly on their own integrity and affect their incomes. The Korean War's outbreak in 1950 sealed their lips.

Pauling did not at first fully understand the dangers ahead. The FBI and other governmental watchdog groups began keeping files on him and tracking his every speech and movement, including trips abroad.

In the postwar period the Paulings had become active members of the Hollywood chapter of ICCASP (Independent Citizens' Committee for the Arts, Sciences, and Professions), a national organization aiming to bring about liberal legislation through lobbying and influencing public opinion. At meetings Pauling—the group's trophy scientist, who was expected to recruit more of his kind—hobnobbed with such celebrity members as James Cagney, Charlie Chaplin, Edward G. Robinson, Olivia de Havilland, Frank Sinatra, and Orson Welles; with authors Thomas Mann and Aldous Huxley; screenwriter Dalton Trumbo (a friend who later was blacklisted among the "Hollywood Ten"); even with actor (and future conservative) Ronald Reagan. By the decade's end, however, ICCASP was being called a "Communist front" group, so Pauling's membership was held against him.

By 1950 Pauling was identified as someone who, possibly inadvertently, was undermining the United States—in part by failing to show a necessary animosity toward the Soviet Union. He believed that communication channels should be kept open between the two ideologically warring camps, particularly in scientific research. Moreover, conservative trustees at the California Institute of Technology were upset by his publicly stated opinions on a number of controversial issues, such as the loyalty oath. By identifying himself as a Caltech professor, he implied that the Institute officially approved of his statements and activities. The trustees began insisting on his dismissal, despite his reputation as a brilliant scientist who brought glory and research funds to Caltech.

In November of 1950 Pauling was suddenly subpoenaed to appear at a meeting convened in Los Angeles before the California State Legislature's Investigating Committee on Education. The committee was interrogating prominent troublemakers in the state's loyalty oath conflict.

A selection of Pauling's remarks shows his forthright words when subjected to hostile interrogators and fierce debate—the first of a number of such occasions in his lifetime. His comments also attest to his strong belief in democracy. But, after all, this was the man who at times would proudly announce, "As a citizen of the United States, I am, of course, a revolutionary; I subscribe to the Declaration of Independence."

I think there is nothing more important than preserving our national security by the proper security measures. . . . However, this must be done in such a way as to preserve our individual liberties. . . . I don't think this oath has anything to do really with communist activities. . . . It is only the people who have strong fundamental American convictions, who believe we must preserve democracy and keep to the spirit of our ancestors who fought at the time of the Revolution, who objected to signing it. . . .

Responding to a state senator who was grilling him, he said:

You believe it is not right to adhere to the principles of democracy. . . . The right decision to be made is from the average decisions of all people without precluding those whom you would suppress because of their opinion and political beliefs.

And to the committee members he observed with touching candor:

It seems to me that as I was thinking about my colleagues at the University of California who were cut off one by one—after thousands of them had voted in opposition to the loyalty oath, they were cut off one by one by the successive advocation of threats that they would lose their jobs and were required to give up their principles as good American citizens, their beliefs—that this was political pressure being imposed, as I have thought about them.

Finally, there were left just this little residue of the original number that were finally fired, a hundred or thereabouts. And as I have thought about them, I have tried to decide how long I would stick to my principles about the loyalty oath. I wasn't able to decide how much strength of character I would have. You never know what you will do until the time arrives for you to do it. I saw man after man, who had spoken strongly against this loyalty oath, sign it when it became evident that he would lose his job if he did not sign it.

Now, I feel that the same principle applies here, and I find it hard to decide myself whether to subject myself, perhaps legalistically, just because of a principle, to the difficulties that might arise. Nevertheless, it seems to me that the beliefs that I have about the proper working of democracy, the way that we can save this nation by preserving democracy against attacks that are being made against it, require that I refuse to answer any question as to my political beliefs and affiliations. And so I say that I shall not answer.

One senator asked Pauling, "Where would we land if every one of us went over and supported those communists, knowing that they were here under the supervision, or whatever you might call it, of a foreign country? Where would we land if we all took the same attitude?" Pauling, true to his trust in the basis of democracy, replied coolly:

You mean all of the people in the nation? . . . Well, then, we would presumably have a different form of government as a result of the choice of the people.

Pauling's testimony dissatisfied the committee, and he was told to return and undergo further interrogation. He was still suspected of being an American Communist Party member or something close to it. Meanwhile, Caltech was widely criticized for harboring such a traitor to the United States—someone who instilled dangerous radical ideas in gullible students. To mollify President Lee DuBridge and (he hoped) avoid dismissal, while also upholding the right to keep one's private political opinions, Pauling wrote a letter further explaining his position. It was the sort of statement he found himself making again and again in future years. He then read it to the committee:

I am not a communist. I have never been a communist. I have never been involved with the Communist Party. . . . I am not opposed to loyalty oaths in general. I have voluntarily taken many loyalty oaths in connection with my services to the nation. . . . [But] I believe that a citizen has the right to announce his political beliefs if he desires, and that he also has a right to keep them to himself if he desires. I may say that I am not personally sympathetic to the extremes of belief and policy that I understand some communists to hold; but I feel that we must staunchly support the basic principles of our democracy, including the right of people to hold even extreme political beliefs.

PASSPORT PENDING

"I was persona non grata in the early 1950s in both the Soviet Union and the United States."

Following his highly public troubles over the loyalty oath, mounting attacks on his character, and investigations of his political associations by Caltech and government agencies, for over a year Pauling mostly retired from activism. He kept busy with his scientific research projects, which included discovering the alpha helix structure of protein substances and identifying the molecular cause of the genetic disease sickle-cell anemia. Ironically, however, he was hauled back into the fray. In 1952, in the midst of the prevailing climate of fear and loathing toward communists, the State Department's Division of Passports refused to reissue Linus Pauling's passport. Notable scientists and political leaders from around the world, even those who disagreed with Pauling's antinuclear and pro-world government stand, protested the ignominious treatment of one of America's leading scientists.

Only after Pauling was chosen for the highest award possible in science, toward the end of 1954, did he obtain a regular passport—as this reminiscence recounts. It was already clear that the receipt of the Nobel Prize in Chemistry finally pushed or embarrassed the State Department into reinstating Pauling's open passport. One serious consequence of this inability to travel abroad was his absence from a crucial 1952 meeting in London that might have disclosed to him the sought-after structure of DNA.

A year after he received an unrestricted passport, Pauling finally gained a legislative hearing on his grievances with the State Department and its Passport Division. Here are some excerpts from Pauling's testimony to the Senate Subcommittee on Constitutional Rights, of the Committee on the Judiciary in November of 1955. Pauling bristled verbally when the senators and their counsel reviewed the Passport Division's argument that Pauling was a security risk because of his history of associations with communist front organizations, which directed his actions. "I don't follow any line. I decide myself what I think that I should do, and I am in a position such that often I am able to do it." Later, with some humor, he admitted that only his wife could tell him what to think or do.

Pauling's experiences and his candid testimony showed ample reason why Congress had instituted a review and appeal process for

Americans who might encounter similarly arbitrary, unaccountable refusals of passports by the State Department.

Here is how he told the story 40 years later to Griffin Fariello, who was preparing an oral history of this notorious witch-hunt period.

In 1952, I wanted to go to a meeting, a symposium arranged by the Royal Society of London to discuss my discoveries on the structure of proteins. I was to be the first speaker and people from various countries working on protein structure were the other speakers. My passport had expired, so I had to apply again. I didn't get the passport. We got as far as New York and Washington, my wife and I, led on by the Passport Office, who kept saying things like, "When you get to New York, you can get the passport," and then I went down to Washington and at the last minute they said, "No, we're not issuing the passport." So we went back to Pasadena. I missed the symposium. Some say that if I'd been there, I would have discovered the double-helix in place of Watson and Crick. I won't go into it, but if I'd gone to that meeting in London and seen Franklin's X-ray photographs, which Watson and Crick saw . . . well, who knows?

I asked on my various stays in Washington why I had been denied, talking to the authorities and the officials in the Passport Department. The first answer I got was, "Not in the best interests of the United States." This wasn't very illuminating. Then they said, "Your anticommunist statements haven't been strong enough." They couldn't say, "You haven't made any anticommunist statements." I was having a fight with the communists at the same time. The Soviets had come out in 1949 with an attack on me, saying that my ideas about chemistry were incompatible with dialectical materialism, that no patriotic Soviet scientist should use them. The professor who had translated my book, *The Nature of the Chemical Bond*, into Russian was fired and never got his professorship back. One of the young professors who attacked me got his professorship. So I was persona non grata in the early 1950s in both the Soviet Union and the United States.

The following year, I was invited by Nehru to visit universities and scientific laboratories in India and to help dedicate a new scientific institute, and I accepted. I also accepted the invitations to give a set of lectures in Greece and then a set in Jerusalem. So, we went to the Passport Office in New York and they said, "Come back tomorrow, we don't have word." And then they said, "You have to go to Washington and see the authorities in the Passport Division." So I sent a cable to Athens canceling my lectures. We went to Washington about the 18th of December, and for several days I went to the Passport Office. And then they said, "Come back after Christmas." So I sent a cable to Israel, canceling. Then I went back after Christmas and they said, "Come back after New Year's." So I sent a cable to Nehru, canceling. By this time my wife and I were so unhappy and discouraged, being in Washington, D.C., on Christmas, you know, with this hanging over our heads we just gave up and went back to Pasadena.

Senator Morse of Oregon introduced legislation that required the State Department to set up a system whereby anyone whose passport was denied could appeal. The State Department went ahead and set up an appeal board. But I couldn't appeal, because Mrs. Shipley, the director of the Passport Division, never refused to issue the passport. She was too smart for me. She never officially denied me a passport: she just wouldn't issue me one. So I had nothing to appeal! [Laughs.]

The next year, 1954, I was reinvited back to India, and I applied again for the passport. I had had one issued a couple of times in between, limited usually to two months. In each case, I had participated in important scientific meetings. So I sent in an application to go to India again, and it was just denied. I thought, "Well, the heck with it. I'll notify Nehru that I can't come." But then it was announced, in late October of 1954, that I was to be given the Nobel Prize in Chemistry. The *New York Times* carried an article—"Is Professor Pauling going to be allowed to go to Stockholm to get his Nobel Prize?" The State Department didn't have the guts to stick to their policy, so I received the passport through the mail. That was the last time I've had passport problems.

PUNISHING ANOTHER DISSENTER

"It may be expected that many thoughtful scientists will decide that it is dangerous to make an important contribution to the national welfare."

Linus Pauling was by no means the only scientist to suffer mistreatment from government bureaucrats and others during the early years of the Cold War. The mean spirit of McCarthyism ran roughshod over America.

Noted physicist J. Robert Oppenheimer had served on the Caltech faculty with Pauling for several years in the late 1930s. When appointed director of the Los Alamos laboratory that would build the first atomic bombs, he asked Pauling to join him there as head of chemistry, but Pauling—busy with other war work and also in precarious health—declined.

After the A-bombs were dropped on Japan, Oppenheimer became a prominent early opponent of nuclear weapons, particularly the hydrogen bomb. (See Part III, pages 105-110.) He promoted civilian control of nuclear power and international cooperation in its peacetime uses in the areas of power generation, industry, and medicine. After serving for six years as chairman of the general advisory board of the new Atomic Energy Commission (AEC), he was dismissed in 1953 as a security risk. His former colleague and friend Pauling leapt to his defense, though he knew that doing so would add further to his reputation as a contemptible "fellow traveler."

At times like this, Pauling possessed one of the few courageous public voices "crying in the wilderness" of a fervid anticommunism. The climate was intensified by the Soviets' success at making their own A-bombs and the apparent triumph of a militant Marxism elsewhere in the world. "A Disgraceful Act" is what Pauling's defense of Oppenheimer was titled when it appeared in *The Nation* in 1954.

The suspension as a security risk of Dr. T. Robert Oppenheimer from his advisory activities with the Atomic Energy Commission constitutes a disgraceful act on the part of the government of the United States. This display of ingratitude toward a man who has been foremost among the scientists of the country in unselfish service to the nation cannot be justified by any rational argument. His reputation has been seriously damaged, and it will remain damaged, no matter what is the outcome of his loyalty hearing.

There is no question about Dr. Oppenheimer's loyalty. It is stated, and he has himself announced, that in the 1930s he had among his friends some who were interested in communism and social and political questions and who may have been communists. In the 1940s and 1950s he spent most of his time, energy, and extraordinary ability in outstanding service to the nation.

Throughout this recent period he has sacrificed his own career as a productive scientist in order to perform a public service. Few men have better deserved the nation's highest award to civilians, the Presidential Medal for Merit, which was presented to him by President Truman at the end of the war.

The conclusion that Dr. Oppenheimer is a loyal and patriotic American must be reached by any sensible person who considers the facts. It must have been reached by the officials of the AEC, and by President Eisenhower himself. We are accordingly forced to believe that the recent action is the result of political considerations—that Dr. Oppenheimer has been sacrificed by the government to protect itself against McCarthyism. This action is sure to have serious consequences to the nation. It may be expected that many thoughtful scientists will decide that it is dangerous to make an important contribution to the national welfare, and that they should not accept employment in government agencies, or should be careful that their contributions are not outstanding.

It has been said that Dr. Oppenheimer opposed the H-bomb program at the time, 1949, when the initiation of this program was under consideration. Dr. Oppenheimer is to be commended if he advanced moral and ethical arguments against the manufacture of that greatest of all weapons of mass destruction, the H-bomb. In 1949, when scientists knew that the bomb could be made, the government might have initiated vigorous negotiation with the rest of the world to achieve a system of general disarmament, abolition of atomic weapons, and settlement of differences between nations through arbitration and the use of a strengthened United Nations.

Now, when hydrogen bombs have been made and exploded, there no longer remains even the slightest doubt that their use in war would cause the end of civilization. Instead of raising trivial questions about Dr. Oppenheimer's loyalty, which he has demonstrated time and again since 1940 through his deeds, the government should be asking him to use his great intellectual ability, in collaboration with many other outstandingly able physical scientists, social scientists, and specialists on international relations and other aspects of the world problem, to find a practical alternative to the madness of atomic barbarism.

DON'T BELIEVE YOUR ELDERS!

"The world progresses, year by year, century by century, as the members of the younger generation find out what was wrong among the things that their elders said."

Linus Pauling always characterized himself as a skeptic. He felt, indeed, that to be a good scientist one had to be skeptical, to always question accepted and entrenched authority; to seek out the facts, organize and consider them objectively, and draw one's own conclusions. In other words, think for yourself. Then, having decided what the truth was, consider what the acknowledged authorities, past and present, said. Perhaps you would agree with them; perhaps not.

"Science is the search for truth," was one of Pauling's favorite sayings. He had learned that too often old truths were based on imperfect observation and evidence. It was crucial to question the established experts—especially when they had been regarded so for many years—and even challenge them if their findings seemed doubtful. Science, like religious beliefs, could harden into dogma. Truth-seekers in history, such as Galileo and Darwin, had often been condemned as heretics and blasphemers. So had religious rebels like Martin Luther and the 18th-century minister-chemist Joseph Priestley (who as a political activist was a Pauling role model; see pages 241-242). Why should this period be any different?

Pauling, the master teacher, always had a special interest in and fondness for the younger generations of students. He regarded them as the torch-bearers for humankind's future. He gave the often-quoted talk below on December 10, 1954, at a torchlight procession outside the government palace in Stockholm, Sweden, where the Nobel Award ceremony had just taken place. Pauling, who had won the Nobel Prize in Chemistry, was delegated by the other Nobelists to address the throng of young people. Not surprisingly, he encouraged a healthy skepticism of authority and activism against any entrenched establishment—a youthful stance that he himself, at the age of 53, retained.

When reading the brief talk below, it is useful to remember that for at least five years Pauling had endured suspicion from colleagues and administrators, and downright persecution from government officials. Pauling was only in Stockholm now because his Nobel Prize had embarrassed the U.S. State Department into finally issuing him the unrestricted passport he had vainly sought for several years.

So here he was—at middle age still young, skeptical, witty, and rebellious at heart. He would need all that as well as his courage, energy, and commitment in the years ahead. More rejection and vilification awaited him because of his widely expressed opinions on world peace, war, and nuclear weaponry. It was inevitable that he would be an ongoing focal point of political agitation.

Young men and women:
On behalf of my colleagues, as well as myself, I thank you for your kind demonstration of friendship and respect.

I am reminded of my own students in California. They are much like you—I have observed that students, young people, are much the same all over the world—and that scientists are the same. There is a worldwide brotherhood of youth and science.

Perhaps, as one of the older generation, I should preach a little sermon to you, but I do not propose to do so. I shall, instead, give you a word of advice about how to behave toward your elders.

When an old and distinguished person speaks to you, listen to him carefully and with respect—but do not believe him. Never put your trust in anything but your own intellect. Your elder, no matter whether he has gray hair or has lost his hair, no matter whether he is a Nobel Laureate, may be wrong. The world progresses, year by year, century by century, as the members of the younger generation find out what was wrong among the things that their elders said. So you must always be skeptical—always think for yourself.

There are, of course, exceptional circumstances: when you are taking an examination, it is smart to answer the questions not by saying what you think is right, but rather what you think the professor thinks is right. . . .

You will have some great problems to solve—the greatest of all is the problem of war and peace. I believe that this problem has been solved, by the hydrogen bomb—that there will never again be a world war—the knowledge that a world war would mean worldwide destruction, perhaps the end of civilization, will surely now lead to permanent peace.

But it is your generation that will have the job of working out the means of preventing disaster, by developing safeguards against paranoiac demagogues who might make nations rabid; you will have this great job to do—and I am confident that you can do it.

THE RUSSELL-EINSTEIN MANIFESTO OF 1955

"Remember your humanity, and forget the rest. . . . If you cannot, there lies before you the risk of universal death."

Pauling was not the only concerned scientist who protested the incessant development and military buildup of nuclear weaponry. Their public protest activities accelerated after the advent of hydrogen and thermonuclear bombs—the two-stage H-bombs and the three-stage "super-bombs" using fission-fusion-fission explosions with one triggering the next. (See Part III, pages 105-120.)

In his lectures and writings Pauling often referred to various antinuclear documents that scientists and other concerned citizens of the world had composed, signed, and published. One of them, the Mainau Declaration, submitted by 52 Nobel Laureates in 1955, warned at its conclusion: "All nations must come to the decision to renounce force as a final resort of policy. If they are not prepared to do this, they will cease to exist."

Another prominent statement made in 1955, also in response to the tremendous assemblage and dispersal of nuclear armaments by both sides of the Cold War, was basically written by Bertrand Russell, the British mathematician, philosopher, and political radical. The document was then signed by nine other notable scientists, including Linus Pauling—who furnished the explanation for it here. Featured among them—his name was on the title—was Professor Albert Einstein, the brilliant German-Jewish physicist who had lived and worked at Princeton University since leaving Nazi Germany in 1933. The Manifesto was, in effect, Einstein's last public statement on behalf of peace. He died several days later.

Einstein inspired Pauling's commitment to world peace and antinuclear activities more than anyone except Ava Helen. After Pauling received the Nobel Prize in Chemistry in 1954, he and Einstein discussed how this great honor could help his work in the political arena. Einstein pointed out to Pauling that "if you want to make an impression on people, then you have to make a somewhat extreme statement"—a tip that Pauling never forgot. Sometimes he appeared to delight in causing consternation by making outrageous remarks or launching attacks on public personages for their actions or opinions.

At the same time, Pauling admired the people who consistently supported peace efforts and argued against nuclear expansion, particularly those in peril for their outspokenness. By quoting other people, Pauling amplified their urgent antiwar messages to the world.

He wrote the following commentary, within a talk to science educators, a decade after the Russell-Einstein Manifesto was published.* The passage is taken from one of his main statements regarding the duty of scientists to improve human society. It provides a glimpse at future changes, many of them positive, attributable to the intense politicizing efforts of internationally respected scientist-activists like Pauling, Russell, and those who attended the famous Pugwash conferences that brought together scientists from around the world. Pauling also commented here on the probable effect that the Scientists' Appeal he initiated in 1957 (see pages 77-83) had on public opinion and government action.

D uring the year after the explosion of the Bikini bomb on the first of March 1954, Lord Russell had given a number of BBC and other talks on the crisis that faced the world when the bombs became a thousand times more powerful than those that destroyed Hiroshima and Nagasaki. On the ninth of July 1955, he issued a statement that had been signed by Professor Einstein a few days before his death and by nine other scientists, along with Lord Russell.

---

* Reprinted with permission from NSTA Publications, Sept. 1990, from *The Science Teacher*, National Science Teachers Association, 1840 Wilson Blvd., Arlington, VA 22201-3000.

In the tragic situation that confronts humanity we feel that scientists should assemble in conference to appraise the perils that have arisen as a result of the development of weapons of mass destruction, and to discuss a resolution in the spirit of the appended draft.

We are speaking on this occasion not as members of this or that nation, continent, or creed, but as human beings, members of the species man, whose continued existence is in doubt. The world is full of conflict, and, overshadowing all minor conflicts, the titanic struggle between communism and anti-communism. Almost everybody who is politically conscious has strong feelings about one or more of these issues, but we want you, if you can, to set aside such feelings and consider yourselves only as members of a biological species which has had a remarkable history and whose disappearance none of us can desire.

We shall try to say no single word which should appeal to one group rather than another. All, equally, are now in peril, and, if the peril is understood, there is hope that they may collectively avert it.

We have to learn to think in a new way. We have to learn to ask ourselves not what steps can be taken to give military victory to whatever group we prefer, for there no longer are such steps. The question we have to ask ourselves is: What steps can be taken to prevent a military contest of which the issue must be disastrous to all parties?

The general public and even many men in positions of authority have not realized what would be involved in a war with nuclear bombs. The general public still thinks in terms of the obliteration of cities. It is understood that the new bombs are more powerful than the old, and that, while one A-bomb could obliterate Hiroshima, one H-bomb could obliterate the largest cities, such as London, New York, and Moscow. No doubt in an H-bomb war great cities would be obliterated. But this would be one of the minor disasters that would have to be faced. If everybody in London, New York, and Moscow were exterminated, the world might, in the course of a few centuries, recover from the blow. But we know, especially since the Bikini test, that nuclear bombs can gradually spread destruction over a very much wider area than had been supposed.

It is stated on very good authority that a bomb can now be manufactured which will be 25 hundred times as powerful as that which destroyed Hiroshima. Such a bomb, if exploded near the ground or under water, sends radioactive particles into the upper air. They sink gradually and reach the surface of the earth in the form of a deadly dust or rain. It was this dust which infected the Japanese fishermen and their catch of fish. No one knows how widely such lethal radioactive particles might be diffused, but the best authorities are unanimous in saying that a war with H-bombs might quite possibly put an end to the human race. It is feared that if many H-bombs are used there will be universal death, sudden only for a minority, but for the majority a slow torture of disease and disintegration.

Many warnings have been uttered by eminent men of science and by authorities in military strategy. None of them will say that the worst results are certain. What they do say is that these results are possible, and no one can be sure that they will not be realized. We have not yet found that the views of experts on this question depend in any degree upon their politics or prejudices. They depend only, so far as our researches have revealed, upon the extent of the particular expert's knowledge. We have found that the men who know the most are the most gloomy.

Here, then, is the problem which we present to you, stark and dreadful and inescapable. Shall we put an end to the human race? Or, shall mankind renounce war?

People will not face this alternative, because it is so difficult to renounce war. The abolition of war will demand distasteful limitations of national sovereignty. But what perhaps impedes understanding of the situation more than anything else is that the term "mankind" feels vague and abstract. People scarcely realize in imagination that the danger is to themselves and their children and their grandchildren, and not only to a dimly apprehended humanity. They can scarcely bring themselves to grasp that they, individually, and those whom they love, are in imminent danger of perishing agonizingly, and so they hope that perhaps war may be allowed to continue, provided that modern weapons are prohibited.

This hope is illusory. Whatever agreements not to use H-bombs had been reached in time of peace, they would no longer be considered binding in time of war, and both sides would set to work to manufacture H-bombs as soon as war broke out, for, if one side manufactured the bombs and the other did not, the side that manufactured them would inevitably be victorious.

Although an agreement to renounce nuclear weapons as part of a general reduction of armaments would not afford an ultimate solution, it would serve certain important purposes. First, any agreement between East and West is to the good, insofar as it tends to diminish tension. Second, the abolition of thermonuclear weapons, if each side believed that the other had carried it out sincerely, would lessen the fear of a sudden attack in the style of Pearl Harbor, which at present keeps both sides in a state of nervous apprehension. We should, therefore, welcome such an agreement, though only as a first step.

Most of us are not neutral in feeling, but, as human beings, we have to remember that if the issues between East and West are to be decided in any manner that can give any possible satisfaction to anybody, whether communist or anticommunist, whether Asian or European or American, whether white or black, then these issues must not be decided by war. We should wish this to be understood, both in the East and in the West.

There lies before us, if we choose, continual progress in happiness, knowledge, and wisdom. Shall we, instead, choose death, because we cannot forget our quarrels? We appeal, as human beings, to human beings: Remember your humanity and forget the rest. If you can do so, the way lies open to a new Paradise. If you cannot, there lies before you the risk of universal death.

RESOLUTION: We invite this Congress, and through it the scientists of the world and the general public, to subscribe to the following resolution:

In view of the fact that in any future world war nuclear weapons will certainly be employed, and that such weapons threaten the continued existence of mankind, we urge the Governments of the world to realize, and to acknowledge publicly, that their purpose cannot be furthered by a world war, and we urge them consequently to find peaceful means for the settlement of all matters of dispute between them.

This Manifesto was signed by Professor Max Born, Professor P. W. Bridgman of Harvard, Professor Albert Einstein, Professor Leopold Infeld, Professor Frédéric Joliot-Curie, Professor Hermann Joseph Muller, Professor Linus Pauling, Professor C. F. Powell, Joseph Rotblat, Lord Russell, and Hideki Yukawa. Nine of them are recipients of the Nobel Prize.

The Russell-Einstein Manifesto attracted great interest at the time, and it led to setting up the Pugwash Conferences, 14 of which have been held. These conferences are on the social responsibilities of scientists. They began in 1957 and have been attended by over 300 scientists from about 30 countries. The topics taken up in the Pugwash Conferences are dangers of nuclear war, arms control, disarmament and world security, biological and chemical warfare, and international cooperation in pure and applied sciences.

Dr. Rotblat, in *The History of the Pugwash Conferences*, says that in the second Pugwash Conference most of the issues, about arms control, disarmament, world security, and bomb test fallout, were highly complex, and that in many instances the scientists in the West received for the first time reasoned objections to their views from scientists from the East, and vice versa.

I have little doubt that the Pugwash Conferences contributed greatly to the achievement of the 1960 treaty on Antarctica as a nuclear-free zone and the 1963 partial bomb test-ban treaty and to the announcement made by nearly all the nations of the world that their goal is the abolition of war. I believe that these treaties would not have been made had it not been for the acceptance of their social responsibilities by scientists in many countries in the world. But this is a slow process, as you recognize from the problems as outlined in the Russell-Einstein Manifesto.

These problems are in large part still with us. We have, I believe, gone through the period of greatest danger. We now have achieved a state of accepted coexistence of the United States and the Soviet Union. No longer does there exist the antagonism that there was 11 years ago or even five years ago. The understanding of the situation exists now. It has been accepted—accepted in government circles. But, still, there is much need for education of the public and also of those responsible for national policy.

THE SCIENTISTS PROTEST

"If testing continues, and the possession of these weapons spreads to additional governments, the danger of outbreak of a cataclysmic nuclear war through the reckless action of some irresponsible national leader will be greatly increased."

It wasn't as if Linus Pauling had nothing to do with his time other than agitate. In 1957 he had plenty of things to keep him busy. Besides teaching and administrative responsibilities at Caltech, his various scientific projects demanded attention—among them medical research. By the mid 1950s, he ended his work with heredity disorders of hemoglobin in red blood cells, and began focusing on genetic and biochemical causes for mental disease and retardation. His knowledge of the prevalence of mental and emotional problems contributed to his acute awareness that in the wrong hands, control over nuclear weapons could result in terrible consequences. (This possibility of course was depicted in 1964 in the popular black-comedy movie *Dr. Strangelove.*) As he said in 1957:

> *Ten percent of the American people spend some part of their lives in a mental hospital. I have been working on the chemical basis of mental disease for many years, and I often wonder how many mentally diseased persons are in the armed forces. I am troubled when I think about the possibility of nuclear war by accident, or by the action of some irresponsible person. Never before have we been in such great danger. Never before has there been the possibility that our great nation would cease to exist and all the American people would be killed. At the same time, of course, the Soviet Union would cease to exist and all the Russian people would be killed; but this thought does not make me feel any better.*

By 1957 Pauling's peace-connected concern had zeroed in on an urgent public health issue: radioactive fallout, coming from successions of bomb tests by the U.S. and the Soviet Union. (See Part III, pages 111-145, for Pauling's more technical discussions about nuclear weapons, tests conducted with them, and the resultant fallout.) During that year Pauling became involved in what was to be the most notable political-activist campaign he ever engaged in: "An Appeal by Scientists to Governments and People of the World"—an international petition effort to ban nuclear testing.

Here is how Pauling told the story of its origin and surprising expansion when talking with an interviewer two decades later.

When it became evident that the testing of nuclear weapons in the atmosphere was causing damage, I began to worry about that and to look into the matter to see how much damage to the pool of human germ plasm was being done—the extent to which human beings were being caused to have a higher incidence of cancer than if the bomb tests hadn't been carried out. I became more and more concerned, the more and more I learned. I had, of course, a background of knowledge in nuclear physics, physics, and chemistry in general, also in biology and medicine, that not many people had. I was able to draw conclusions on the basis of a rather limited amount of information.

I gave a lecture in a symposium on this subject in Washington University in St. Louis, for the honors graduates of the university. It received an astounding reception, and I decided—together with Barry Commoner [a botany professor] and Ed Condon, a professor of physics—to prepare an appeal to the United Nations to stop the testing of nuclear weapons in order to stop damaging the pool of human germ plasm and increasing the number of cancer cases. We got 2,500 signatures from American scientists within a month or two. A few months later I decided to distribute it over the world, and we got altogether 13,000 signatures from scientists in 50 different countries. My wife and I presented these signatures to Dag Hammarskjöld at the United Nations. President Kennedy finally decided that the thing to do was to stop the nuclear testing and the partial bomb-test treaty was made.

Pauling's later recollections of this large-scale effort varied somewhat in their details and often left out certain stages of the story. In early June the American scientists' petition, with its more than 2,000 signatures obtained in 10 days, was sent to a joint Congressional subcommittee investigating atomic radiation. It also went to President Eisenhower and was issued as a press release. As soon as some European scientists set eyes on the American scientists' test-ban petition, they began crossing out the word "American." Circulating copies among their colleagues, they sent the signed petitions to Pauling.

By September, the Paulings decided to widen the appeal. They mailed out some 500 letters and unsigned petitions to scientists they already knew and to professors of science, particularly chemistry and biology, located in many other nations. By the end of the year they had received over 7,500 foreign signatures from 48 countries. They decided to present the petition with all the signatures, including the American ones, to the United Nations in mid January, when they were scheduled to be in New York for a special program. (In the months afterward more signatures arrived. The final total was over 13,000 signatures from 50 nations.)

Among the signers were 37 Nobel Laureates, 105 members of the National Academy of Sciences (one-fifth of the membership), 95 Fellows of the Royal Society of London, and 216 of the Soviet Union's leading scientists. "It is significant," Pauling commented, "that most of the leading geneticists of the country [U.S.] signed the appeal. It is, of course, the geneticists who understand best the damage that radiation can do to the human race by its action on the genes, and who are most concerned about this aspect of the bomb tests and of nuclear war."

Here is the full text of the famous Appeal:

W e the scientists whose names are signed below, urge that an international agreement to stop the testing of nuclear bombs be made now.

Each nuclear bomb test spreads an added burden of radioactive elements over every part of the world. Each added amount of radiation causes damage to the health of human beings all over the world and causes damage to the pool of human germ plasm such as to lead to an increase in the number of seriously defective children that will be born in future generations.

So long as these weapons are in the hands of only three powers an agreement for their control is feasible. If testing continues, and the possession of these weapons spreads to additional governments, the danger of outbreak of a cataclysmic nuclear war through the reckless action of some irresponsible national leader will be greatly increased.

An international agreement to stop the testing of nuclear bombs now could serve as a first step toward a more general disarmament and the ultimate effective abolition of nuclear weapons, averting the possibility of a nuclear war that would be a catastrophe to all humanity.

We have in common with our fellowmen a deep concern for the welfare of all human beings. As scientists we have knowledge of the dangers involved and therefore a special responsibility to make those dangers known. We deem it imperative that immediate action be taken to effect an international agreement to stop the testing of all nuclear weapons.

DEFENDING THE RIGHT TO PETITION

"The danger is not from peace or from the workers for peace, or from the circulators of petitions urging international law and international agreements. It is from the stockpiles of nuclear weapons that exist in the world."

Linus Pauling's determination to circulate a test-ban petition among the international scientific community and turn it over to the United Nations brought him a new set of troubles. The Senate Internal Affairs Subcommittee (the Senate's equivalent of Congress' HUAC) wanted to call him in because they suspected his motivation. Some believed that this was part of a communist plot to embarrass the U.S. and interfere with its weapons development. But the interrogation was delayed for two years. In the meantime, disarmament and nuclear test-ban negotiations had begun and were proceeding, slowly and painstakingly, in Geneva. And there had been a welcome hiatus in nuclear testing, apparently brought on by Pauling's petition and other protests to the Soviet and American governments. (See pages 132-140.)

The subpoena summoning Pauling finally came in 1960, more than two years after the petition's delivery. It became clear that the subcommittee members hoped to find out which persons and organizations had helped Pauling in his efforts. But Pauling refused to identify any of his assistants. The subcommittee told him to think it over for a few months, implying that if he still refused he would risk being found in contempt of Congress and subject to imprisonment.

By 1960 the anticommunist demagogue Joseph McCarthy was gone, destroyed by alcoholism and his own zealotry. In any case, most Americans no longer believed his vicious, unfounded attacks on supposed communists and communist sympathizers, especially after the Korean War ended. He had also been humiliated during televised hearings conducted by his own Senate investigative subcommittee, and by a candid TV profile by Edward R. Murrow. Still, the Red-baiting mood remained in the Capitol and elsewhere. The Hollywood blacklist of writers and other creative persons still was in force, and the FBI under J. Edgar Hoover's vigilant direction spied on people involved in the civil-rights and other liberal movements. By now, however, there were significant objections to the persecution of Pauling.

After four months Pauling came back to the subcommittee and told its chairman, Senator Thomas Dodd, why he was not going to give any names other than those who signed the petition itself. Because of Pauling's efforts and protests by many other people, including journalists, a firestorm of outrage would have resulted from sending Pauling to jail for contempt. Instead of using the Fifth Amendment to account for his refusal, as a number of people in similar interrogations did, Pauling chose to use the First Amendment, focusing on the right to petition the government. Dodd and his attorney then subjected him to a series of leading questions about his membership or support of various organizations, causes, and individuals—apparently intent upon showing that Pauling's antinuclear efforts were communist-directed. Finally, Pauling was permitted to leave, a free man still, and pleased that the United States was seriously involved in negotiations with the Soviet Union to end nuclear testing. He did, however, contest Dodd's "editing" of the published sessions.

The circulating of petitions is an important part of our democratic process. If it were to be abolished or greatly inhibited, our nation would have made a step toward deterioration—perhaps toward a state of dictatorship, a police state.

I am very much interested in our nation, the United States of America, and in the procedures that were set up in the Constitution and the Bill of Rights. Now, no matter what assurances this subcommittee might give me about the use of the names of the people who circulated the petition that I wrote, I am convinced that these names would be used for reprisals against these believers in the democratic process, these enthusiastic, idealistic, high-minded workers for peace. I am convinced of this because I myself have experienced the period of McCarthyism and to some extent have suffered from it, in ways that I shall not mention. I am convinced of it because I have observed the workings of the Committee on Un-American Activities of the House of Representatives and of this Subcommittee on Internal Security of the Judiciary Committee of the Senate.

I feel that if these names were to be given to this subcommittee the hope for peace in the world would be dealt a severe blow. Our nation is in great danger now, greater danger than ever before. The danger is not from peace or from the workers for peace, or from the circulators of petitions urging international law and international agreements. It is from the stockpiles of nuclear weapons that exist in the world, which have the capability of destroying the world. . . . This danger, the danger of destruction in a nuclear war, would become even greater than it is now if the work for peace in the world, peace and international law and international agreements, were hampered.

A terrible attack is being made now in the United States on the efforts of our government to achieve international agreements on stopping the bomb tests and for disarmament. This attack is being made by representatives of defense industries who benefit financially from the Cold War. . . .

If two nations, the USSR and the United States, were to try to follow the policy of each striving to exceed the other in the power of destruction year after year, then we would truly be doomed to catastrophe. Then the nuclear war that will destroy civilization surely would come.

I believe that the work for peace and morality and justice in the world needs to be intensified now, and I plan to do whatever I can in working for peace in the world, working for international agreements about disarmament; always, of course, such that they increase the safety of the United States and do not decrease it, and involving controls and inspection. . . .

I am responsible for my actions, and I wrote the petition and I sent it out to people, asking that they get signatures to it. I have selected the many people to whom these petitions were to be sent. I think that my reputation and example may well have led these younger people to work for peace in this way. My conscience will not allow me to protect myself by sacrificing these idealistic and hopeful people, and I am not going to do it. As a matter of conscience, as a matter of principle, as a matter of morality, I have decided that I shall not conform to the request of this subcommittee.

In Part III, Linus Pauling expands on the main issues in the test-ban petition. The harnessing of atomic energy—and the nuclear weapons made as a result—transformed the way he and many other people regarded the prospect of another great war.

But first an "interlude" to acquaint readers with the person and the relationship that pushed and pulled Pauling into political activism. He invested a significant amount of time, mental effort, and physical energy in causes relating to world peace and other humanitarian concerns. Since many of these coincided with the peak discovery period of his professional career, the work came at a cost to his scientific achievements, and he knew it. But perhaps Pauling, intensely creative and astoundingly productive, could afford to do it more than most. He did this work, he said, for humankind—and for Ava Helen Pauling.

Ava Helen Miller and Linus Pauling at a party at her mother's house in Corvallis after Linus' college graduation. The couple would marry the following year. (Photo courtesy of Linda Pauling-Kamb)

Interlude

A Partnership in Life . . . and Peace Work: Ava Helen and Linus Pauling

Anyone who knew Linus Pauling, either personally or from his political activities, was aware that he attributed his humanitarian views and social activism to his wife's early and pervasive influence. In their longstanding peace campaign the Paulings worked together—giving speeches and attending conferences, talking with reporters and interviewers, writing letters and articles and public statements. All of this required time-consuming preparatory research, effective responses, intense strategy talks, and correspondence with like-minded people.

During the 1980s Pauling began considering where to consign his lifetime accumulation of papers and other memorabilia—including his many medals, particularly the two gold Nobel awards. He thought so highly of Ava Helen's work, especially her contributions to the world peace movement, that he set the condition that the recipient repository must welcome his wife's papers as well. The only institutional archive that agreed to his wish was Oregon State University. Appropriately, the OSU campus was the alma mater of both Paulings, and of course was where they had originally met and fallen in love. Moreover, in 1982 OSU had initiated the Ava Helen Pauling Lectureship for World Peace; Linus Pauling delivered the first lecture. Among its internationally renowned speakers over the years have been Helen Caldicott, John Galbraith, Noam Chomsky, Arun Gandhi, and Oscar Arias Sanchez.

This section, featuring Linus Pauling's own words about his wife, is an edited composite of several published conversations, transcribed but unpublished interviews, and a few "notes to self" and unsent letters to his children written after Ava Helen's death in 1981.

I have so many memories of my wife that it is hard to know where to begin talking about the ways she helped me. I distinctly remember the first time I ever saw her. I had been asked to take over in instructing a class of 25 girls in first-year college chemistry at Oregon Agricultural College, where I was studying chemical engineering. After introducing myself, I selected a name at random from my class roster and asked the girl a question: "Will you tell me what you know about ammonium hydroxide, Miss . . . Miller?" She made a good answer. This chance meeting has determined the nature of my life.

The girl was Ava Helen Miller, who later became my wife. She was the smartest girl in the class, also by far the best looking. Perhaps even more important, for some reason when she saw me she took a liking to me, and of course I wasn't able to resist! At the time, I was impressed by her wide knowledge and interest in many subjects, including world affairs. She was majoring in home economics and, I am sure, had already set as her goal the development of a successful family.

In 1922 I began graduate work at the California Institute of Technology in Pasadena, California, which eventually led to my Ph.D. in chemistry, with minors in physics and mathematics. My life was changed very much for the better on June 17, 1923, when Ava Helen and I were married in Salem, Oregon. My wife was 19 and I was 22. We had wanted to marry the year before, but practical considerations prevented us. I was fortunate in having been selected by the right young woman. Young men and women must strive to find and marry the right person early.

A self-administered intelligence test we both took early in our marriage proved her to be in some ways smarter than I. Not only was she quicker, but she had more correct answers. By then, of course, it was too late for me to seek a mate over whom I might feel mentally superior, as some men seem to want to do!

Ava Helen had great interest in the family—her own family, consisting of her mother and her 11 brothers and sisters, several of whom were married, and her new family, which at first consisted of her and me, and later included our four children. Having studied chemistry, she was interested in the work that I was doing as an advanced student of chemistry, and then as a teacher of chemistry and a scientific researcher at the California Institute of Technology.

When we were married, my wife decided that her job was to see that I was not distracted from my course of thinking about scientific problems. She strove to take as many burdens as possible from my shoulders, in order that I could devote myself to my scientific and educational work as effectively as possible. So for many years she tried to protect me from being distracted by taking care of all the problems that arose. I'm reminded of the story of the man who said that he and his wife had made an agreement in which she would decide all of the minor problems and he would decide the major ones, and so far there hadn't been any major problems.

The Paulings in the 1960s. Pauling, who greatly admired his wife's intelligence and strong character, sometimes called her his "auxiliary memory" and humorously recommended that others acquire a mate for this convenience. She served as his auxiliary social conscience as well.

I think that every person should be able to enjoy life. Also, every person should contribute to the work that has to be done in order that the world and human beings go on. Some people are able to earn their living by doing work that they enjoy. My recommendation to all young people is to try to decide what you most enjoy doing, and then look around to see if there is a job for which you could prepare yourself that would enable you to continue having this sort of joy. Most of the interesting jobs require a considerable period of education. Moreover, if you are educated you are put in a position to enjoy reading and other intellectual activities, which can make your life better and happier.

New ideas, which may give the solution to a difficult problem, originate in the whole body of knowledge that you have come into possession of. Whenever I hear a student say that it is not important to remember facts, that all you need to know is where to look things up in a book, I am astonished by his lack of understanding. It is the knowledge that you have in your head, what you can call up in your memory bank, that is important. I have been especially fortunate for many years in having two memory banks available. Whenever I can't remember something I ask my wife, and thus I am able to draw on this auxiliary memory bank. Moreover, there is a second way in which I get ideas. I listen carefully to what my wife says, and in this way I often get a good idea. I recommend to you young people that you make a permanent acquisition of an auxiliary memory bank that you can become familiar with and draw upon throughout your lives.

It is my belief that Ava Helen is largely responsible for my success. I think her own greatest success was in her role as a wife and mother. For many years, Ava Helen devoted herself to taking care of me and our children. As far as women are concerned, I am old-fashioned enough to like the idea of a woman's managing the household. This is an important activity. A woman does not have to be a bank vice-president to find happiness. I should think routine work like sitting at a desk writing letters, making reports, or punching data into computers would be much less interesting and satisfying than running a home. My wife was happy making a home for me and the children. Later she found considerable happiness in being a public figure active in such causes as human rights and world peace.

The Paulings with their four children at their Pasadena home in the early 1940s. From left to right: Linda, Crellin, Linus Jr., Peter, Ava Helen and Linus Pauling. (Photo courtesy of Linda Pauling-Kamb)

During the Second World War, I continued my teaching, but also was engaged in many investigations of scientific and medical problems relating to the war effort, including work on explosives. I had been asked by Robert Oppenheimer to join him in the work on the atomic bomb at Los Alamos, but had decided not to do that, and instead to continue the work that I was doing in the California Institute of Technology and as a member of war research committees in Washington, D.C.

Ava Helen had been interested in social, political, and economic problems ever since she was a teenage girl. She used to argue with a friend of the family, one of the judges of the Oregon State Supreme Court. She had a general interest in science and was very able, very smart, but she was really concerned about human beings. The humanistic concern she had was very great. I'm sure that if I had not married her, I would not have had this aspect of my career—working for world peace. It was her influence on me and her strong support that caused me to continue.

In 1945 there occurred an episode that changed my life. It consisted of a remark made to me by my wife after I had given a public lecture.

In August 1945 atomic bombs were exploded by the United States over Hiroshima and Nagasaki, Japan. Each of these bombs, involving only a few pounds of nuclear explosive, had explosive power equal to 15,000 or 20,000 tons of TNT. The nuclear explosive, plutonium or uranium-235, has 20 million times the explosive power of the same weight of TNT or dynamite. These two small bombs destroyed the cities and killed about 250,000 people.

Someone who knew that I was an effective lecturer about chemical subjects invited me to speak at a luncheon before the members of the Rotary Club in Hollywood, to tell them about the nature of this tremendously powerful new explosive, involving fission of the nuclei of the atoms. I did not have any classified information about the atomic bombs, and so I was free to speak.

Later I gave a similar talk before another group, in which I discussed not only the nature of nuclear fission but also the change that had occurred in the nature of war, through the development of atomic bombs. I quoted Albert Einstein, who had said that the existence of these bombs, so powerful that a single bomb, lobbed over by a rocket, could destroy a whole city, required that we give up war as the means for settling disputes between the great nations, and instead develop a system of world law to settle these disputes. I also quoted statements by various politicians and students of international relations.

After this lecture, when my wife and I had come home, she made the following statement to me: "I think that you should stop giving lectures about atomic bombs, war, and peace. When you talk about a scientific subject you speak very effectively and convincingly. It is evident that you are a master of the subject that you are talking about. But when you talk about the nature of war and the need for peace, you are not convincing, because you give the audience the impression that you are not sure about what you are saying and that you are relying on other authorities."

These sentences changed my life. I thought, "What shall I do? I am convinced that scientists should speak to their fellow human beings not only about science, but also about atomic bombs, the nature of war, the need to change international relations, the need to achieve peace in the world. But my wife says that I should not give talks of this sort because I am not able to speak authoritatively. Either I should stop, or I should learn to speak authoritatively."

I had by this time begun to feel so strongly about these matters that I decided to devote half of my time, over a period that has turned out to be nearly four decades, to learning about international relations, international law, treaties, histories, the peace movement, and other subjects relating to the whole question of how to abolish war from the world and to achieve the goal of a peaceful world, in which the resources of the world are used for the benefit of human beings, and not for preparation for death and destruction.

During the next years I gave hundreds of lectures about nuclear weapons, the need for world peace, and, from 1957 on for several years, the damage to the pool of human germ plasm and to the health of living people by the radioactive fallout from the atmospheric testing of atomic bombs. My life, ever since that day many years ago, no longer involved my wholehearted efforts in teaching science and carrying on scientific research.

I think that my wife was pleased that I had taken her remark seriously enough to devote myself, in at least half of my time, to world peace and world problems generally. I was not alone in this effort. She was also very active in the peace movement, serving as an officer of the Women's International League for Peace and Freedom and of Women Strike for Peace, and she gave a great many lectures about world peace during the remainder of the nearly 59 years of our marriage. She was involved too with the American Civil Liberties Union.

Over the years, my wife and I supported numerous organizations whose goal was world peace. For a while, many other scientists did the same. Then, in about 1950, the Republican senator from the state of Wisconsin, Joseph R. McCarthy, began scandalous investigations into the private lives of leading citizens suspected of communist subversion. As a consequence of the influence of what came to be known as McCarthyism, advocates of cooperation with the Soviet Union were criticized as un-American. In this environment, a number of scientists stopped making public appearances altogether. But, perhaps out of stubbornness, I refused to allow McCarthy and the anticommunists in the United States to silence me.

I felt compelled to earn and keep Ava Helen's respect. She always understood the reasons for all my actions. And I did not want her to think I was a coward. In addition, I had my own self-respect to consider. I was determined McCarthy would not succeed in browbeating me.

I think my wife's work and mine can be said to have enjoyed considerable success. For instance, when she and I were in Europe, we learned that "An Appeal by American Scientists" had demonstrated to scientists in other countries that Americans were concerned about the dangers of nuclear war and nuclear testing. The petition we submitted to the United Nations calling for a halt to testing was ultimately signed by 13,000 scientists, perhaps the largest group ever to sign such a statement. In 1961, my wife and I continued our task by circulating among scientists and nonscientists a petition against the spread of nuclear weapons. About 200,000 people signed it.

On 10 October 1963 I was notified that I had received the Nobel Peace Prize. Reporters asked me which of the two Nobel prizes I valued the more: The Nobel Peace Prize, or the prize in chemistry, which I had received in 1954. My reply was that the Nobel Prize in Chemistry pleased me immensely, but that it was given to me for enjoying myself—for carrying out researches in chemistry that I enjoyed carrying out. On the other hand, I felt that the Nobel Peace Prize was an indication to me that I had done my duty as a human being—my duty to my fellow human beings.

It was a great surprise. At the time, I said my having received it made working for peace respectable. Of course, my wife, my children, and I had all suffered considerably during the years of our pacifist work.

The Paulings often worked together in their office at home for world peace and antinuclear causes. (Photo courtesy of Linda Pauling-Kamb)

Ava Helen Pauling In Her Own Words

The Pauling Papers at Oregon State University contain sufficient materials by and about Ava Helen Pauling and her involvement with the peace movement and humanitarian work of her times, whether directly or indirectly through her husband's work, to merit a book. Here is a small sample of Ava Helen talking: an edited excerpt from an interview she had in 1977 with documentary filmmaker Robert Richter.

I suppose that I am responsible to some degree for Linus's deciding to put so much of his effort into peace activities. In talking with him, I said I thought that it was of course important that he do his scientific work. But if the world were destroyed, then that work would not be of any value—so he should take part of his time and devote it to peace work, as we called it.

I felt a little guilty about this because I knew very well what great and deep pleasure he got from his scientific work, and how competent and enthusiastic he was in it. But he also realized that there was a need for people to know and understand the different means of waging war. So he did devote a good bit of his time during those years—the late '40s and the '50s and on into the '60s—to working for peace. And I worked with him in doing much of the mechanics—writing letters, getting names, routine things.

We also went on lecture tours together where we both talked, attended peace congresses, and took part in activities for peace. We thought, and still do, that the world is surely going to have to cooperate much more than it does now if it is to survive. Of course Linus carried on his scientific work, too, but only put about half of his time in it, so that it was a genuine sacrifice.

I hope that Linus Pauling will be remembered as a good man and an honest man, a man of great integrity—that is perhaps his best quality. What I have admired and liked in him is the fact that he has worked with such passion and eagerness and truth in science regardless of the awards and honors that he has received. He has had confidence in himself, and in his knowledge that if he thought of a problem and solved it, it would be for the good of mankind. He has continued to have very many ideas and he works at them with a deep conviction and courage and integrity.

So I want people to remember him in that way, as I believe they will if enough of what he is can be passed on to future generations. What to me means the most is the kind of work he did, how he worked . . . and the help that he was to so many people.

Ava Helen Pauling in Greece in 1964, on a marathon peace march to Athens. "LP not there," her husband wrote on the back of the photo. Ava Helen increasingly went out on her own by the '60s as a speaker and strategist with organizations such as Women Strike for Peace.

In the early years of the Paulings' marriage, Ava Helen focused much of her attention and time on the home front. This included gaining a reputation as a winsome and intelligent hostess—a decided social advantage for an ambitious professor of science. In 1927 the young Mrs. Pauling summarized her traditional view of a married woman's life in this way:

> *If a woman thinks honestly and clearly, she must soon reach the conclusion that no matter what life work she chooses, it could be done better by a man; and the only work in which this is not the case is the work involved in a home with children. In this way she contributes truthfully and substantially to the career of her husband and through her children to the improvement of the world.*

As her children grew older and less dependent on her presence, Ava Helen was freer to travel with Linus to scientific meetings and peace conferences, as well as lecture tours interspersed with tourism. (In several early instances, though, she left them for extended periods in others' care while accompanying her husband on long stays in Europe and the East Coast.) She began to gain more confidence in her own voice, in her ability to influence audiences and readers even when Linus was not present.

On the basis of considerable observation, Ava Helen was also concluding that many brilliant men of science of her acquaintance depended almost totally on their practical wives' willingness to create stress-free domestic environments that allowed them to focus almost entirely on their own intense work and competitive professional progress. Where would such men be without the helpmeets whose services they usually took for granted? And what other satisfactions might these women have achieved with their own lives? She certainly did not regret having helped her husband gain worldwide recognition for both his scientific accomplishments and his work for peace. At least she knew that Linus fully appreciated her contributions to his success and her influence on his thinking—he often said so, publicly. But she was also aware that her own innate intelligence and capabilities had not been fully utilized.

By the mid 1960s Ava Helen Pauling, always independent-minded, was paying close attention to the newly resurgent Women's Movement, stirred up in good part by the national attention to civil and human rights generally. Here are excerpts from a moderately feminist talk, or sermon, that Mrs. Pauling gave to the congregation at the First Unitarian Church of Los Angeles. It was entitled "The Second X-Chromosome."

By this point in her life Ava Helen had become a full-fledged civil libertarian and peace activist in her own right. During some years she actually had more speaking engagements than Linus, and traveled to more countries. One can detect an undercurrent of regret in her talk. Probably Ava Helen often considered what path she might have taken in an era that encouraged intelligent, capable, and ambitious women to seek their own professional fulfillment, whether or not they married and had children.

But just by influencing her husband politically over the years, Ava Helen Pauling made a significant contribution to world peace and health. And earlier than that, through the careful application of a special diet over many years, she kept Linus alive, then enabled him to recover from a life-threatening illness—thereby making it possible for him to continue his scientific work. His unique and wide-ranging accomplishments in science, after all, were the means by which he could gain the attention and respect of audiences and readers, and of other scientists, when he talked about nuclear weapons, peace, and humanism, those topics of intense interest and special concern to her.

W hy do we have two sexes—man and woman? An asexual or one-sexed organism is simpler, one might even say less trouble, but it has been shown normally to lack the necessary capacity for recombination of genes to meet the conditions of a radically changed environment. An asexual organism depends on mutation, a change in the gene structure, for its variability. This is too slow a process except in a most stable environment. Accordingly, the evolutionary process has required that there be the possibility of great exchange of genetic material and recombination of characters in order to cope successfully with rapid changes in the environment of the organism. . . . Sex then is necessary and the two sexes provide the almost limitless recombination of genes and crossing over of characters that have provided the human race with its evolutionary potential and its ability to cope with even drastic changes in its environment. . . .

We now have woman and man each with a special role determined by nature and with special characteristics and talents to carry forward the human race. Nature assigned to woman the role of the repository of the embryo, thus ensuring her a more sedentary part, making her observant, wary, cautious, tough, and persevering. I believe woman to have been the first scientist. She must in her cave have been aware of the effect of temperature, water, and the storage of food—the gathering of edible grains and fruits must have been her job as the warriors were off to battle.

In all primitive cultures women played an equally important role to man in the affairs of the family. . . . The superior strength of man was equaled by the toughness and stamina of woman. As civilization progressed, women, before gaining legal status and equal rights, had become chattels and completely subservient to man. As she was recognized as being valuable property and indispensable, great effort was made to keep her completely under subjection, which continues in many forms even today.

The freedom which women are supposed to enjoy in the U.S. is more fancied than real, far from being equal. You have all seen the advertisement which places a woman high on a column and below her a foolish looking man. The caption reads, "Every man wants his woman on a pedestal!" This is the silliest, most disgraceful insult to women! No woman wants to be up on a pedestal (substitute shelf for pedestal), where she can be easily ignored and neglected. She wants to be taking and doing her part in the affairs of the world with her feet on the ground and sharing in and contributing to the life around her. . . .

We need a re-evaluation of woman and her special attributes. We need to place value on all work and those who do it. We need to examine the jobs and the careers open to women. . . .

Two great changes are necessary if women in the United States are to attain the place of dignity and respect to which their capabilities entitle them. Better education and a better preparation for adult life; and nursery and child care centers. State nursery schools are needed to help care for her small children so that women may work and develop their capabilities. Intellectual curiosity must be encouraged and fostered in young women and all discrimination against women must be removed. Careers other than marriage are possible and profitable.

Today women can vote and can be a political force in most of the countries of the world. Can women resume authority and restore sanity to the world? I believe that they can and that they must. The very existence of mankind depends on it. We know that mankind's cooperative instincts have led to his survival in the evolutionary struggle, and women learned early the value of cooperative effort. Now the world community is so small that man must cooperate with the entire world. Women have begun in a substantial way to bring about this world cooperation. . . .

The solution of women's problems is the solution of society's problems and it lies in their own hands. Perhaps I should say that when women have solved the problems of today's social structure, they will have solved their own problem. And it is a larger, more complex problem than merely whether or not a woman has a job outside her home.

Women can create the kind of world they need for their men, for their children, and for themselves. This requires the full use of their political rights and privileges. It requires the full employment of their capacities and their abilities. They must make use of their knowledge and they must demand the right to gain knowledge. . . .

Women, American women, must prepare themselves and their female children for a constructive role in the world of the future. I believe the participation of hundreds of women in the peace movement is a healthy sign and a hopeful one, but much more needs to be done in the economic field. Women in the United States are still coming off second best. . . .

We can expect much more participation by women in the future, and once we realize that the fault of women's unhappiness lies in our culture itself, we can correct the error. We must get over our hostility toward women holding a place in society commensurate with men.

After Ava Helen died in 1981, Linus felt unbearably bereft for some while as he struggled to reconcile himself to her departure from his life. In a poignant letter written several months afterward to their children (never sent, but found after his own death in 1994), he reported:

> *I am getting along moderately well, and also moderately poorly. . . . I get along most of the time by managing to forget that Ava Helen has died. When I am traveling I think that she is at home in Portola Valley, waiting for me. When I am in the Institute I think that she is at home, and that I shall soon see her. When I am in our house in Portola Valley, I think that she is in another room. When I am at the ranch, too, I think that she is in another room.*
>
> *But then, several times a day, something happens to make me realize that these thoughts are not true, and that my dear companion is indeed dead. I usually then experience a paroxysm of grief, such as I never have experienced before. I usually begin to cry.*

Several years after Ava Helen's death, Linus still deeply missed her. In attempting a philosophical resolution of his predicament, he wrote in one of his "notes to self":

> *Just before she died (at age 77, when I was 80), my wife said to me, "Our molecules are together." She was, I am sure, happy with this thought—the thought that she and I, as unique individuals, had not lost completely the uniqueness of our association by her death—by the fact that her body, like that of Julius Caesar, would soon be turned to clay, or rather for her, to molecules of carbon dioxide, water, nitrogen, and inorganic ash. Instead, some of the molecules that had determined her nature and some of those that had determined my nature were present together in the bodies of our four children, and had cooperated in determining their natures; and they had cooperated also, somewhat diluted, in determining the nature of our 15 grandchildren and of our great-grandchildren, then three in number. She was very very [repeated 10 times] fond of me, just as I was very very [repeated 10 times] fond of her, through the 60 years of our association, and I am sure that despite her feeling of sadness that our life together was ending, she found some consolation in the knowledge that our cooperation was not being ended by her death.*

Ava Helen's permanent absence from Linus's life inevitably diminished his attention to the humanitarian and peace-serving work that they had done effectively together for so long. Still, he knew that he could extend into the future the meaning of his wife's beliefs about humanity and her devotion to peace by continuing onward, on his own or in combination with other people. When called out to battle, he usually went forth—hurling words against the makers of war, the destroyers of Earth and the life upon it.

Ideas and ideals, so far as we know, do not possess elemental substances and DNA. And yet they grow, find mates, and live on in new forms. So the peace-promoting spirits of Ava Helen and Linus Pauling achieve their own immortality. They have been transmuted, and will be transferred anew to others' lives as the years and centuries go by.

Words carry them along.

The Paulings in 1978 at Deer Flat Ranch, their home on the central California coast. Ava Helen died three years later. (Photo courtesy of Barclay Kamb)

Pauling protested President Kennedy's decision to resume nuclear testing in 1962 after an international moratorium ended with France's move to "join the nuclear club" by conducting its own tests. In 1963 the Limited Test-Ban Treaty was signed, inspiring the Nobel Peace Committee to honor Pauling for his unrelenting campaign to educate people about the dangers of radioactive fallout. (World Wide Photos)

Part III

In the
Nuclear Age

A new epoch for humankind arrived dramatically with two huge atomic bomb blasts over the Japanese cities of Hiroshima and Nagasaki. Ever afterward would come fierce debate over the moral issue of whether or not the United States was justified in committing this immense act of aggression against a civilian population—killing or severely injuring several hundred thousand people. It was argued, however, that as many or more persons, including American G.I.s, would have been killed in a conventional ending of the war through the intense bombardment and invasion of Japan.

Various American scientists who had participated in the atomic bomb's development and had then seen the first one explode over New Mexico (notably physicist Leo Szilard) had tried to persuade the government and military to do otherwise—for instance, demonstrate nuclear fission's astounding explosive force in a remote Pacific area. But their advice did not prevail.

When Linus Pauling was first asked to give talks to the public about atomic energy, he couldn't help but show a certain enthusiasm for the amazing positive potential in nuclear energy—as when he described it in 1946 to members of the Caltech Women's Club:

> *The discovery of methods of controlled release of atomic energy is the greatest discovery that has ever been made. The discovery of fire is comparable—but it was accidental, it involved no understanding, no reasoning—just the acceptance of the gift from the gods, with thousands of years passing before the nature*

of the phenomenon was understood. Atomic energy, nuclear energy, has been released as the consequence of penetrating thought, powerful logic, many delicate experiments.

Ordinary fire and ordinary explosives involve chemical reactions between molecules, the rearrangement of atoms. Nuclear energy comes from reactions involving the nuclei themselves— the atoms becoming other atoms. It need not astound us that these reactions occur—we've known that the sun's heat had to come from this source. But scientists were skeptical that man could release this energy so easily. Everyone, I think, was surprised.

Pauling knew that Americans were both fascinated and repelled by these new bombs that had brought the war with Japan to a swift close. Giving talks to acquaint people with the basics of atomic energy would provide an opening to discuss the important implications of these powerful weapons. Though their creation had brought about the wonderful discovery of a new source of power, Pauling felt that they were immoral and should never be used again against people anywhere. Perhaps they would actually induce nations to end violent threats and warfare as the primary means of settling territorial disputes and other problems.

In his talks and writings, Pauling would quickly make the transition from technical explanations to discussing the need for permanent world peace. "Atomic energy now means so much more to everyone in the world that my talk must be mainly about social and political matters," he might announce at the start. Frequently, he got quite specific about how people should make their opinions and concerns known to their leaders, legislators, and policy-making organizations.

If Linus Pauling worried about nuclear weapons, so did many other scientists. In this postwar period Pauling joined the Federation of Atomic Scientists, whose campaign to get Congress to remove nuclear research from military control and turn it over to a civilian agency resulted in the Atomic Energy Commission. (For years FAS's publication, the *Bulletin of the Atomic Scientists*, provided an outlet for debates over nuclear weapons development and test radiation.)

MEET THE ATOM BOMBS

"A big one, which the atomic bomb scientists say could be made, could flatten the whole of New York and kill its millions of inhabitants."

In the autumn of 1945 Pauling began giving lectures to introduce nonscientists to basic information about the atomic bombs recently dropped on Japan. On the day following one of his talks, he was visited in his office

by an FBI agent, who asked how he had obtained the technical information about the two types of bombs. He was obviously suspected of
obtaining classified information from a loose-tongued scientist who had
worked on developing them at Los Alamos. Already the government
seemingly had evidence that Soviet spies were trying to obtain the secret
for making atom bombs. Pauling assured the agent that because he was
a chemist and knew a great deal about atomic physics already, he had
just figured it out for himself—making a few educated guesses about
things he wasn't sure about. (He might have ventured to say that probably it wouldn't take the Russians long to figure it all out, either.)

Pauling must have given the 1945 talk excerpted below several
times, because he had marked for removal some information that the
federal agent must have identified as classifiable. (The less technical
part of his lecture appears in Part II, pages 51-54.) It shows how he could
simplify scientific concepts and phenomena when talking to lay persons.

I have never seen an atomic bomb explode, but several of my friends
have, and have told me about it. The limited experience which I have
had during the war with ordinary explosives has not been of much help to
me in appreciating the power of atomic explosives, because ordinary
explosives are hardly worth mentioning in the same breath with fissionable atoms. And yet we used to think of nitroglycerine and TNT and RDX
and PETN as pretty powerful substances, worthy of respect: a pound of
TNT, in the form of a shaped charge, can blow a hole through six inches
of armor plate; a hundred pounds, which might be carried into this room
by one man, could kill everybody in the room; a few tons, which might be
dropped as a bomb, could destroy this building or devastate a whole block
of houses.

TNT and similar molecular explosives are powerful because the
atoms in their molecules are combined in such a way that a large amount
of energy is stored up, which can be suddenly released as a detonation
wave causing the atoms in the molecules to rearrange themselves into
new product molecules, which fly apart with great velocity, impinging on
surrounding molecules and producing the shattering shock wave which
spreads out from the center of the explosion.

The energy of TNT is stored up between the atoms in the molecule,
and not within the atoms. Only six years ago was it discovered that there
is stored up in the minute nuclei of heavy atoms themselves an almost
unbelievably great amount of energy which can be released at the will of
man. These heavy nuclei are themselves unstable, in the same way that
molecules of TNT are unstable; under the influence of neutrons these

nuclei can split in two, with the evolution of an incredible amount of energy, which causes the split products to fly apart with terrific velocity.

It is in the nature of this reaction, its dependence upon a supply of neutrons, that it proceeds slowly if there are not too many fissionable atoms around—uranium-235 or plutonium—but that it proceeds explosively, in a millionth of a second, whenever more than a certain amount, a pound or two, of the material is brought together. Suppose that we had two pieces of plutonium, each shaped like half of a golf ball and weighing perhaps a pound (the density of plutonium is very great—about 20 times that of water), and a mechanism for suddenly clapping them together: this would be an atomic bomb, like that which devastated Nagasaki, and if it were to explode here, it would destroy Hollywood.

This, then, is an atomic bomb—the smallest that we know how to make now—a couple of pounds of plutonium, equal to 40 million pounds of TNT, and capable of wiping out a city 10 square miles in area and killing hundreds of thousands of people. Yesterday Harold Urey testified that three such bombs exploded in Washington could cause our federal government to vanish. And these are little atomic bombs, the smallest that will explode. A big one, which the atomic bomb scientists say could be made, could flatten the whole of New York and kill its millions of inhabitants.

We must not think that because only three atomic bombs have been exploded there are only a few in existence. I can make a guess about this, on the basis of the order-of-magnitude figures quoted in the Smyth report—and my guess is that there are perhaps a hundred or two in existence—enough to kill perhaps 50 million people, if each were dropped on a different city—and by next year there may be 500. My colleague Robert Oppenheimer, whose opinion is based on knowledge of the situation, has stated that he expects tens of thousands possibly to be used if there is an atomic war.

Nor must we think that atomic warfare will be expensive. The atomic bomb program cost two billion dollars, and only two bombs were dropped on Japan—but Oppenheimer has said that in mass production these bombs would cost not a billion dollars apiece, but only a million dollars. This is terribly cheap—a million-dollar atomic bomb has the power of 40 million pounds of TNT, which in bombs would cost perhaps $100 million. For a given amount of money we can do a hundred times as much damage to the enemy as in preatomic days. The next war should be a real one, indeed; perhaps it will be equal to 100 like the one we have just gone through.

HERE COME THE SUPERBOMBS

"Most scientists predict that hydrogen bombs a thousand times more powerful than an old-fashioned atomic bomb can be designed and constructed in a few months or years."

Pauling's early public talks about atomic energy increasingly emphasized the importance of changing the way international conflicts are resolved so as to avoid future wars involving nuclear weapons. Probably because he had already demonstrated his ability and interest in educating people about atomic energy and its dangers to humankind in warfare, in 1946 Pauling was invited to join the Emergency Committee of Atomic Scientists—better known as the Einstein Committee. This small, elite group of scientists was guided by renowned physicist Albert Einstein, who had become a confirmed and alarmed peace advocate. The great physicist, who had left Germany in 1933, now seemed to regret his urgent advice to President Roosevelt prior to the war's outbreak that the U.S. undertake a crash atomic research program to develop controlled nuclear fission, based on his famous equation $E=mc^2$. The Manhattan Project had led to the two A-bombs dropped on Japan. Einstein's cautionary public messages had encouraged other scientists to speak out on the dangers of any future world wars that would inevitably utilize nuclear bombs.

Living on the West Coast, Pauling was unable to attend many of the Committee's meetings, which took place at Princeton, though he visited Einstein there as often as he could. But in the next few years, Pauling helped raise funds and made some lecture tours, talking about atomic energy and the need for peace. Sometimes he toured with Leo Szilard, and they showed a film prepared by the Einstein Committee that revealed to American viewers for the first time the horrible devastation of Hiroshima and Nagasaki—impressing upon them the need to ban any future use of such weapons.

In 1949 the Truman administration announced that it would go along with a recommendation made by military strategists and various atomic scientists, based on a concept put forward earlier by nuclear physicists, notably Edward Teller. The U.S. intended to develop an advanced new weapon to add to its existing nuclear arsenal: the hydrogen bomb. This decision was protested by numerous scientists who understood the ghastly potential of this device. By then the Einstein Committee had disbanded, and one of its members, Harold Urey, even favored creating the new bomb. It was viewed by him and others as a matter of maintaining national security by continuously keeping ahead of the Soviet Union in the quality and quantity of nuclear arms, now that the Russians had started producing their own A-bombs. Some scientists were curious to know whether this bomb would even work—and if so, just how powerful it might be.

Here is Pauling's explanation to lay audiences about the differences among ordinary explosives, atomic fission, and the nuclear fusion in the hydrogen bomb. This talk on "The Ultimate Decision," which he first gave at Carnegie Hall in New York on February 13, 1950, was part of an intense drive to pressure the administration into canceling its decision to proceed with constructing and testing the "H-bomb." Pauling's lecture was received with praise, even by the *New York Times* reporter covering the event. Pauling and other scientists and political activists traveled around the nation delivering the same message. But when the Korean War erupted in early summer, adding to the great concern over the communist takeover of China in the previous year, all hope of stopping production of the new superbomb ended.

Pauling typically would start his talk with some background science and then move into discussing the bigger issues involved.

I like to talk about atoms, and to think about them. We know a great deal about atoms and molecules now, and the physical scientists who have investigated this part of our world have done a good job. . . .

It is these tiny particles—our knowledge of and control over these tiny particles—that have made the world of today crucially different from the world of 10 years ago.

A few pounds of uranium-235 or plutonium-239 and machinery for detonating it constitute an old-fashioned atomic bomb, of the Hiroshima-Nagasaki type. The reaction of these nuclei liberates in a millionth of a second as much energy as is liberated by the detonation of 20 million pounds of TNT. We know that at Hiroshima one of these old-fashioned bombs killed 80,000 people. A member of Congress has stated that 1949-model bombs are six times as powerful as the earlier bombs. And now we, and presumably the Russians too, are working on hydrogen bombs.

A hydrogen bomb consists of an old-fashioned atomic bomb surrounded by a ton, or perhaps 10 tons or more, of hydrogen or other light elements, the nuclei of which can fuse together to form heavier nuclei, with the liberation of around five times as much energy, on a weight basis, as in a fission bomb. There may be present a hundred or a thousand or ten thousand times as much explosive material as in the old-fashioned atomic bomb (which serves simply as a detonator for the hydrogen bomb, by raising the temperature to several million degrees), and most scientists predict that hydrogen bombs a thousand times more powerful than an old-fashioned atomic bomb can be designed and constructed in a few months or years. There seems to be no theoretical limit on the size of these terrible weapons.

One hydrogen bomb would wipe New York out of existence, another Washington, another Chicago, another Los Angeles, another London, another Paris, another Moscow. What will there be left on Earth then? Still hundreds of millions of people—if a billion people were to be killed by the detonation of two score hydrogen bombs in the first phase of an atomic war, there would still be a billion left.

But the atmosphere over the whole Earth would be filled with radioactive products of nuclear reactions. No human being, no animal, no plant over the surface of the Earth would in future years be safe from the insidious action of these great quantities of radioactive materials. Even though, by centuries of effort, the physical destruction caused by these hydrogen bombs might conceivably be repaired, the biological effects never could be averted.

Terrible as the situation is, we need not succumb to despondency. The decision about the future has not yet been made—and we, the people, can by the pressure of our opinions determine it. When, three years after John J. McCloy first brought the hydrogen bomb to public attention, interest in it became great; our leaders brought forth one plan: they said that the solution is for this country to "arm itself with the hydrogen superbomb to preserve the peace of the world." These were the words of Chairman Tom Connally of the Senate Foreign Relations Committee. They were subscribed to by senator after senator; and even a distinguished scientist, Harold Urey, expressed the firm belief that we would have to keep the rest of the world under control by force, by fear of the hydrogen bomb.

President Truman announced that he had ordered production of the bomb "to see to it that our country is able to defend itself against any possible aggressor." But strong opposition developed at once. Twelve leading atomic scientists asked for a pledge against use of the bomb. Senator Brien McMahon proposed a new approach—a recovery program for the world, eliminating the causes of war. Senator Tydings suggested that President Truman propose an international disarmament conference to end the world's nightmare of fear. James Warburg called for outlawing all weapons. Professor Einstein asserted that the solution of the problem is formation of a supra-national judicial and executive body, and a declaration of the nations to collaborate loyally in the realization of such a restricted world government.

It is now evident to everyone that our State Department is not omniscient, that our foreign policy is not perfect and incapable of amendment.

We must instead find the solution—it has not been given to us—and we must all help.

MEGATON MADNESS

"There is no effective defense against these great weapons of destruction."

Two years after Linus Pauling and other scientists and peace activists had tried to stop the hydrogen bomb program, the first of the new H-bombs (fission-fusion devices) were set off in the Marshall Islands. This was a U.S. territory in the South Pacific where areas with small islands or atolls were given over to atomic weapons testing, the native inhabitants being relocated to new homes elsewhere, far from their ancestral dwellings. The blasts were kept off limits and in a news blackout, so the public at first didn't learn much about the bombs. Soon the Russians showed that they too had an H-bomb. Then in 1954, at Bikini, a more complex three-stage version of the superbomb (fission-fusion-fission) was first detonated. Its outside shell of uranium became fissionable during the intense heat and fusion of the hydrogen atoms, giving it a considerably higher explosive yield.

An apparently unexpected outcome of this new "U-bomb," as it was sometimes dubbed, was the large production of rare or unnatural radioactive isotopes of various elements that had taken on additional neutrons, such as strontium-90, which does not occur in nature. The addition of protons from the hydrogen fusion caused some elements in the atmosphere to be transmuted into others (such as nitrogen into a radioactive form of carbon, carbon-14). Measurable "fallout," as these radioactive particles were called, was detected in many far-distant places. It was impossible now to hide evidence of such testing, so the government began to release informative yet reassuring news about these superbombs, intending to dispel the public's fear and quiet scientists' concerns.

In this 1954 talk on "The World Problem and the Hydrogen Bomb," evoked by the news about this potent new weapon and given initially at the First Unitarian Church of Los Angeles, Pauling ended his self-imposed exile from political activism. Now he reentered the fray and began focusing major attention on the health and environmental hazards of radioactive fallout—a concern that would occupy the center of his anti-nuclear campaign through the rest of the '50s. Here he also acknowledged that even worse weapons than the H-bomb might someday be created to kill people in war.

D uring the last few months some hydrogen bombs were exploded, and information about the destructive power that they have been shown actually to possess has been released to the public.

We—everybody in the world—must consider this information, and decide what its significance is, and what must be done if the world is to be saved for posterity.

The time has come when man must show whether he is properly called "Homo sapiens," or whether he is still an unthinking brute. First, I may mention that the hydrogen bomb itself is not the worst weapon that could be built—it is outdone as a death-dealing instrument by the cobalt bomb, which has not yet been tried out on a large scale. But the hydrogen bomb itself is enough to force us to consider the direction in which the world is moving, and to reach a decision about the future of the world. . . .

Scores of atom bombs have been detonated in the United States, the South Pacific, Australia, and Russia. It has been reported that the latest models of atom bombs are around 10 or 20 times as destructive as the original ones.

No announcement has been made as to the number of atom bombs that are stored up in the arsenals of the leading countries of the world, but a recent newspaper report said that the informed guesses lie in the region of 5,000 atom bombs in the United States, 500 atom bombs in Russia.

Scientists recognized early that still more destructive bombs could be made. The energy radiated by the sun arises not from the fission of the nuclei of heavy atoms, but from the fusion of light nuclei—the reaction of four protons, the nuclei of hydrogen atoms, to form a helium nucleus. . . . The ordinary atom bomb is to serve simply as the detonator of the hydrogen bomb—to raise the hydrogen to a high enough temperature to cause it to react. The reaction leads to the formation of helium, and to the evolution of energy, for about a ton of hydrogen, one thousand times as great as that for an atom bomb. . . .

I have seen a statement that the hydrogen bombs that have already been exploded in the South Pacific have an explosive power between 2 and 14 million tons of TNT; the largest one is thus described as a 14-megaton bomb, meaning equivalent to 14 million tons of TNT.

This bomb would destroy practically everything within an area of 1,000 square miles—that is, within a circle about 35 miles in diameter. One of these bombs detonated over New York would destroy the whole city, out to the suburbs, and might kill 5 million people. One of them detonated over Los Angeles would destroy this city, perhaps killing 2 million people. . . .

Part of the danger from atom bombs and hydrogen bombs lies in the radioactive material that they produce. Japanese fishermen 80 miles from the hydrogen bomb explosion were burned by radioactive ash that fell on their ship. Many radioactive fish had to be destroyed in Japan—every fish caught by fishermen two thousand miles from the scene of the explosion. The effect of radioactivity can be very greatly increased by a simple process—just the addition of some cobalt to the atomic bomb or hydrogen bomb. For 2 or 3 billion dollars enough cobalt bombs could be made to kill everybody—animals too—in the United States, simply by detonating them off the western coast, and in other suitable places, and allowing the winds to carry the products of detonation across the country. Probably some millions of people would be killed elsewhere too. . . .

There is no effective defense against these great weapons of destruction. We might hope that 50 percent of the airplanes or guided missiles carrying atom bombs or hydrogen bombs that are launched against American cities could be shot down. The most optimistic estimate that I have seen is that possibly 90 percent could be shot down. If we accept this, all that would be necessary would be for around 10 or 20 missiles carrying hydrogen bombs to be launched toward New York; probably one or two of them—more probably still, several—would escape being shot down and would explode over the city. Then New York would be destroyed. While we were losing our major cities, we might be able to cause equally great damage in Russia. . . .

The atom bomb and the hydrogen bomb have become powerful weapons of destruction in the hands of powerful nations opposed to one another. If international affairs continue along the lines characteristic of the whole past history of the world, we shall sooner or later see the outbreak of a hydrogen-bomb war. No nation will benefit from such a war—it may be expected confidently that a hydrogen-bomb war, if it comes, will result in the destruction of most of the cities in the world, the death of hundreds of millions of people, the end of the present civilized world.

There is only one way in which this end can be avoided. This way is to work for peace in the world. In the past each great nation has attempted, in its diplomatic negotiations with other nations, to achieve results which benefit itself preferentially over other nations. Negotiations between nations have not in general been carried out on a high ethical plane. The representatives of a nation do not ask whether an agreement that is being made—or a declaration of war—will benefit the world as a whole, but only whether the act will benefit one's own nation.

The time has now come when it is to the advantage of everybody in the world, of every nation in the world, to solve international problems in

a peaceful manner—which necessarily means in a just and ethical manner—and not to solve them by force, by that ultimate resource of powerful injustice, war.

A SLOW DEATH FROM THE SKY: FALLOUT

*"A number of people were raising the question of whether this
radioactive material might not be quite damaging both genetically and
somatically to the human race."*

The nuclear testing that had been conducted by the United States in the
late 1940s produced harmful radiation, but usually these substances
remained within relatively circumscribed and remote regions. Much of
the fallout released into the atmosphere was dissipated before reaching
populated areas. However, the situation dramatically changed in the
early 1950s, when different types of nuclear bombs began to be
exploded by the United States at the desolate Nevada Test Site, a huge
military area previously used for artillery and aircraft training and testing.
Not only were protective bunkers tested for withstanding nuclear attack
in combat situations, but replicas of towns were built so as to study the
effects of different types of blasts on civilian facilities. This activity took
place on America's home soil, not in the faraway South Pacific.

The much larger explosive yields of the new thermonuclear bombs
generated intensely radioactive substances, either from matter on the
ground or in the atmosphere itself. These were carried to distant loca-
tions by wind and rain. Some had a very long half-life—the time it takes
for the radioactivity to disappear. Measurable fallout was detected in
many places around the world, inevitably causing alarm among those
who understood the implications to health. Especially troubling were
those radioactive byproducts of nuclear explosions that could be incorporated into living matter—into plants and animals—and people.

By the mid 1950s it had become clear that the U.S. government, particularly through its regulatory organization, the Atomic Energy Commission (AEC), was not telling the whole truth about the hazards of intensive
nuclear testing. Instead, bland assurances of safety were combined with
a concerted public-relations campaign that appealed to patriotism and
even promoted the entertainment potential of witnessing nuclear blasts.
In the postwar period Las Vegas, 75 miles southeast of the Nevada Test
Site, was becoming a tourist boomtown. Residents and visitors would go
outside to watch the latest atomic blasts (usually announced in advance)
light up the night like gigantic fireworks. So did people living in small
towns and ranches bordering the military reservation, who would gather
on hilltops for a good view.

After a while, however, stories leaked out about how civilian residents—children especially—as well as livestock got sick and even died after flakes of radioactive fallout from the tests had rained down in their areas. Over time, many persons experienced deteriorating health, usually some form of cancer; these included soldiers who had lived near or been on maneuvers at the test site. The AEC, however, refused to acknowledge any connection, and for years lawsuits brought against the government were dismissed. Concern, even panic, periodically ensued when fallout, monitored and measured by Geiger counters, got carried to regions far away from the nuclear explosions, descending on cities and, in agricultural lands, even getting into the milk supply when dairy cows were exposed to irradiated fodder.

By the mid 1950s, Pauling too was focusing much of his attention on the insidious dangers of fallout, especially carbon-14, a radioactive isotope of carbon, the element contained in all organic molecules. Here is how Pauling summarized his motivation and experience in studying the fallout problem, in an interview conducted in 1977.

The problems that I work on are almost always rather complicated ones where there is a mass of information that hasn't been clarified. I like to find order, to find an answer to the questions. With the nuclear weapons I really became deeply interested when the question of the biological effects of the high radiation from the nuclear weapons came up, and I realized that this was something that had not been discussed to any great extent. I had some books about the effects of nuclear weapons, and in the '40s and '50s I pored over them hour after hour, month after month, year after year, when I was working hard to have some effectiveness to educate the people about the danger of nuclear weapons.

The Einstein Committee was set up to inform people about the nature of nuclear weapons—the devastating power of nuclear weapons and the need for finding an alternative to war. Despite the effort, the nuclear weapons arsenals became more and more complicated. The AEC hadn't released any information yet about radioactive fallout—and other people hadn't thought very much about it at that time.

When it became evident that the testing of nuclear weapons in the atmosphere was causing damage, I began to worry about that. I looked into the matter, to see how much damage to the pool of human germ plasm was being done—the extent to which human beings would have a higher incidence of cancer than if the bomb tests hadn't been carried out. I had, of course a background of knowledge in nuclear physics, physics, and chemistry in general, and in biology and medicine, that not many people had.

I became more and more concerned, the more and more I learned. I was able to draw conclusions on the basis of a rather limited amount of information. Actually there was some information, but it wasn't available. It had been kept secret, kept away from the public. I had some hints about damage done to the germ plasm—high energy radiation from the radioactive substances, and of course some statements were made by the Atomic Energy Commission that the amounts weren't great enough to cause any damage. But it hadn't been made quantitative enough for me. So I began checking to find out as much as I could to see if I could answer the question to my own satisfaction about just how much damage is done by the radioactive fallout.

Some people had begun making calculations about the biological effects of nuclear testing. There was uncertainty about how great they were, at that time. A number of people were raising the question of whether this radioactive material might not be quite damaging both genetically and somatically to the human race. A study was being made of survivors at Hiroshima and Nagasaki, especially the incidence of leukemia among these survivors. A professor of genetics in the California Institute of Technology, Ed Lewis, was especially interested in just this question, and he calculated the greater incidence of leukemia in people who had been exposed to high energy radiation of Hiroshima and Nagasaki when compared with the estimated number of cases of leukemia and other forms of cancer caused by the natural background radiation.

I made one contribution. I got a hint that it wasn't just fission products—the radioactive fallout itself that could cause damage—but also the carbon-14 produced by the reaction of the neutrons liberated in a nuclear explosion with the nuclei of the nitrogen molecules in the atmosphere. I had run across a paper published by a Russian who said that carbon-14 had caused a lot of gene mutations and a lot of cases of cancer. I got worried about this. But the spokesman for the Atomic Energy Commission had published a little paper that said that the amount of carbon-14 wasn't great enough to do any damage.

When I started checking up on this, it was a very complicated business. I realized that, so far as I could tell, the carbon-14 would do as much damage as radioactive fallout to the pool of human germ plasm and to persons living at the time that carbon-14 got into their bodies, either in this generation or a future generation. It seemed to me to be a serious matter.

I had a strong feeling about the morality of carrying out these problems. I settled down to try to work this out, and finally did write a paper on how much damage the carbon-14 from the bomb tests would do. I decided that the carbon-14 would in the course of time have done as much damage as the fission products, so that the total amount of damage would double the amount that had been calculated in the fission products. I felt confidence enough in my own estimates to be willing to talk about it.

The estimates were necessarily rather rough. I said a factor of five either way. I ultimately reached the decision that the 600 megatons of bomb tests that had been carried out up until 1963 by the United States, the Soviet Union, and Great Britain would altogether cause 15 million infants to be born with gross physical or mental defects, who otherwise would have been normal if the bomb tests hadn't been carried out; and that probably about 15 million people would be caused to have cancer who would not have cancer otherwise. Pretty big. And so if you test one 20-megaton bomb, that would be at the sacrifice of one-thirtieth of those numbers—that would be 500,000. Five hundred thousand unborn children, 500,000 cases of cancer per 20-megaton bomb tested.

It took me eight months, I think, to get that paper published in *Science*. The editor kept sending new memos to people in the atomic energy business, who wrote back saying that there was something wrong, that my estimate of testing at the rate of what I think I said of 60 megatons a year was off by an astronomical amount. In fact it turned out that when the figures became known later, my estimate was almost exactly right about the rate of testing that had been going on. And the recent estimates about genetic and somatic effects of high energy radiation, using new information, were not far off from the ones I made—well, perhaps three times lower, but I'm willing to accept that the bomb tests were carried out at the sacrifice of five million rather than 15 million unborn children.

I think I could have contributed more in the way of scientific discoveries, and have thought that I made a real sacrifice in this work for peace. I started the study of radioactive fallout; I was interested in that as a scientific question. I was serious to know what the answer was. But then I was sort of stuck with it. I felt that it was my duty to continue to work along these lines. Some scientists said that they considered me a spokesman for science in these matters, as I was to some extent with respect to the bomb test treaty. There were many other scientists working on this problem. . . . I happened to be the one who stirred up public feeling about it.

I gave over 500 public lectures about radioactive fallout and nuclear war and the need for stopping the bomb tests in the atmosphere and the need for eliminating war ultimately. I didn't enjoy giving these lectures especially. I had to take half my time for a decade working on these problems of international affairs, the nature of radioactive fallout, and the prospect of nuclear war in order that I could handle the subjects in a proper way and be able to meet my critics. I would have preferred to be doing scientific work instead. So when I received word in 1963 that I'd been given the Nobel Peace Prize for 1962, I felt that that showed that the sacrifice I had made was worthwhile, that it was proper for me to have done that.

THE FALLOUT DEBATE

"There is a widespread belief among scientists that the AEC has not been honest with the public in its pronouncements about the biological effects of fallout radioactivity."

The scientists, pacifists, and other members of the public who objected to the continuing technological development of nuclear bombs found their greatest immediate public-relations weapon in the radioactive fallout issue. No one became better known for his tenacious opposition to the extensive nuclear testing being done by the U.S. and the Soviet Union than Linus Pauling. For his determined activism he would pay a large penalty in both his personal and professional lives.

Many individuals and organizations did not want people to hear or read what he had to say. If they could not actually restrict (or even eliminate) his right to say it, they could at least try to make it difficult for him to speak out effectively in prominent places. The mainstream's popular magazines would not publish Pauling's articles or many of his rebuttal letters. They mirrored the official "disinformation" and attacks on Pauling's credibility and loyalty as an American. He was rarely invited to talk about the issues on in-depth TV news programs. And when he did, he often encountered biased reporting and outright defamation. For instance, when he appeared on the Sunday morning program "Face the Nation," he was subjected to blistering innuendoes attacking his character and implying that he was really a Communist.

Angry over misstatements in a major *Life* magazine article calculated to reassure the public about nuclear weapons research, partly by deliberately distorting Pauling's test-ban petition yet not quoting it, Pauling arranged to confront its coauthor, physicist Edward Teller, the "father of the H-bomb," in a much-publicized television debate. But his initial arguments, pointing out errors and misstatements in the article, often sounded quibbling and shrill. They were smoothly countered by his clever adversary, who "kept his cool" while Pauling emoted angrily. (Pauling's sense of outrage seems justifiable when one reads how Teller actually speculated blandly during the debate that radioactive fallout

might even be good for some people, and speed up the progress of evolution—slyly adding that Pauling, as a "progressive," should appreciate
that possibility.)

A number of viewers considered the widely and repeatedly shown
debate a draw. (The full transcription was later published in *Daedalus*,
the journal of the American Association for the Advancement of Science
(AAAS). It became part of the important permanent record of the fallout
controversy.)

Pauling kept insistently telling the public what he knew and feared,
and discussing what he had figured out, about radiation and fallout. But
he was denied a direct voice in the major media, though journalists could
attack him with impunity. An important antinuclear testing article entitled
"Every Test Kills" was published in 1958 in *Liberation*, a politically radical
magazine with comparatively few readers. And of course Pauling would
only be preaching there to a choir of dissidents. Here are excerpts from
it, showing how Pauling often felt disposed to argue with "the authorities"
and was apt to attack them as much on moral grounds as scientific ones.

I t is difficult to imagine what a war fought with great nuclear weapons
would be like—a war fought with 10,000 times as much explosive
energy as was used during the whole of the Second World War. It can be
estimated that in a third world war as many as 800 million people would
be killed by the blast, fire, and immediate radiation effects of the nuclear
bombs, and that many, perhaps most, of the large cities of the world
would be completely destroyed. In addition, the release of radioactive
materials would do serious harm to the pool of human germ plasm, in
such a way that hundreds of millions of seriously defective children
would be born in succeeding generations, and the human race as we know
it might cease to exist. . . .

In addition to the effects of blast and fire caused by these bombs,
there are the effects of radiation. These effects are insidious, and hard to
understand and evaluate. Like many other scientists, I have been making
use of my background of knowledge and experience in the fields of physics, chemistry, biology, and medicine in the effort to determine from the
published material what the probable estimates are of the effects of
atomic radiation on the health of human beings now living and on future
generations.

I have reached the conclusion, in agreement with most other scientists, that even the tests of nuclear bombs that are now being made are
harmful, because they spread an added burden of radioactive elements
over every part of the world. Let me discuss this point in some detail. The

effects of radiation are different in their nature from those of ordinary chemical poisons. A very small amount of an ordinary chemical poison will do no harm whatever to a person; but a very small amount of radiation may harm him in such a way as to cause him to die or to have a seriously defective child.

The rays of high-energy radiation are like little bullets that shoot through the body, damaging some molecules, breaking them in two, tearing away some atoms.

Some of the new molecules that are produced by radiation are poisonous. If enough of them are made in the body of a human being, he will die in a few days. He is said to have died of radiation sickness. Many thousands of people died in this way at the time of the Hiroshima-Nagasaki bombings.

The amount of radiation that causes death of a human being, acute radiation sickness, is about 300 to 600 rad (radiation units). There is an amount that does not cause death. But this does not mean that the human being is not hurt by a small amount of radiation, because, unlike ordinary poisons, radiation also has another effect that may be serious even if the amount of radiation is small. In each cell of the human body there are, among the billions of molecules of many different kinds, a few very important ones. These are the molecules, probably of deoxyribonucleic acid [DNA], that govern the behavior of the cell, that control the manufacture of other molecules, and the process by which the cell divides to form new cells, and that determine the nature of the children who are born to the person.

If one of these special molecules happens to be damaged by a single little bullet of radiation, from a single radioactive atom, it may be changed in such a way as to cause the cell to divide much more rapidly than the other cells of the body. This cell will then produce a colony of rapidly dividing cells, and the human being may die from cancer—perhaps leukemia, bone cancer, some other kind of cancer—caused by the single radioactive atom.

This is the reason why even the small amounts of radioactive atoms, such as strontium-90 and cesium-137, that are being spread all over the world by bomb tests, can cause people to die and can cause defective children to be born. There is no safe amount of radiation or of radioactive material. Even small amounts do harm. . . .

About 15 percent of the people who die of leukemia, the total number being about 150,000 per year, die because of the action of cosmic rays and natural radioactivity. There is nothing that we can do to escape these

natural radiations. Most of the rest of the cases of leukemia may be attributed to heredity or to chemical causes that have not yet been discovered.

But now people also are dying of leukemia caused by man-made radiation, including that of the fallout radioactivity of the nuclear bomb tests.

Some people say that the number of deaths from leukemia caused by
fallout is negligible. . . .

But I do not consider the effects negligible. I believe that each human
being is important, and that even a few thousand or a few million human
beings, a small fraction of all those now living in the world, are important.
Dr. Albert Schweitzer has said that "A humanitarian is a man who
believes that no human being should be sacrificed to a project—especially
to the project of perfecting nuclear weapons to kill hundreds of millions
of people." The leader of a nation testing nuclear weapons should know
that when he gives the order to explode a superbomb with 5 megatons
equivalent of fission he is probably dooming 1,500 people to die of leukemia, tens of thousands more to die of bone cancer and other diseases, and
100,000 seriously defective children to be born in future generations.

Do you think that I am exaggerating the effects of fallout from the
nuclear bomb tests? Do you think that scientists of the world are in serious disagreement about this matter, that some of them contend that no
damage whatever is done? If you were to think that I am seriously exaggerating, and that there are some scientists who contend that no damage is
done, I could not blame you, because you could easily have been misled
by statements published in the newspapers, in particular by the statements
that have been made by some scientists, some representatives of the
Atomic Energy Commission. . . .

Professor [Kenneth] Pitzer is a former student of mine, who is now
Dean of the College of Chemistry of the University of California in Berkeley, and who was for a time Director of Research for the Atomic
Energy Commission. Professor Pitzer, in his letter to me, said that the
tests are necessary to improve our nuclear weapons, and that "the risks to
human life from nuclear bomb tests are very small—much smaller than
the risks we take in our everyday living." He and Dr. Willard F. Libby,
the scientist who is a member of the Atomic Energy Commission, have
said that the number of deaths due to nuclear bomb tests is small compared with the number, 40,000 per year, due to automobile accidents.

To this argument I may reply that we strive to cut down the number of
people killed each year in automobile accidents, and that I believe that we
should strive also to cut down the number killed by bomb tests—which
we can do by stopping the tests.

The suggestion that is made in the comparison of the bomb-test damage with the 40,000 deaths per year from automobile accidents is that it would be all right to carry on bomb tests so long as the number of Americans killed by bomb tests is less than the number killed by automobiles, 40,000 per year. I consider this suggestion to be highly immoral. Dr. Libby has also compared the chance that a person takes of dying from leukemia or bone cancer or other disease caused by fallout radioactivity from the bomb tests with the chance that he takes of drowning if he goes swimming in the ocean. I believe that it is immoral also to make this comparison, and I am shocked that Dr. Libby should have made it.

We believe in freedom of the individual human being, freedom to decide for himself to take the chance of drowning if he wants to go swimming. It is an entirely different matter for a few national leaders in Washington, Moscow, and London to decide to subject every one of the two and one half billion people in the world to the action of radioactive poisons that can cause leukemia, bone cancer, and other diseases. . . .

There is a widespread belief among scientists that the Atomic Energy Commission has not been honest with the public in its pronouncements about the biological effects of fallout radioactivity. Scientists think that the public statements by spokesmen for the Commission, such as Dr. Libby, do not correctly express the beliefs of the biologists employed by the Commission itself.

There is no doubt that many of the public statements of the Commission are worded in such a way as to be seriously misleading. For example, according to the *New York Herald Tribune* of 9 June 1957, Dr. Libby on the day before had said that "There is no single provable case of any person being injured or seriously affected by any of the slightly extra radiation created in the United States by the tests."

I myself believe that this statement is true; but it is seriously misleading because it suggests that the fallout radiation does no harm. When a man dies from leukemia or bone cancer, there is no way of telling whether his disease was caused by fallout radiation or by cosmic rays or heredity or some other natural cause. Hence no one person can be pointed out as having died from leukemia or bone cancer caused by fallout—there is no provable case, as Dr. Libby says. Even statistical methods fail, because medical statistics are not good enough to detect a small increase, of one or two percent in the number of deaths by leukemia (about 150,000 per year). But it is not right to make the statement that there is no single provable case, and then say no more.

Another misleading statement made by Dr. Libby and other AEC spokesmen is that "the amount of fallout radioactivity is much smaller (a thousand times smaller, a hundred times smaller, many times smaller) than the maximum permissible amount." This statement is misleading because people in general think that the "maximum permissible amount" is an amount set by health authorities such that the risk of serious health damage is not so great as to make it necessary to forbid workers to be subjected to it. It is a limit of danger set for a hazardous occupation, an occupation that may be selected by a few individual workers, by their own decision; but it is an entirely unsuitable limit for the whole of the people in the world, with no choice of their own. The present "maximum permissible amount" of radiation for workers in hazardous industry is 200 rad (200 radiation units) in a lifetime, 5 rad per year.

Many biologists, such as Dr. W. L. Russell of the Oak Ridge National Laboratory, have estimated the amount of shortening of life expectancy that radiation produces. There is rather general agreement that the decrease in life expectancy is approximately what Professor Hardin Jones of the University of California has estimated, two weeks per rad. I calculate from this estimate that 200 rad of radiation, the "maximum permissible amount" that is now allowed, would, on the average shorten a man's life by about eight years.

The effect of radiation is a random one—some people are caused to die, others are not. Hence I estimate that if fallout radioactivity is as great as one two-thousandths of the "maximum permissible amount," as in fact it is (it probably is considerably higher than this figure), about one person in 2,000 in the world would have his life cut short by about eight years and that hence over one million people living in the world may be expected to have serious damage done to their health by the bomb tests.

I am more critical of Dr. Libby and of Professor Pitzer than I am of the nonscientists who make incorrect and misleading statements. I think that scientists, who have a background of knowledge and experience that permits them to know what the truth is, what the facts are, and who, despite this, make misleading statements which seem to be intentionally misleading, are really guilty of seriously improper behavior. . . .

Science is search for truth—it is not a game in which one tries to beat his opponent, to do harm to others. We need to have the spirit of science in international affairs, to make the conduct of international affairs the effort to find the right solution, the just solution of international problems, not the effort by each nation to get the better of the other nations, to do them harm when it is possible.

We must make a start. Let us start by stopping the bomb tests.

CAN'T WE HALT THE ARMS RACE?

"In the course of time . . . there can be built up around these agreements a system of international law and mutual trust and confidence that will be a boon to mankind."

If the mainstream media in the United States chose to ignore what Linus Pauling was saying, or else report it unfavorably, he could at least write a book. In late 1957 he began working on one. *No More War!* was written quickly. He began tape-recording the text (he often dictated the first draft of publications), then combined the material with various statements and statistics that he had made earlier, or was working on at the time.

When the book was published in 1958 he gave out many copies to help publicize his warning messages. Each U.S. senator got one, including John F. Kennedy, who in two years would become president. Whether or not JFK actually read it, Pauling always felt that he had been influenced by the nuclear test-ban campaign and its science-based reasoning, and possibly by some of the book's suggestions and pragmatic humanism. Among Pauling's warnings was his concern that supplying other nations with fissionable material for use in nuclear reactors to generate power could enable them someday to produce nuclear bombs. His reasoning remains relevant four decades later.

Here is a selection from the first part of the chapter on "The Need for International Agreements."

I dread any national policy that depends upon ever greater power of destruction, ever greater arsenals of nuclear weapons. Such a policy, followed by two great nations, is sure to lead to catastrophe for the world.

The United States and the USSR now have stockpiles of nuclear weapons that can destroy the world. Great Britain also has a stockpile.

So long as these weapons are in the hands of only three powers an agreement for their control is feasible. If testing continues and the possession of these weapons spreads to additional governments, the danger of outbreak of a cataclysmic nuclear war through the reckless action of some irresponsible national leader or through a technological or psychological accident will be greatly increased. . . .

The possibility cannot be ruled out of the existence, at some time in the near future, of a unified Germany. A prosperous German nation might, before many years have gone by, have its own stockpile of thousands of great nuclear weapons, enough to destroy the world—comparable in size to the American and Russian stockpiles. If the future world were to be a world of power politics, a world of world anarchy, as in the past, rather than of world government, there might arise in it a Germany armed with nuclear weapons and controlled by a successor to Hitler, a madman who would sacrifice the world to his nationalism.

With stockpiles of tens of thousands of nuclear weapons in the world, presumably some of them small ones, similar to the Hiroshima and Nagasaki bombs, there is the possibility that a considerable supply of the small weapons, so called tactical weapons, would be stored ready for use in some nation, an ally of the United States or the USSR, where they could be captured by an unscrupulous national government. The job of manufacturing fissionable material for these bombs, uranium-235 or plutonium-239, is a moderately difficult one, which might not be undertaken lightly by a small nation. However, these small atomic bombs can easily be converted into superbombs. All that is needed is a supply of the fusionable materials lithium and deuterium and a supply of ordinary uranium, easily available in ton lots.

An additional danger is introduced by the possibility of development of power plants based on controlled fusion. Much research is now being carried out on this problem, and significant progress was reported a few months ago by groups of workers in Great Britain, the U.S., and other countries. This effort, if successful, would result in a great boon to the world, because the supply of fuel (deuterium) is inexhaustible, and, moreover, the operation of the power plants would not be attended by the serious problem of disposal of the immense quantities of radioactive materials as a result of accident that attends the operation of fission power plants. But controlled-fusion power plants would introduce the danger that small nations could use the neutrons supplied by them to convert uranium into plutonium. The chemical process of purifying the plutonium is so simple that a small nation could undertake it, and in this way make its supply of fission bombs.

It might turn out in the course of time that scores of nations in the world would be able to develop good-sized stockpiles of weapons of 20-megaton size, capable of destroying the greatest cities in the world. There is the possibility of outbreak of nuclear banditry.

The nature of nuclear war is such that delay by even a few hours in meeting an attack might make retaliation impossible. Decision about initiating the counterattack cannot be postponed until the time when the commander-in-chief can be informed; it must be invested in the various subordinate commanders. With increase in the number of people with power to launch the planes and missiles with their loads of superbombs, there comes greater and greater chance that a mistake will be made, that a nuclear war will be started because of an error.

Already, two planes loaded with H-bombs have crashed. In one case there was an explosion of the molecular explosive that serves to compress the fissionable material and initiate the nuclear explosion, but the nuclear explosion, fortunately, did not occur.

Even though great care is taken there is danger that, in the course of time, an accident will take place resulting in the detonation of a super-bomb over a city or other target, and initiating the nuclear attack and counterattack that would bring disaster to the world.

An international agreement to stop the testing of nuclear weapons could serve as a first step toward a more general disarmament and the ultimate effective abolition of nuclear weapons, averting the possibility of a nuclear war that would be a catastrophe to all humanity. . . .

One argument sometimes given against making international agreements is that we cannot trust the Russians.

We do not trust the Russians at the present time—we have great stockpiles of weapons, designed to be used against them. But we live in the same world with the Russians and, now that the world has become a nuclear world, we must learn to get along with them.

The proposed international agreement for stopping all testing of nuclear weapons does not involve our trusting the Russians or the Russians' trusting us. In the discussions, both the USSR and the U.S. have accepted the plan of having an effective system of inspection stations within the countries involved, manned by inspectors from other countries.

I am reminded of the time when I was with Lord Boyd Orr, former head of the Food and Agriculture Organization of the United Nations, and he was asked the question "Do you trust the Russian Foreign Office?"

His reply to this question was "I do not trust any foreign office, not even my own!"

The world of nations at the present time is largely anarchistic. Nations make agreements, treaties, with one another, and each nation keeps these agreements, its treaties, so long as they are of benefit to it—then it breaks them. In the past there has been no penalty.

The stage of development of the world now is such that it is becoming more and more important to every nation in the world that international agreements be made and be kept. There are many agreements that can be made that would benefit all of the nations in the world, for all time.

One of these agreements is the agreement to stop the testing of all nuclear weapons. Another is an agreement to stop further stockpiling of nuclear weapons, with an effective system of international controls. Another, of equal importance, is an agreement about development and control of missiles, especially intercontinental ballistic missiles. These missiles, by decreasing to a quarter of an hour the time elapsing between the pressing of the button that initiates the attack and the wreaking of destruction on the enemy, make essential, in the absence of international control, a finger-on-the-trigger attitude, with its great danger of accidental start of nuclear war.

In the course of time, as other agreements about disarmament are made, agreements such as to benefit all of the nations and all of the people of the world, there can be built up around these agreements a system of international law and mutual trust and confidence that will be a boon to mankind.

The development of such a system of international law has, of course, already been begun. The United Nations in its operation is an illustration of it.

With every year of successful operation of the United Nations the system of international law becomes more effective. As more nations are added to the group within the United Nations—especially when China becomes a member nation—the United Nations will become more powerful, and the system of international law will become more and more effective.

As more and more agreements about disarmament and other international problems are made, we must at first continue to mistrust Russia— and Russia must continue to mistrust us. Each step toward the world of the future must be taken carefully—yet it must be taken.

STOP THE SPREAD OF NUCLEAR WEAPONS!

"Restriction of loyalty to within national boundaries is obsolete, and loyalty to the whole of mankind is now a necessity."

Aided by his wife, Ava Helen, Pauling pushed onward to promote international peace through conferences such as one they organized for Oslo in May of 1961, primarily to prevent nuclear weapons from being turned over to the control of other nations. Among its sponsors were a number of Nobel laureates and eminent scholars. Some months earlier, the Paulings had drafted the statement, which was initially circulated worldwide through the network of connections begun during the test-ban petition— eventually to be signed by some 200,000 people around the world. In Oslo it was signed by the 60 conference attendees—peace activists all.

At the time of the conference, the three nations with nuclear arsenals—the U.S., the Soviet Union, and Great Britain—had abstained for several years from atmospheric testing of new devices. There was no formal agreement in place, but an attempt to negotiate one was taking place in Geneva. Pauling was hopeful that a test ban would soon be accomplished, so was focusing more now on another agreement need that he felt was also urgent.

The problem of the spread of nuclear weapons was later taken up within the United Nations, and in 1970 a temporary nonproliferation treaty was signed; it was made permanent in 1995, when about 180 nations signed it—with the notable exceptions of India, Pakistan, and Israel, all of them now known to have developed nuclear capabilities. (See pages 257-261.)

THE OSLO STATEMENT: Adopted Unanimously by the Participants in the Conference Against the Spread of Nuclear Weapons, Oslo, Norway, 2 to 7 May 1961

We, 35 physical and biological scientists and 25 social scientists and scholars from 15 countries, have met for five days in Oslo to discuss the increased danger of nuclear war and world destruction that might result from the spread of nuclear weapons to further nations or groups of nations.

There is an imminent possibility of the acquisition of nuclear weapons by several nations. It is our conclusion that this constitutes a grave risk to the world:

1. Each addition to the number of nations armed with nuclear weapons drives its neighbors toward acquiring similar arms.
2. As nuclear weapons pass into more hands, the chance increases that a major war will be started by some human error or technical accident.
3. The spread to more nations increases the chance of deliberate initiation of nuclear war.
4. Increase in the number of nuclear powers would further increase the difficulty of achieving disarmament.
5. After it obtains nuclear weapons, a nation becomes a more likely target in any nuclear war.

There are further deleterious consequences of the acquisition, either by transfer or development, of nuclear weapons by other countries. The manufacture of nuclear weapons requires secret scientific research. This is against the tradition of science, interferes with personal freedom and international cooperation, and inhibits the use of science for the welfare of mankind. Weapons of total destruction concentrate great and often decisive political influence in military, industrial, and managerial groups.

Furthermore, the means of delivery associated with nuclear weapons make it practically impossible to exercise political control over their use.

For these and other reasons the spread of nuclear weapons must be stopped. The time for this action is limited.

We urge that the present nuclear powers immediately bind themselves by treaty not to transfer nuclear weapons to other nations or groups of nations, and that all nations not now possessing these weapons commit themselves to refrain from obtaining or developing them.

The Goal of General and Complete Disarmament: Preventing the spread of nuclear weapons is an essential part of the struggle to end war. For more than a decade scientists have been in agreement that the development of nuclear weapons has made it possible for man to destroy civilization. There is no adequate defense against nuclear weapons that could not be overcome by increasing the scale of the attack. There is no way of arranging international agreements to limit war between the great powers to the use of conventional weapons or of "small" nuclear bombs. Over and over again the leaders of nations, scientists, students of international relations, and other informed people have said that the stockpiles of nuclear weapons must not be used and that the only future for the world is one in which war between nations is abandoned and disputes are resolved by recourse to law.

Yet, despite the negotiations in Geneva for a bomb-test agreement, despite the efforts to achieve disarmament, the nuclear stockpiles have multiplied. The nuclear weapons of the great nations have explosive energy many thousands of times that of all of the explosives used in all past wars. These bombs in a war would kill a large part of the world's people.

We consider that no dispute can justify nuclear war. Even small wars today are extremely dangerous, because of the likelihood that a small war would grow into a world catastrophe.

In view of the danger and instability of the present arms race, the only sane policy for the world is that of achieving general and complete world disarmament with suitable international control and inspection. That is the proclaimed goal of the nuclear powers and of all other nations.

General and complete disarmament can and must be achieved. Its ultimate level should be that of international and national police forces. The problem of finding ways of eliminating nuclear weapons and arriving at general and complete disarmament is complex, but if it is given a fraction of the attention now devoted to military matters, we believe that it can be solved, and we urge that great efforts be expended on this at once.

Demilitarized Zones: Ways of relieving the pressures that cause the spread of nuclear weapons must be explored. The successful completion in 1960 of a treaty among many countries making all of Antarctica an atom-free zone affords a promising precedent. We urge that negotiations be started on the much more complex problem of extending the principle of demilitarization to the areas of greatest tension, beginning with Central Europe.

The Test-Ban Agreement: Since 1958 the three nuclear powers have sought to draft an agreement to stop the testing of all nuclear weapons. Many technical complications relative to inspection have arisen. Great progress has been made, but the negotiators are now finding it difficult to complete their task.

We oppose the carrying out of any further tests of nuclear weapons by any nation. We urge that the drafting of the test-ban treaty be swiftly completed by reasonable compromise on the few questions remaining unsettled.

Economic Consequences of Disarmament: Disarmament will provide a great opportunity to raise the standard of living throughout the world, but will also pose major problems of reorganization. We urge that detailed studies of these problems be undertaken now on both a national and an international scale. Such plans will positively encourage the effort towards disarmament. Considerable numbers of scientists, engineers, workers, and industrial managers are employed in research organizations or in work related to armaments. These men and women will be stimulated to support disarmament by the existence of practical plans to convert their employment from military to peaceful uses.

Moral Responsibility: Those who advocate the spread of nuclear weapons are making an understandable but archaic response to a radically new situation. This new situation demands a new understanding of moral responsibility. Restriction of loyalty to within national boundaries is obsolete, and loyalty to the whole of mankind is now a necessity. Individuals must bear personal responsibility for acts contrary to the interests of mankind.

Scientists and scholars have a unique responsibility to make plain the full significance of the revolutionary weapons development of the past decade. This requires presentation of factual information about the effects of atomic and hydrogen bombs, the overall consequences of nuclear war, and the brutalizing effects of preparation for nuclear war upon the values of our society. At the same time, their constructive proposals for coping with these grave problems are essential. Both wisdom and skill are needed to build movements capable of wresting our future from destruction.

Since we not only seek self-preservation, but also want to allow full lives for future generations, we must by example and teaching bring our children and youth to grasp world events, to realize their common interests with people in all countries, to reject hatreds and fears which some use to divide them, and to appreciate that no dispute between nations justifies nuclear war.

Science and scholarship are by tradition international undertakings, in which men work together in many parts of the world toward goals transcending their personal lives. This continuity of effort is now essential to prevent war and to seize our opportunities for freeing the world community from hunger, disease, illiteracy, and fear, for achieving economic, political, and social justice, and for contributing to a culture worthy of man.

A World Without War: Modern weapons transform man's dream of a world without war into a practical necessity. It is possible to organize the world community on principles of freedom and justice under law and mutual trust.

We must act on this conviction, with words and deeds aimed against the spread of nuclear weapons and toward disarmament.

NO HAVENS FROM FALLOUT

"My own estimate is that all of the people in the United States would be killed in a nuclear war, if we do not build fallout shelters, and that if we do build them and train the American people, all of the American people would be killed in a nuclear war."

Beginning in the late 1950s the American government, partly through the Atomic Energy Commission, began promoting the idea of "fallout shelters." These would be below-ground structures of varying sizes that might accommodate anywhere from one family to many inhabitants of a neighborhood or community. Food, water, lighting, cooking devices, and other emergency goods were to be stocked in them—in sufficient quantity for people to stay in safety and relative comfort for several weeks before venturing above into a devastated landscape. As in the air-raid drills of World War II, school children were instructed how to take cover under their desks in schoolrooms, in the event of an attack. People who survived the initial attack would have a brief period of time to get into a shelter that would protect them from the blast's descending fallout.

During this period elaborate settlements—virtual small cities with homelike furnishings—were being constructed deep within the earth to house key personnel (military commanders, scientists, and civil authorities) and support staff in the event of an all-out nuclear attack, thus guaranteeing the survival of at least some of the nation's people. Within these subterranean command posts were nuclear weapons for retaliating against the enemy who had launched a first strike, or a countering second strike.

Having one's very own bomb shelter became almost a status symbol of the early 1960s. Various magazines even gave explicit instructions for building one, from the simple to the elaborate and luxurious. (Some people later converted them into wine cellars.) Special contracting firms advertised for the chance to make them for families. Communities designated civil defense shelters that could house a number of persons without their own facilities for survival. During the fallout-shelter mania, Linus Pauling could be expected to give a sharp "reality check" in his evaluation of the entire endeavor, which he regarded as expensive, misguided, and futile. Much better, he thought, was putting an equivalent effort into banning the bombs and the bomb tests altogether—the bottom line of this article published in *Liberation*.

A great effort is now being made to get the American people to build a great number of fallout shelters. President Kennedy, in his letter to his fellow Americans of September 7th (published in *Life* magazine of 15 September 1961), says that there is much that the American people can do to protect themselves, and that in doing so we strengthen our nation. *Life* itself, in its accompanying article, makes the statement that if Americans took precautions against fallout, only about 5 million would die in a nuclear attack. "You could be among the 97 percent to survive if you follow advice on these pages. . . . How to build shelters. Where to hide in cities. . . . What to do during an attack."

The president in his letter states that:

> The government is moving to improve the protection afforded you in your communities through civil defense. . . . We are providing fallout shelters in new and in some existing federal buildings. We are stockpiling these shelters with one week's food and medical supplies and two weeks' water supply for the shelter occupants. In addition, I have recommended to the Congress the establishment of food reserves in centers around the country where they might be needed following an attack. Finally, we are developing improved warning systems which will make it possible to sound attack warning on buzzers right in your homes and places of business.

Can any reasonable person contend that these measures to protect ourselves in case of nuclear war should not be taken?

My answer is the following: I have made a study of this great problem, and have reached the conclusion that for the United States to embark upon a great program of shelter construction would not provide protection, but instead would increase the already great danger to our nation and to the American people.

There is no doubt that fallout shelters would provide some protection for some people, in case of a nuclear attack, and, moreover, that a populace that had been trained in methods of seeking protection would have a somewhat larger number of survivors than an untrained populace.

But the protection provided by a great system of fallout shelters and by training the populace could be and no doubt would be completely negated by the increased scale of the attack that would be delivered, if the arms race continues.

An atomic bomb explodes, perhaps 50 or 100 miles from you—far enough so that you are able to reach your shelter without having been vaporized, incinerated, or irradiated in such a way that you will die in a few days from acute radiation sickness. After two weeks in your shelter you are forced to leave it, or die of thirst and hunger. Then another bomb explodes. What is your fate?

Or you are 50 or 100 miles from the place where a bomb explodes: but instead of a 10-megaton bomb, it is a 100-megaton bomb. If you are 50 miles away, you will probably be burned to death. If you are 100 miles away, you might well receive a lethal dose of high-energy radiation before you achieve the protection of your shelter. But even if you do achieve the protection of your shelter, you will have to emerge sooner or later, and the environment will be so unfavorable that you will die.

The palliative effects of shelter construction and training the populace can be completely neutralized by increasing the scale of the attack by a factor of 4.

The statement made by *Life* magazine that all but 5 million Americans could be saved in a nuclear war is ludicrous. It is not worth discussing, except as an example of the extent to which militarists will go in misleading the American people. I find it shocking that President Kennedy should have written, "I urge you to read and consider seriously the contents of this issue of *Life*."

Professor Edward Teller is a person who can speak with greater authority than *Life* magazine. Although I think that Professor Teller is not reliable in these matters, because of his emotional and professional involvement with nuclear militarism, I shall quote him and discuss his statements.

Professor Teller (*U.S. News and World Report*, September 25, 1961) has said, "If we don't prepare, 100 million Americans could die in the first days of an all-out nuclear war. Thirty to 40 million more could die from starvation and disease. The United States would cease to exist. But I firmly believe 90 percent of our population could be saved. It means 20 million would die, and this is terrible to contemplate. But why not try to give 90 percent a decent chance for survival?"

I think that Professor Teller's estimate that 130 or 140 million Americans would die in a nuclear attack, if unprepared, and 20 million, if prepared with fallout shelters, is low. My own estimate is that all of the people in the United States would be killed in a nuclear war, if we do not build fallout shelters, and that if we do build them and train the American people, all of the American people would be killed in a nuclear war. . . .

I think that it is probable that, after two years of continued large-scale manufacture of additional bombs, the United States could in fact deliver 20,000 megatons of bombs over the Soviet Union, and that the Soviet Union could deliver a 10,000-megaton attack against the United States. These attacks, carried out in such a way as to maximize the number of deaths, would leave 94 percent of the people in each of the two countries dead at the end of 60 days, with 80 percent of the survivors so badly injured that they probably would die before many months had gone by.

My estimate of the effect on the United States of a nuclear war carried out in the near future is the following: the attack on the United States would involve 10,000 megatons of bombs. At the end of 60 days, 170 million of the 180 million American people would be dead. Of the remainder, 8 million would be injured and 2 million uninjured, except for some effects of radiation. They would have to cope with such delayed effects as the disorganization of society, disruption of communications, extinction of livestock, genetic damage, and the slow development of radiation poisoning from the ingestion of radioactive materials in the air that is breathed, the water that is drunk, and the food that is eaten—these factors were not taken into account in the RAND-Everett-Pugh studies. I judge that there would be no survivors in the United States at the end of a year, and no survivors in the Soviet Union.

Now let us assume that the populace is well trained and has built shelters of the sort assumed by the RAND Corporation (not those assumed by Professor Teller, which probably portray an unjustified optimism about the effectiveness of shelters). According to the RAND-Everett-Pugh studies, the same effects could be achieved in a 40,000-megaton attack on a prepared United States as in a 10,000-megaton attack on the unprepared United States.

Although, in case that the arms race, including the construction of shelters, continues, it is conceivable that the United States might gain some advantage over the Soviet Union or vice versa, such that the one nation or the other would have a slightly greater number of survivors in a nuclear war, the development of nuclear weapons has, I believe, now reached the stage where the great majority of the people in both countries would be killed, if a nuclear war were to be fought, and it has become irrational to plan to fight a nuclear war.

I think that the threats of nuclear attack that are made by the leaders of both countries are not seriously meant. No national leader would initiate the war that would end in the destruction not only of the enemy nation but also of his own. So long, however, as this period of extreme militarism continues, there will be great danger that a nuclear war will be initiated through some psychological or technological accident or through some series of catastrophic events such that even the wisest national leaders are unable to avoid the process that would result in the destruction of civilization.

I believe that the only rational course for the world to follow is that of working toward the goal of general and complete disarmament with the best possible system of controls and inspection, and with the development of an improved system of international law, such as to permit the solution of international problems in the way that represents the maximum of justice to all nations and all people.

THE IMPORTANCE OF A TEST-BAN TREATY

"No dispute between nations can justify nuclear war. . . . For the first time in the history of the world self-interest, selfishness, operates in the same direction as morality."

In the midst of disarmament and test-ban negotiations that began in 1958—pushed no doubt by the tornado of worldwide public opinion that Pauling had helped to stir up—the nuclear powers had been persuaded to declare a temporary moratorium on testing. "The Most Important Thing in Our World Today" was the apt title Pauling gave to a 1959 article about the Second Geneva Conference on the Testing of Nuclear Bombs.

But in 1961 France, eager to become a full-fledged nuclear power, broke the abstention period by conducting nuclear tests in the South Pacific, immediately altering the international climate. Both the USSR and the U.S. now said they would do whatever they chose to do regarding testing. Pauling sent a letter to Nikita Khruschev imploring the government not to resume nuclear testing. It elicited a lengthy, detailed response explaining the Russian rationale for new testing—national security. (Pauling's similar letter to President Kennedy went unanswered.)

In the autumn of 1961 the Russians set off in Siberia a series of atmospheric tests, including their most potent, "dirtiest" superbomb yet—and simply ignored the great outburst of criticism. The U.S. itself began preparing to conduct some long-delayed underground weapons tests. Wherever he could gain entry in the media, Pauling kept up a barrage of protests against both sides. And on March 1, 1962, he sent a scathing telegram to JFK, asking:

> Are you going to give an order that will cause you to go down in history as one of the most immoral men of all time and one of the greatest enemies of the human race?
>
> In a letter to the New York Times I state that nuclear tests duplicating the Soviet 1961 tests would seriously damage over 20 million unborn children, including those caused to have gross physical or mental defects and also the stillbirths and embryonic, neonatal and childhood deaths from the radioactive fission products and carbon-14.
>
> Are you going to be guilty of this monstrous immorality, matching that of the Soviet leaders, for the political purpose of increasing the still imposing lead of the United States over the Soviet Union in nuclear weapons technology?

Many years later, Pauling recalled that break in the moratorium period this way:

> I sent a very strongly worded telegram to Kennedy when the United States resumed nuclear testing in 1962, emphasizing the fact that every nuclear bomb tested in the atmosphere is exploded at the cost of the wellbeing of thousands of unborn children. This was after the Soviet Union had begun testing again and there had been a period of a couple of years when bomb tests hadn't been carried out—the result of an agreement between the United States and the Soviet Union to stop testing the nuclear weapons. The Soviet Union said so long as no Western country carries out bomb tests, we shan't carry out any. Then France exploded a couple of nuclear weapons in the atmosphere, and a couple of months later the Soviet Union resumed nuclear testing, saying that this agreement had been brought to an end because of a

violation by France. And then the United States resumed nuclear testing.

On April 25 of 1962, the day after Kennedy announced that the U.S. would soon resume nuclear testing, a blast went off in the South Pacific. Several days later the Paulings joined a large group of demonstrators who were picketing the White House in protest. On the evening of the second day they both went to dinner inside the presidential mansion, where the Kennedys were giving a dinner party honoring American Nobel laureates. When Jacqueline Kennedy met Dr. Pauling, she remarked how their daughter Caroline, noticing the picketers, had asked, "Mummy, what has Daddy done wrong now?" As for President Kennedy, he graciously told him, "I hope you will continue to express your feelings." There was little chance, of course, that Pauling would not.

Linus and Ava Helen Pauling break White House protocol and dance together at the banquet given in 1962 by President John F. Kennedy to honor America's Nobel laureates. Earlier that day they had picketed outside, to protest JFK's resumption of nuclear testing.

The sense of impending nuclear threat was greatly increased during the Cuban Missile Crisis in October of 1962, when the United States confronted the USSR over the latter's intention to install nuclear missiles in nearby Cuba, now headed by the revolutionist Fidel Castro and an outright communist government. The U.S. imposed a naval blockade—which Pauling called "an act of the utmost irresponsibility." "That was the most dangerous day in the history of the world," Pauling commented later. "President Kennedy threatened that we would use nuclear weapons if there was any resistance to the quarantine we imposed on that day." Warfare seemed imminent as Soviet ships approached the island less than 100 miles from Florida. Finally, Premier Khrushchev backed down and ordered the ships' return. Kennedy had taken a huge risk—and won. At another time in history the tense situation would have ended in outright war, as had happened in Cuba between Spain and the U.S. in 1898. But nuclear weapons might well have been launched, precipitating a third world war, perhaps this one truly "the war to end all wars."

Doubtless this hot crisis in the Cold War propelled the alarmed leaders and diplomats on both sides into seeking some accord over nuclear tests, which might in time even lead to a succession of disarmament agreements. Thus it appeared as if the two sides' possession of nuclear weaponry had indeed acted as a deterrent. Yet some peace advocates continue to believe that viewing the nuclear deterrence as an asset to peace-keeping has been a major roadblock in total disarmament efforts.

Naturally Pauling was greatly pleased in the following year when the American negotiating team in Geneva, under Kennedy's encouraging leadership, finally committed the U.S. to a limited test-ban treaty, covering the atmospheric tests that were the main source of radioactive fallout.

The following text was initially given as a speech in late spring of 1963, before the final test-ban agreement had been reached. As the speech was being printed for October publication, this welcome news could only be noted in a parenthetical insertion. The magazine, however, came out ahead of two important events: the announcement on October 10, 1963 that Linus Pauling had been selected to receive the Nobel Peace Prize—the very date the test-ban treaty was to take effect; and the assassination on November 23 of President Kennedy. Despite his willingness to resume America's nuclear testing in the previous year (to match the Russians'), and his involvement in other political decisions for which Pauling publicly chastised him, Kennedy had genuinely wanted to end the barrage of widespread radioactive fallout that had been going on for over 10 years.

Here, as elsewhere, Pauling considered the role of unilateral actions by nations that could prompt their adversaries to respond negatively—with increased militarism—or positively—with diminished belligerence and competitiveness.

T hese are extraordinary days that we are living through. If the world survives, we, or our children or grandchildren, may look back on them and say that they were the most important days in the history of the world. What we do now may determine the whole future of the human race.

I am going to talk about the problem of achieving peace and disarmament from the scientific point of view. After all I am a scientist—a human being, too—and I shall talk as a scientist and a human being. Scientists have had much to do with achieving the situation that we are in now and to which we must find a solution. They have changed the nature of the world in every respect: our means of transportation and communication, our food, everything about the world, but especially the means of waging war. That is the first way in which science is related to the great world problem.

The second way is this: To solve this great world problem we have to apply the attributes of science, which are honesty and objectivity. A scientist cannot make discoveries unless he is honest and unless he is objective—free from dogma, from bias. These attributes are, of course, the same as those of morality. In the old days the scientists and the moral leaders were the same men.

As for honesty, we must search for and accept the truth—the truth about the world . . . about everything.

Objectivity is the other attribute we must use—freedom from bias. . . .

I believe we must accept these ethical, scientific principles in our attack on the great world problem if the world is to be saved. . . .

No dispute between nations can justify nuclear war. And, with the knowledge about nuclear war existing in the world, we cannot eliminate only nuclear war; we have to eliminate war itself. For the first time in the history of the world self-interest, selfishness, operates in the same direction as morality. We now must rid the world of the immorality of war.

You can understand how happy I was on the 25th of September, 1961, to hear President Kennedy's great words before the General Assembly of the United Nations. He said,

> We challenge the Soviet Union not to an arms race but to a peace race. The disarmament program that we shall propose will involve the following steps: First, an agreement to stop the testing of all nuclear weapons, with a satisfactory system of international controls and inspection. Second, an agreement forbidding the transfer of nuclear weapons to nations or groups of nations that

*do not now have them, because the danger of outbreak of nuclear
war increases rapidly with increase in the number of nations having these weapons. Third, the cessation of manufacture of nuclear
weapons. Fourth, the gradual dismantling and destruction of nuclear weapons. Fifth, the cessation of manufacture of the vehicles
for delivering weapons, and the gradual destruction of the existing
vehicles.*

These are great words, but what about deeds? Very shortly thereafter,
President Kennedy announced that our military budget would be
increased by three billion dollars—a unilateral action by the United States
in the direction of increased militarism. It was followed a month later by
an announcement that the Soviet Union would increase its military budget—and these increases have continued. At that time, the Soviet Union
had already begun the testing of nuclear weapons.

Before 1961 the United States had tested 110 megatons altogether,
and the Soviet Union had tested 55 megatons. The Soviet Union's 1961-
62 series of tests of great weapons has raised her total megatonnage to
over 400, and the tests carried out by the United States now total 200
megatons. The Soviet Union is now responsible for twice the amount of
contamination of the atmosphere with radioactive materials that cause
cancer in human beings who are now alive, and in unborn human beings,
and cause damage to the pool of human germ plasm that I estimate will, in
the course of time, result in the birth of 15 million grossly defective children, children with gross physical or mental defects. (This is a very uncer-
tain estimate, based on the best information that I could get from the
Federal Radiation Council.)

The first item on President Kennedy's program was to make a bomb-
test agreement. Negotiations have been going on for four years. One matter under negotiation is the number of veto-free, on-site inspection trips,
where it is thought that a small atomic bomb might have been tested, but
might have escaped detection. It is not possible to test big atomic bombs
underground and escape detection, only bombs smaller than the
Hiroshima and Nagasaki bombs.

The Soviet Union has tested very few of these small bombs, although
she has had plenty of opportunity to do so; her tests have been almost
entirely of megaton bombs. Nevertheless, there is a fear that she might
carry out some underground tests, which would be undetected by seismo-
graphic instruments because they would be confused with earthquakes.
Four years ago we contended that there would be about 100 earthquakes
per year with which these bomb tests might be confused, whereas the

Soviet Union said there would be only 35. We wanted to have 20 percent as many tests as earthquakes, and accordingly we asked for 20 free, on-site inspection trips per year. The Soviet Union said she would allow only three per year, which would be 8 percent of the 35, but, of course, only 3 percent of a hundred. Nobody proposed a compromise between 3 and 20.

Now is a crucial time. The negotiations have been resumed, and the situation has changed. . . .

The *London Times*, on the 10th of September . . . said, "There is probably no other subject on which people in all countries are so nearly unanimous as the need to put an end to nuclear testing."

Secretary General U Thant of the United Nations said, "Stop haggling over the number of inspections. We must renounce war, or we shall see the end of the human race." If we do not work to apply pressure on our government and the Soviet government to accept the compromise proposed by the neutral nations, the bomb-test agreement may not be made.

What about President Kennedy's second point, to make an international agreement preventing the spread of nuclear weapons to other nations or groups of nations, thus decreasing danger from the outbreak of nuclear war? There is no doubt that the spread of nuclear weapons would be accompanied by an increased probability of nuclear war as a result of some psychological or technological action or some deliberate action of an irresponsible national leader. . . .

President Kennedy has, I think, tried to support the policy he announced on the 25th of September, 1961, but he has not done it, and I surmise that, as a politician, he has decided that he is not able to do it. His recent actions were, I think, the result of pressures from the military and industrial complex that have turned out to be more powerful than the pressures from the people who are concerned about themselves, their lives, their children, their children's children, and about the hundreds of billions of dollars over the years wasted on armaments. . . .

I think that the president has striven to follow a course of sanity, and that we, the American people, have failed him in not providing him with support. When my wife and I went to Geneva during the bomb-test negotiations and talked with Ambassador Wadsworth, Semyon Tsarapkin, and Ambassador Sir Michael Wright, Ambassador Wadsworth said that he was discouraged. "Go back home to the United States," he said, "and get your organization, SANE, to work harder to alert the American people, to get them on the job, to stand up, to say what they want. Nobody in Washington can stand up against public opinion." But public opinion has not yet become effective. . . .

I would like to see some senator stand up in the Senate sometime and say, "We must do this because it is the moral thing to do," rather than to ask, "What will the United States gain from this action, from this appropriation, from this aid from the Alliance for Progress?" The characters of politicians are just the opposite of those of men of science and morality. Most of the immorality in government is associated with the institution of war. I shall be happy when we get rid of this institution, when our nation, along with the other nations of the world, becomes moral.

In a December issue of the *Saturday Evening Post* was an article reporting an interview by Stewart Alsop with Secretary of Defense Robert McNamara that illustrates this point. Alsop: "What do you think of the proposition that the price of any kind of nuclear war is so high that the nuclear weapon is not a rational instrument of national policy?" McNamara: "No sane man wants nuclear war or any kind of war, but war has to be conceivable in support of vital national interests; otherwise you have no real national power."

Let me interpret this; what does it mean? It means that if what we want is contrary to the principles of justice, so that we can't go to the United Nations and ask that the matter be resolved, then we have to be able to threaten nuclear war. . . . This is the basis of our foreign policy; this is how irrational we are.

I think we can see that it is not the Soviet Union that is the enemy of the United States, the enemy of the American people; it is not the United States that is the enemy of the Soviet Union, the enemy of the Russian people. It is war that is our common enemy. War and militarism may lead to the death of all of us—all the Russian people and all the American people—to complete destruction of our nations and much of the rest of the world. And it is the military-industrial complex that President Eisenhower talked about in his last speech, that is the great enemy of the American people. These militarists want to keep the Cold War going.

It is profitable to keep the Cold War going; the system of investments we have in foreign countries almost requires that we keep it going. These are the enemies of the American people, and of President Kennedy; they are the ones who are winning out, are causing President Kennedy to act in a direction contrary to his expressed policy, to increase the intensity of the Cold War, to rearm West Germany, to promote the spread of nuclear weapons, to prevent the bomb-test agreement from being made, because it might lead to other agreements that would decrease the intensity of the Cold War.

It is our task now to defeat these forces of evil. We have to be working hard right now; this is the time, perhaps the last time when it will be
possible for a bomb-test agreement to be made. . . .

The world has been changed in an astounding way by the discoveries
made by scientists. Never again shall we have the world of William
Shakespeare, the world of Queen Victoria, the world of President
Roosevelt—never again. This is a new world in which we live. It is possible to eliminate war from the world, and it is our task, now, to do our part.

We must work—bombard the senators, our local senators, Senator
Fulbright, the chairman of the Foreign Relations Committee, and the president, with telegrams, urging that the proposal of the neutral nations about
the bomb-test agreement be accepted, that nuclear weapons not be turned
over to NATO, that we not take unilateral actions of increasing the military budget, which are always followed by similar unilateral actions by
the Soviet Union. These actions cannot increase our safety; instead, they
increase our danger.

The balance of terror that now exists will continue to exist in the
future no matter how much money is spent. No effective defense except
that of peace can be achieved. We shall remain in great danger, from now
until the day when the world is destroyed, unless we make the international agreements leading to disarmament and peace. It is our task—your
task and my task—to do our part in achieving this great goal.

THE NOW-PROVEN HAZARDS OF HIGH-ENERGY RADIATION

*"The best course that we can follow with respect to exposure to high-
energy radiation is still . . . keep the dose as low as you can."*

In the years after Pauling delivered his warnings about the effects on
public health of radioactive fallout from nuclear tests, he and many scientist colleagues, physicians, and other activists insisted on gaining
more explicit and honest information from the government about the
weapons tests results along with other data about radiation. Whatever
they could not find out from the AEC itself or the Nuclear Regulatory
Commission, which replaced it in 1975, they sought to obtain elsewhere.
This included the health histories and records of Hiroshima and
Nagasaki survivors; of "downwinders"—individuals and families unknow-
ingly exposed to the most intense fallout from the U.S. tests because
they lived close to the Nevada Test Site; of persons who had worked in
the development laboratories; and of workers at the industrial sites—

primarily Oak Ridge, Tennessee, and Hanford, Washington—where enriched uranium and plutonium were produced from uranium ore.

Furthermore, a number of scientists conducted experiments on laboratory animals using varying amounts of radiation and exposures over time, and studied the results in terms of cancer incidence and genetic damage transmitted to offspring. This data could be extrapolated to estimate the likely consequences to humans of equivalent amounts of high-energy radiation, even if given in very low doses over a long period of time. It is generally agreed that any amount of radiation (including "background" radiation coming from the environment) can be detrimental. Opponents in the U.S. of nuclear reactors as an energy source—once enthusiastically seen as a replacement for fossil fuels—are often successful in arguing their case with the public by pointing to the health hazards of workers and populations exposed to radiation; the problem of safe disposal of nuclear wastes; and the possibility of a nuclear accident (as at Three Mile Island in Pennsylvania in 1979 and the far worse one at Chernobyl in the USSR).

From the mid 1960s until his death in 1994, Pauling occasionally wrote papers about radiation, but more often made statements to interviewers who sought his opinions. He no longer supported the use of nuclear reactors and instead urged scientists, engineers, industry, and nations' governments to develop alternative sources of generating power—solar, wind, geothermal, and tidal energy.

Popular prejudice against the installation of nuclear reactors is stronger in the U.S. than in most other countries. The thorny issues of health and public safety has made the enthusiastic promotion of nuclear reactors politically incorrect, and the "anti-nuke" attitude Pauling helped engender in the '50s lingers on.

In his 1983 addendum to the chapter in the 25th Anniversary Edition of *No More War!* on "Radiation and Health," Pauling acknowledged the painstaking and heroic efforts made by John Gofman, a former physician with the AEC, to educate the public about the long-term consequences of exposure to high-energy radiation, including X-rays.

T he best course that we can follow with respect to exposure to high-energy radiation is still the one recommended by the Committee on Genetic Effects of Atomic Radiation of the United States National Research Council–National Academy of Sciences: Keep the dose as low as you can. Since 1958 additional information about the biological effects of high-energy radiation has been obtained. This information does not invalidate the statements and conclusions that were presented in Chapter 7, 25 years ago. Discussions of the recent work can be found in a number of books. An especially thorough and detailed discussion is in the book *Radiation and Human Health*, by Gofman.

In the years after 1958 the United States Atomic Energy Commission continued with its efforts to suppress the public's knowledge of the damage done by fallout radioactivity and carbon-14 produced in the tests of nuclear weapons. Discussion of these efforts is presented in a number of books, including *Killing Our Own: The Disaster of America's Experience with Atomic Radiation*, by Harvey Wasserman and Norman Solomon.

Dr. John W. Gofman has become one of the most active and responsible authorities about the biological effects of high-energy radiation. He was associate director of the Lawrence Livermore Laboratory, where research and development on nuclear weapons is carried out, from 1962 to 1969, and he was the founder of the Laboratory's Biomedical Research Division, where he carried on a program of evaluating the role of ionizing radiation and chromosome injury in causing human cancer, at the request of the Atomic Energy Commission. He is now professor emeritus of Medical Physics at the University of California, Berkeley.

Wasserman and Solomon in their book refer to Gofman in the following words:

> *Gofman had since become a medical doctor and a nationally known health researcher, holding a number of prestigious awards for his work on heart disease. Most important of all—from the AEC's standpoint—Gofman was an atomic loyalist. During the days of the test-ban campaign he had served on the Commission's "Truth Squad," which toured the country in the path of Linus Pauling and others, attacking their anti-testing opinions. But soon after taking charge of the AEC's radiation health program, Gofman was submerged in controversy. Summoned to Washington to discuss "radioactive iodine," he found himself in the midst of a heated discussion about Harold Knapp, an AEC scientist whose study of fallout in southern Utah had shown levels of radiation far in excess of Commission standards. The real purpose of the meeting, Gofman said later, was to find a way to suppress Knapp's findings, which would "in effect, make the AEC reports over the past 10 years look untrue." After dissecting Knapp's research, Gofman and three other committee members could find nothing wrong with it. They recommended publication of his paper.*

Gofman and his associate Dr. Arthur Tamplin had by 1967 become convinced that the entire approach of the AEC to the handling of public health and the safety aspects of the development of nuclear energy was erroneous. In 1969 they stated that if the average exposure of the United States population were to reach 0.17 rads per year average, which was then allowed by the government regulations, there would be in time an excess of 32,000 of fatal cancer plus leukemia per year, and that these deaths would occur year after year. They recommended that the legal exposure limit be reduced immediately to one-tenth the amount, that is to 0.017 rads per year average. The support for their work was soon cut off by the AEC, and they resigned their positions in the Lawrence Livermore Laboratory.

In his 1981 book *Radiation and Human Health* Dr. Gofman presents an analysis of the existing evidence about radioactive fallout that provides quantitative support for the conclusions stated in the first edition of this book, especially with respect to cesium-137, strontium-90, and carbon-14. In addition, he discusses another cause of damage to human health by nuclear weapons and nuclear fission power plants. This is the element plutonium, which is a powerful poison.

Plutonium is the element whose nuclei undergo fission in most atomic bombs—uranium is the other element that undergoes fission. When a nuclear bomb is exploded, not all the plutonium experiences destruction by the process of nuclear fission; instead, some of it remains as the element plutonium, mainly plutonium-239. The plutonium attaches itself to dust particles in the atmosphere, and these particles fall to earth as part of the local fallout or worldwide fallout. While they are falling through the atmosphere they are inhaled by human beings. A fraction of the inhaled plutonium is retained permanently in the lungs. The amount of this fraction that is retained in the lungs is much larger for cigarette smokers than for nonsmokers, mainly because the smoking of cigarettes damages the cilia in the bronchi of the lungs, which have the function of removing particulate matter from the lungs. The plutonium nuclei decay by radioactive decomposition, producing alpha particles, which cause cancer.

Gofman estimates that 328 kilograms of plutonium-239 or other plutonium isotopes had been released upon the 48 coterminous states of the United States by 1972 as the result of fallout from atmospheric testing of nuclear weapons, and that about 10 times that amount had been deposited over the whole world, mainly in the Northern Hemisphere. Experimental studies with dogs (beagles) had shown that 0.38 microgram in the lung is enough to cause fatal cancer. Only a small part of the plutonium that is falling toward the surface of the earth gets into the lungs of human beings, but Gofman's calculations of the amount that is inhaled have led him to the conclusion that the plutonium from the bomb tests carried out up to 1972 have caused cancer that has been fatal or will ultimately be fatal in more than 100,000 people in the United Stales and a total of more than 950,000 in the world as a whole. Accordingly, plutonium must be taken into consideration, together with the radioactive fission products and carbon-14, in estimating the damage to human beings caused when nuclear warheads are detonated on the surface of the earth or in the atmosphere. We must also be similarly concerned about plutonium from the operation of nuclear power plants.

Dr. Gofman also points out that misleading statements about the danger of plutonium are sometimes made by spokesmen for the government or for the nuclear power plant industry. The statement is made that no person has ever been shown to have died of cancer caused by plutonium. The reason that this statement is misleading is that after a person has contracted cancer it is, with rare exceptions, impossible to say what caused the cancer. Lung cancer caused by plutonium is indistinguishable from lung cancer caused by carcinogenic substances in tobacco smoke or some other carcinogenic agent. It is accordingly usually impossible to say that a particular patient who died of lung cancer had died as a result of the plutonium that he had ingested. Every person in the world now has some bomb-test plutonium in his or her lungs, so that every person is at risk from this cause of cancer as well as from cesium-137 and other substances produced by the explosion of nuclear weapons. Whenever a person dies of cancer, there is a chance that death was caused by the plutonium that was inhaled and that had remained deposited in the lungs.

Moving on to Linus Pauling's receipt of the Nobel Peace Prize for 1962, awarded for his efforts to propel international leaders and diplomats into achieving a nuclear test ban, it is important to understand the humanitarian and ethical motivations behind these efforts.

Pauling saw value in the lives and wellbeing of individuals and their future offspring, and did not regard them as mere statistics and something easily expendable. This viewpoint ultimately won out, both in nuclear treaties and in a dramatic change in the public's attitude. What kind of person nowadays would encourage atmospheric nuclear testing, complacently put up with fallout, or face the prospect of nuclear warfare with equanimity, secure about holing up in some "fallout shelter"? When reading through Pauling's speeches, articles, and correspondence of the long and arduous pre-test ban period, one is likely to feel amazed that there was any debate at all—and to be impressed anew with Pauling's unwavering determination, despite constant calumny.

Linus Pauling had a favorite quotation from an American of the past who possessed great practical and moral wisdom—the printer, author, inventor, and statesman Benjamin Franklin. Beginning in the early 1950s, through the years Pauling often used it in talks and writings, including it even as an epigraph to a new edition of his *General Chemistry*, doubtless hoping that students would absorb the message along with the dense information he had provided about his favorite science. Franklin had written the words in 1780 in a letter to his friend and Philadelphia neighbor, Joseph Priestley, the radical minister and ingenious chemist who had emigrated to the United States, chased from England because of his support of the principle of democratic revolution. It would seem only fitting to give Franklin's telling observation here, at the close of this section on Pauling's concerns about nuclear weaponry and nuclear warfare, to precede the next section on Pauling's humanitarian perspective.

The rapid progress true Science now makes occasions my regretting sometimes that I was born so soon. It is impossible to imagine the height to which may be carried, in a thousand years, the power of man over matter. O that moral Science were in as fair a way of improvement, that men would cease to be wolves to one another, and that human beings would at length learn what they now improperly call humanity.

The Paulings admire the 1962 Nobel Peace Prize gold medal. When the award was announced, Pauling's only regret was that it was not given in Ava Helen's name, too. (Photo courtesy of NTB, Oslo, Norway)

Part IV

Peace Through Humanism

In the 15 years following the end of the Second World War, Linus Pauling, in holding up the banner of peace, had proved courageous in dealing with the secrecy and persecutions that characterized his own nation's response to the USSR's Iron Curtain. He persisted in trying to calm unreasonable fears of communist recruiting activities and alert the public to offenses of civil rights, which frequently were directed by the government and protected by bureaucracy. He continued to proclaim the value of the United Nations as an international problem-solving and governing entity—even though the expanding New York-based organization was increasingly attacked by American conservatives who wanted to preserve the unregulated autonomy of the United States and objected to any criticisms of its policies and actions.

Pauling thereby put his professional reputation in peril and disrupted his personal life again and again. But why? Because he felt impelled by a sense of duty to humanity, not just to his own society. Although he had the reputation of enjoying the spotlight and adulation, it would have been far easier on him to get them in less arduous and time-consuming ways, as he could have just by being a notable scientist engaged in a number of frontier areas of research.

When Pauling talked about the scientific aspects of nuclear weapons, both with scientists and the lay public, he almost always introduced humanitarian considerations. As he worked for world peace throughout the 1950s, he had been moved to stake out and express what might be considered a philosophical position, or at least a set of statements that would summarize what he thought and felt about humankind.

Accustomed to dealing with science topics, he might start with the facts as he knew them, which related to nuclear warfare and testing. But then he would introduce terms such as morality and ethics that are usually associated with religion.

The spiritual realm was not familiar territory to Pauling. He had received the customary Sunday school training in childhood. But in early adolescence he became an agnostic, having seen no evidence of a supreme being who, while presiding over the world and a vast universe beyond it, was concerned not just with human individuals' fates in life, but with their thoughts and behavior.

Pauling tended to get quickly impatient with philosophers' wordy speculations—though he appreciated the blunt verbal activism of elderly British mathematician-philosopher, Bertrand Russell, who several times got himself jailed for participating in antiwar protests. He often quoted the eloquent peace manifesto written by Russell in 1955, which Einstein had signed two days before his death, and which was also signed by Pauling and eight others (pages 72-77).

Linus Pauling considered himself a humanist, particularly after joining the Unitarian Church in 1950. Humanism, the form of philosophic thought that focuses on the interests, needs, and idealistic goals of humanity, dates back in Western civilization to the classical times of Ancient Greece and Rome. Revived as the anti-authoritarian "free-thinking" rationalism of the 18th century's Enlightenment period, humanism for many people has now replaced the formal belief system offered by organized religions—notably Christianity, in the West—while still espousing strong codes of personal and communal ethics. Humanism maintains that one does not need to believe in God in order to live a moral life, which entails doing good for other people, as well as avoiding doing harm to anyone—a near-universal precept usually called the Golden Rule.

Pauling practiced humanism through his long involvement with educating the public about the perils that would come from a future nuclear war, about the damage to public health caused by bomb testing, and about the wasteful expenditure of money, human effort, and the Earth's resources on military armaments. Pauling's humanism was also expressed in his repeated insistence on the need for setting up and enforcing a system of world law that would effectively deal with nation-states who violate human and civil rights within their own boundaries, or who in some way violate other nations.

In the course of discussing nuclear weapons, Pauling over time gradually set his own cohesive ethical values, as this section shows. His increasing grasp of the technology of nuclear weapons was always balanced by his humanistic messages to audiences and readers. Pauling would apply the morality system he created in the period after World War

II to many more circumstances than those engendered by the existence of nuclear weapons.

I BELIEVE IN THE POWER OF THE HUMAN SPIRIT

"I believe that there is a greater power in the world than the evil power of military force, of nuclear bombs—there is the power of good, of morality, of humanitarianism."

From time to time Pauling produced passages in his discourse that were rhapsodic in tone. Often the statements were simple—seeming almost childlike in expressing a sense of wonder at nature and the universe, especially when amplified by scientific knowledge. Notably beginning in the late 1950s and early 1960s, this expression of awe preceded or accompanied an emphasis on ethics and morality—but not, for this avowed nonbeliever, from a traditionally religious point of view.

Here, for example, is just such an inspirational passage from Pauling's influential 1958 book, *No More War!* This book combined technical information—nuclear weapons, their destructive potential in warfare, and the radioactive hazards to health from testing them—with specific proposals about how successful negotiations and lasting peace might be achieved among nations.

Sometimes I think that I am dreaming; I can hardly believe that the world is as it is. The world is beautiful, wonderful—scientists every year uncover, discover, more and more wonders of organic and inorganic nature. Man is a wonderful organism—the human body, with its millions of millions of cells, molecules of many different kinds entering into chemical reactions with one another; the human mind, capable of feats of complex calculation, of abstract reasoning infinitely beyond those of even the greatest giant electronic calculator.*

Man has developed admirable principles of morality, which in large part govern the actions of individual human beings. And yet, we are murderers, mass murderers. Almost all of us, even many of our religious leaders, accept with equanimity a world policy of devoting a large part of our world income, our world resources—one hundred billion dollars a year—to the cold-blooded readying of nuclear weapons to kill hundreds of

---

* *Editors' note:* When this book was published in 1958, computers of course were only just beginning their amazing evolution into much smaller, faster, more powerful and versatile data-processing and communication devices.

millions of people, to damage the pool of human germ plasm in such a way that after a great nuclear war our descendants might be hardly recognizable as human beings.

Does the Commandment "Thou shalt not kill" mean nothing to us? Are we to interpret it as meaning "Thou shalt not kill except on the grand scale," or "Thou shalt not kill except when the national leaders say to do so"?

I am an American, deeply interested in the welfare of my fellow Americans, of our great nation. But I am first of all a human being. I believe in morality. Even if it were possible (which it is not) to purchase security for the United States of America by killing all of the hundreds of millions of people behind the Iron Curtain without doing any harm to anyone else, I would not be willing that it be done.

I believe that there is a greater power in the world than the evil power of military force, of nuclear bombs—there is the power of good, of morality, of humanitarianism.

I believe in the power of the human spirit. I should like to see our great nation, the United States of America, take the lead in the fight for good, for peace, against the evil of war. I should like to see in our cabinet a secretary for peace, with a budget of billions of dollars per year, perhaps as much as 10 percent of the amount now expended for military purposes. I should like to see set up a great international research program involving thousands of scientists, economists, geographers, and other experts working steadily year after year in the search for possible solutions to world problems, ways to prevent war and to preserve peace.

During the past hundred years there have been astounding developments in science and technology, developments that have completely changed the nature of the world in which we live. So far as I can see, the nature of diplomacy, of the conduct of international affairs, has changed very little.

The time has now come for this aspect of the world to change, because we now recognize that the power to destroy the world is a power that cannot be used.

May our great nation, the United States of America, be the leader in bringing morality into its proper place of prime importance in the conduct of world affairs!

TRANSITION TO PEACE

"Science is the search for the truth—it is not a game in which one tries to beat his opponent, to do harm to others."

Pauling's book *No More War!* allowed him to expand upon and expound a number of the concerns he had about the future of humankind. The technological advances that had gradually produced civilization over millennia had been greatly accelerated in the past several hundred years, particularly during the 20th century. Now we were confronting for the first time, the possibility—even the probability—of annihilation. But Pauling still had hope that this terrifying prospect might finally instill some sense in national leaders, who would decide in favor of peace.

Pauling often thriftily reused statements he had made that he particularly liked because they expressed well what he wished to convey. Thus his book held echoes of previous writing—and would provide material for new texts in the future, including his Nobel Peace Prize lecture.

W e live now in a period of rapid change—a period of revolution, of nuclear revolution. Everything in the world has been changed as a result of scientific discoveries. I think that the greatest change of all is that in the ways of waging war—the change from old-fashioned molecular explosives, the one-ton TNT bomb, to the great nuclear weapon, the superbomb that is 20 million times as powerful.

This change, from molecular explosives to superbombs, has caused war to rule itself out.

Even the politicians and diplomats are changing, although they are slow to show it. They still behave at times as though war were the method to solve international disputes, but it is clear that the leaders of the great nations know that a nuclear war cannot be allowed to wreak its destruction on the world.

The time has now come for war to be abandoned, for diplomacy to move out of the 19th century into the real world of the 20th century, a world in which war and the threat of war no longer have a rightful place as the instrument of national policy. We must move towards a world governed by justice, by international law, and not by force.

We must all, including the diplomats and national leaders, change our point of view. We must recognize that extreme nationalism is a thing of the past. The idea that it is just as important to do harm to other nations as to do good for your own nation must be given up. We must all begin to work for the world as a whole, for humanity.

Science is the search for the truth—it is not a game in which one tries to beat his opponent, to do harm to others. We need to have the spirit of science in international affairs, to make the conduct of international affairs the effort to find the right solution, the just solution of international problems, not the effort by each nation to get the better of other nations, to do harm to them when it is possible.

I believe in morality, in justice, in humanitarianism. We must recognize now that the power to destroy the world by the use of nuclear weapons is a power that cannot be used—we cannot accept the idea of such monstrous immorality.

The time has now come for morality to take its proper place in the conduct of world affairs; the time has now come for the nations of the world to submit to the just regulation of their conduct by international law.

THE NEED FOR PEACE *NOW*

"We believe in morality, and yet we are cold-bloodedly preparing to kill, to murder hundreds of millions of people."

By the end of the '50s and into the early '60s Pauling's sense of urgency regarding the Cold War's nuclear arms race reached a fever pitch. He was pinning his hopes on what he called "the most important activity in the world today"—the Second Geneva Conference on Bomb Tests, begun at the end of October of 1958. He believed that if an accord could be reached on the cessation of testing, further negotiations could then take place among the nuclear nations on halting the building, stockpiling, and intercontinental transporting of nuclear bombs on submarine patrols and bombers ready to drop payloads whenever they received an appropriate sequence of doomsday signals from the highest military command.

Pauling felt he could not get his desperate message out too often or to too many people. Here is an excerpt from a talk he gave to a Los Angeles-area church congregation in 1959, in which he emphasized the need to conduct research on achieving peace. This talk shows how simply and vividly he could speak to ordinary citizens about the dangers involved in either using or testing nuclear weapons. Inevitably—particularly considering his audience—he brought in the issue of morality, as in desensitizing public reactions to "body count" in warfare.

I t is hard to understand what the world situation is now. I can hardly believe that such great changes have taken place in the last 15 years. The Second World War was fought almost entirely with one-ton block-busters—one ton of TNT, equivalent to 2,000 sticks of dynamite. *One* stick of dynamite, of course, can do quite a bit of damage, can kill people who are close by. Two thousand of them—2,000 pounds of TNT—could smash this building and kill everybody in it. During the Second World War about 3 million one-ton blockbusters, 3 million pounds of high explosive, were used. Then came the atomic bomb—the Hiroshima and Nagasaki bombs—each one equivalent to 20,000 tons of TNT—20,000 one-ton blockbusters, killing 100,000 apiece at Hiroshima and Nagasaki.

We are guilty, of course, of having used these weapons without warning. It is astounding how people's ideas change. Twenty years ago everyone was horrified at the bombings of Guernica, where thousands of innocent women and children were killed by Franco's bombers. And then when tens of thousands—40,000—were killed at Amsterdam by Hitler's bombers we were again horrified. Yet, before long, *we* had adopted the policy of mass bombardment of the German cities, and mass bombardment of Tokyo with fire bombs. And then we dropped the atomic bomb. This just shows how the immorality of nations has increased in recent decades.

And that was not the end. On the first of March 1954 we detonated, at Bikini, the first modern bomb—the first superbomb—a three-stage bomb with 10 pounds of plutonium as its trigger, about 200 pounds of lithium deuteride as its fusion stage, and a thousand pounds of ordinary uranium metal for the third stage. The bomb had the explosive energy of 20 million tons of TNT, equal to a thousand Hiroshima or Nagasaki bombs. This *one* bomb was the equivalent of seven times all of the explosive used in the whole of the Second World War.

I heard Norman Cousins illustrate what these bombs are like—these bombs that are now the standard weapons, piled up in the stockpiles of the great nuclear nations. In 1942 a thousand great bombers flew over the German city Cologne. Each carried four great bombs, each bomb one ton of TNT. Four thousand great one-ton blockbusters were dropped on the city that night, and destroyed the city. Now, suppose that another thousand planes, each with four great bombs, had come over the next night, and another thousand the next night, and the next night, and the next night—for *14 years*. Then the total would be the equivalent of the bomb that we exploded at Bikini, of *one* of the 20-megaton bombs that are stockpiled by the thousands by the nuclear nations of the world. This is the situation that we face now with respect to war.

It is not even necessary to hit the target with a superbomb. A 20-megaton bomb hitting New York would smash it flat over an area 20 miles in diameter. It might kill 10 million people, just by the blast, fires, and immediate radiation effects of the first second of the explosion. But it would not need to *hit* New York in order to kill the 10 million people. It could *miss* New York by a hundred miles, and still do the job. If the wind were blowing toward New York, the people would all be killed by fallout radioactivity. Great amounts of fallout are produced by these bombs. This is the reason that they are called "dirty bombs."

If the fallout from a 20-megaton bomb is spread out over an area of 10,000 square miles—100 miles by 100 miles, or 50 miles by 200 miles—the people will receive in the first day 10 times as much radiation as is needed to cause them to die of acute radiation sickness.

Fallout is of two kinds. There is the local fallout, which I have been talking about, and worldwide fallout. A certain percentage, perhaps 20 or 30 percent of the radioactive fission products, gets into the atmosphere, or even the stratosphere—upper atmosphere—and then slowly, in a month, for that which is still in the troposphere, and some years for that in the stratosphere, the radioactive materials that have not yet undergone radio-active decomposition will fall to earth, and irradiate people. The fallout is spread all over the Earth, although the United States gets more fallout than other countries.

Everybody in the world is being subjected to fallout radioactivity from the worldwide fallout. The strontium-90 gets into our bones. There is no human being on Earth who does not have strontium-90 in his bones, strontium-90 that is irradiating his bones and causing leukemia and bone cancer, whereas 20 years ago there were *no* human beings on Earth who had *any* strontium-90 in their bones. Carbon-14 gets in their bodies. Carbon-14 is produced in the upper atmosphere by cosmic rays. There is now 10 percent more in the atmosphere of the world than there was before 1954. It was in 1954, when we exploded the first superbomb, that the amount of carbon-14 in the atmosphere went up by a detectable amount. It has been going up by about 2 percent per year during the last five years. Carbon-14 is a radioactive material that causes damage. . . .

What are we doing? I can hardly believe that I am here, giving this lecture. We believe in morality, and yet we are cold-bloodedly preparing to kill, to murder hundreds of millions of people. Each of us contributes a large fraction—10 percent of the money that he earns—to increase the armaments that our country has, which could kill hundreds of millions of people. This behavior is irrational. I think that the world has been changing too fast for the diplomats to keep up with it. They are still back in the old period of power politics of the 19th century, carrying out the same old diplomatic actions, depending on war and the threat of war.

The time has come when not only the representatives of nations, but the nations themselves, must be moral. The time has come now when we are *forced* to cooperate in attacking the problem of war.

Professor C. Wright Mills, of Columbia University, has said in his book *The Causes of World War Three*:

> *What scientist can claim to be a part of the legacy of science and yet remain a hired technician of the military machine? What man of God can claim to partake of the Holy Spirit, to live the life of Jesus, to grasp the meaning of that Sunday phrase "the brotherhood of man" and yet sanction the immorality, the spiritual irresponsibility of the Caesars of our time? What scholar can claim to be part of the big discourse of reason, and yet retreat to formal trivialities and exact nonsense in a world in which reason and freedom are being held in contempt, being smashed, being allowed to fade out of the human condition? The answer is quite plain. Very many scientists, very many preachers, very many intellectuals are in default. Scientists become subordinated parts of the science machines of overdeveloped nations. These machines are among the prime causes of war. Thus scientists become helpful and indispensable technicians of the thrust toward war. Preachers, rabbis, priests, standing in the religious default, allow immorality to find support in religion. They use religion to cloak and to support impersonal, wholesale murder, and the preparation for it. They condone the attempt to murder millions of people by clean-cut young men flying and aiming intricate machineries toward Euro-Asia, zeroing in on cities full of human beings.*

For the first time in the history of the world, realism and selfishness—personal and national selfishness—now work on the same side as morality. The selfish, purely selfish, task now for the human race is also the moral one: the abandonment of war. We have now to accept international law, international agreements, such as to operate with the maximum amount of justice done to all of the nations and all of the people. We are fortunate to live at this unique epoch in the history of the world, the demarcation in time between the past, when we have had wars, ever increasingly brutal and horrible wars with their accompaniment of death and suffering, and the future, when we are going to give up war, to use the resources of this beautiful world for the benefit of human beings. We are now entering on a period of continuing peace in the world, of peace and morality.

ALBERT SCHWEITZER, PHYSICIAN AND HUMANITARIAN

"He was concerned that this beautiful world, with all its myriad forms of life, was being slowly and permanently altered. . . . He determined to use the voice given him by the award of the Nobel Peace Prize to speak loudly and clearly to all who would listen."

Linus Pauling's humanitarian bent was undeniably strengthened by his in-depth exposure in 1959 to the world-famous medical missionary, Albert Schweitzer. Awarded the Nobel Peace Prize in 1952, Dr. Schweitzer had become greatly concerned about both the prospect of nuclear war and the health hazards of nuclear testing. He was among the thousands of scientists who signed Pauling's petition to ban nuclear tests. He and Pauling, both interested in peace issues, had corresponded in German prior to his inviting the Paulings to visit him at his clinic in the interior of Africa, at Lambaréné in French Equatorial Africa (now Gabon).

After the evening meals Dr. Schweitzer would ask Pauling to stay and talk with him for several hours. Pauling spoke German fluently, since he had lived in Germany for over a year as a postdoctoral student in the mid 1920s. This brief personal contact with a man whose core belief lay in "the reverence for life" indelibly affected him. So too did his impressions of the clinic buildings and grounds, filled with Africans suffering from many types of parasites, infections, and degenerative diseases (including sickle-cell anemia, whose molecular cause Pauling had discovered in the late 1940s).

After Schweitzer's death in 1965, Pauling collaborated with his friend and former research associate Frank Catchpool (John Francis Catchpool, M.D.) to write a profile of him. As a young physician, Catchpool had spent three years (1956-59) on the medical staff of Schweitzer's clinic. When the Paulings visited there for a week in 1959, he showed them around and told them a great deal about Schweitzer and his work. Later that year he joined Dr. Pauling as a medical researcher at Caltech, and left in 1964, not long after Pauling's exit. He was associated again with Pauling as clinic director at the Linus Pauling Institute of Science and Medicine. For some years Dr. Catchpool has been a family physician in private practice in Marin County, California.

With Albert Schweitzer at his clinic in Lambaréné, West Africa, in July 1959. Schweitzer, who had won the Nobel Peace Prize in 1953, was concerned about nuclear testing and had signed Pauling's Scientists' Appeal in 1957. (Photo courtesy of Linda Pauling-Kamb)

Of the thousands of millions of human beings who have lived during the first half of the 20th century, we may expect that the memory of only a few will be preserved in history—of Einstein, whose new ways of looking at the world brought about a revolution in scientific thinking; of Bertrand Russell, who by application of his incisive intellect brought clarification to mathematics, philosophy, and politics; and, with little doubt, of Albert Schweitzer, who will be remembered as an outstanding musician and musicologist, philosopher and moralist, physician and humanitarian, and leader of and active participant in the effort to save civilization from destruction in a nuclear war. Schweitzer's humanitarian work is symbolized by the hospital in Lambaréné, the product of 50 years of sweat in the torrid, waterlogged, equatorial West African jungle—50 years of frustration, 50 years of heartbreak as the unending stream of suffering humanity washed up to the doors of the hospital like the tides on the shores. No case was ever refused, no sufferer was ever turned away.
. . .

In his book *Out of My Life and Thought* Schweitzer recalls that when he announced his intention to leave for Africa his friends, colleagues, and relatives "expostulated with him on the folly of his enterprise." For one who had so much to give, and who was then at the pinnacle of three careers, this epic gesture must have seemed like an act of renunciation that could only be described as foolhardy and absurd.

By the time that he was 30 years old Schweitzer had earned three separate doctorates. . . . As a scholar, lecturer, and organist he was acclaimed and honored throughout Europe, and worldwide fame seemed to be assured to him. Then, at the height of his vigorous career as writer, concert organist, and university lecturer, he took up the study of medicine. . . .

Why did he renounce all this to go to Lambaréné as a doctor? . . . Because he was tired of talk and wanted action. He chose Africa because of early conversations about Africa with his father and because as a child he had been deeply impressed by a statue by Bartholdi of a Negro in chains that stood in the market place in Colmar.

Europe at this time was just beginning to hear of the atrocities being committed by white men in Africa, about the baskets of human hands collected by Leopold's agents in the Congo, about the appalling suffering and wastage of life that had been inflicted by the slave traders, who counted themselves lucky if 20 percent of their catch was brought alive to the coast . . . and about the plantation managers who were thought to be not making adequate use of their investment if the slaves survived more than three years. The European conscience was stirring, the time for words was past. Medicine had made such progress that doctors could honestly say they were doing more good than harm. The hideous tropical afflictions were being catalogued and effective chemotherapy was being developed.

Schweitzer chose Lambaréné because it was one of the most inaccessible areas of the world, an area heavily infected with sleeping sickness, elephantiasis, malaria, schistosomiasis, Framboesia, leprosy, and many other terrible diseases—a large area without a single doctor.

Schweitzer had to promise the Paris missionary society that in Africa he would remain "as silent as a carp" on theological matters. His religious thinking was held by many to be dangerously heterodox. . . . Since childhood he had been in the habit of asking rational questions such as "If the wise men brought such precious gifts, why were the parents of Jesus always so poor?"

In 1913, before leaving for Africa, Schweitzer had said to friends that he credited himself with health, sound nerves, energy, practical common sense, toughness, and prudence, and that he believed himself to be quite capable of enduring the eventual failure of his plan. These qualities were soon tested. Arriving at Lambaréné, he set up his first consulting room in an empty chicken hut in the grounds of the Protestant mission. Then in 1914 the war started, and Schweitzer was promptly placed under house arrest by the French as an enemy alien. He could only watch as all his supplies and equipment so carefully purchased with his life's earnings and the gifts of his skeptical friends were looted by those whom he had come to help. Later on, as the war became more bitter, he was transported back to France and interned in a concentration camp, where he became sick for the first time in his life.

In 1925 he returned to Africa with supplies to build a new and better hospital, purchased with the royalties of six more books and the honorariums of many lectures and concerts. Working to an undrawn master plan, he built the hospital that stands today. By the mid 1930s it was probably the most modern bush hospital in all Africa. It stands today, just after Schweitzer's death, still pulsing with activity, a total of 56 galvanized iron-roofed sheds, many already rusty with age, a monument to Schweitzer's incredible energy and ingenuity.

Schweitzer, the intellectual, pushed back the forest, planted the fruit trees, dug the well. (He told us how, after a certain depth had been reached, the walls were in danger of collapsing; he ordered his men out and finished the well himself.) Schweitzer, the intellectual, taught the convalescent patients how to make string from cactus leaves and how to forge nails from old scrap iron, for in the jungle everything is precious. It was a prodigious effort to supervise the sawing of lumber from the huge ironwood logs, the mixing of concrete with hand-broken stones. His vegetable gardens were a source of amazement to the old African hands. Boats incongruously resembling Rhine River punts were built under his supervision; they still ply the Ogowe today.

The trickle of patients soon grew to a steady stream, and Schweitzer, the mason and carpenter, labored also as surgeon and dentist, as obstetrician and pharmacist, compounding his own drugs and teaching the patients how to knit bandages. . . .

In later years, as the hospital grew and more doctors and nurses came to assist him, Schweitzer would . . . turn with renewed energy to build more accommodations for the patients and staff. Schweitzer always managed to keep his eye on the main objective—to treat suffering Africans. The treatment remained the first priority; no one should be turned away. Even in a visitor to the hospital, in his normal state of health, several parasitic diseases could be found and treated.

No payment was asked other than a "coup de main" from those fit enough to work, and a token gift to the hospital. The tasks were tailored to suit the Africans' ability. The wives of the operated man were requested to help scrub the operating room floor. Other members of the family would haul water for the vegetable garden. Squads of the patient's relatives would be put to the endless task of keeping the jungle at bay. Others would help with the construction of new buildings. The effort required to organize and direct these work teams, often recruited among Africans whose physical and mental powers and will to work had been eroded by years of malnutrition, anemia, and repeated fevers, absorbed a large amount of Schweitzer's and his assistants' energy. The exhortations to accomplish the task at hand often led casual observers and transitory visitors to the impression that Schweitzer was autocratic in his manner and dictatorial in his administration of the hospital. . . .

The criticism has often been voiced that Schweitzer did not move with the times. Visitors to the hospital in recent years were astonished that Schweitzer had no power boat to move supplies and visitors to the hospital. In the early days of the hospital there were one or two passenger boats a year reaching the west coast of equatorial Africa; then came a dangerous two- or three-day motor boat trip up the Ogowe river to Lambaréné.

Now one can reach an airfield near the hospital, by airplane. From the dirt runway hewn out of the jungle there is a short ride by truck, if it is running, to the south bank of the southern fork of the river. Visitors to the hospital find the hospital canoe waiting for them at the river's edge. This venerable craft has outlasted a dozen motor boats, and its motor has never failed. It is powered by four or five lepers from the Leper village. These men, long-time residents of the hospital, have feet so eroded by repeated injuries and infections resulting from their disease that they are barely able to walk. The paddling of the canoe provides them with the ideal occupation. They are seated in the fresh air, and the trip downstream is really no effort at all; the trip back gives them three-quarters of an hour of good, solid exercise. The long wait at the river's bank keeps them off their feet. For this work they are provided with a hut, treated with medicines, fed, and clothed. . . .

It has been said that Schweitzer denied his patients modern drugs and treatment and that the standards of hygiene were bound to prejudice the patients' recovery. However, it should be remembered that the principal factor in a surgical operation is the skill of the surgeon rather than the complexity of the instruments. Sterility depends on the care with which the instruments and the linen are sterilized rather than on their color and polish. At Schweitzer's hospital the preparation of patients for operation and the sterilization of linen and instruments were conducted in an elaborate ritual carefully worked out 30 years ago, and modified only as proved innovations were introduced into practice.

Africa is no place for experimentation, because the press of routine, life-preserving surgery makes it seem almost criminal to waste time on unproved techniques. New techniques cannot easily be evaluated in Africa because of the multiplicity of diseases and the uncertainty of environmental factors. When the first miracle antibiotics were introduced Schweitzer questioned their routine use and suggested that they be reserved for occasions when a miracle is required. Indiscriminate use of these miracles must, he argued, diminish their effectiveness. "Hospital Staph," now the scourge of civilized hospitals, has proved his judgment correct. . . .

Reverence for life and a compassion for all living things are amply manifested by the teeming animal and human life that assails the eyes, ears, and nose of the visitor to his hospital. One wonders how the patients could be nursed in such surroundings. Africans often pass up the government hospital to come to Doctor Schweitzer's hospital, where they can be treated by European-trained nurses but continue to be surrounded by their wives, chickens, goats, and children, and to be fed with food cooked in the traditional manner by their own womenfolk, with the cooking pots balanced on three large stones and heated by a handful of burning sticks.

It has often been asked why Schweitzer did not train Africans to staff his hospital and other hospitals. One answer may be that he came to wash their feet and to bind up their wounds himself, and not to train others to do the task that he had taken up in the name of all white men; but there is also the suggestion in some of his writings that he doubted that the Africans had reached the stage in their development when this training would be successful.

As one strolls through the hospital one is buffeted by conflicting impressions—repelled by the hideous afflictions of some of the patients, but heartened by the sound of laughter, since the hospital is surely one of the happiest of hospitals; appalled by the squalor and filth, then reassured by the thought that the hospital dormitories closely approximate an average African's village; shocked by the meager rations, but chastened by remembering that few "civilized" hospitals provide free food.

Schweitzer wrote that "A single doctor in Africa, even with the most modest equipment, can mean very much for very many. The good which he can accomplish surpasses a hundred-fold what he gives of his own life and the cost of the material support that he must have. With a few simple drugs, and sufficient skill and apparatus for the most necessary operations, he can, in a single year, free hundreds of men from the grip of suffering and death."

If this be true, can a doctor justify taking time out from the struggle with suffering and death to labor with an air-conditioning plant for his operating room? Can he divert funds from the purchase of lifesaving drugs to purchase the comforts of civilization for himself or his patients? Today in other parts of Africa there can be found several white-elephant hospitals, beautiful to look at, but understaffed and underprovided with drugs because the cost of building has been so great that there was nothing left over.

On one notable occasion, in April 1957, Schweitzer did take time off from his medical and administrative duties in the hospital. For many years he had become increasingly concerned about the nuclear arms race and concerned about the havoc being wrought on the genetic material of all life. He was concerned that this beautiful world, with all its myriad forms of life, was being slowly and permanently altered. Mutations of genes were taking place at a rate considerably higher than before the advent of man-made ionizing radiations. Recognizing that there was a real risk that the unrestrained arms race would degenerate into a cataclysmic holocaust that could terminate all life on Earth, he determined to use the voice given him by the award of the Nobel Peace Prize to speak loudly and clearly to all who would listen.

In order that he could not be accused of speaking like a dotard, he set himself to understanding the mechanism of creation of radioactive elements in a nuclear explosion, the injection of the radioactive dust created in atomic explosions into the upper atmosphere, the patterns of fallout of this radioactive dust, the routes of assimilation of radioactive isotopes into living tissue, the modes of genetic and somatic damage by high-energy radiation, and the half-lives of the radioactive elements. He also set himself to studying the available information about the probable effects of the explosion of megaton bombs in heavily populated areas in a nuclear war, studies which only a few military men had bothered to make.

On 24 April 1957 Schweitzer dramatically added his name to the growing list of those world leaders who had publicly taken a position against the continued testing of nuclear weapons. From Radio Oslo in Norway there was issued, and rebroadcast all over the world, his now famous statement "Peace or Atomic War." This statement, reviewing the discovery of radioactivity and X-rays at the end of the 19th century and the realization that these rays can damage living tissue, echoed President Eisenhower's call for a "gigantic leap into peace rather than a leap into space," and called for an end to atomic testing on the grounds that "We of this generation cannot take responsibility for the consequences of a raised background level of radioactivity on the generations to come." "We must muster the insight, the seriousness, and the courage to leave folly and face reality," he said. "The end of further experiments with atomic bombs would be like the early sun rays of hope which suffering humanity is longing for."

Two years ago, after six years of uncertainty and after a period of renewed nuclear testing and further contamination of the atmosphere with radioactive fission products and carbon-14, the bomb-test treaty advocated by Schweitzer was formulated and then subscribed to by most of the nations of the world. This act has led to reduction of tensions and to an increased hope for the abolition of war and its replacement by world law.

The award of the Nobel Peace Prize for 1952 to Albert Schweitzer was presumably made on the basis of the reference of Nobel's will to work for fraternity among nations; Schweitzer's labors since 1952 provide the additional justification of effective work toward the abolition of standing armies. One of his last acts, one month before his death, was to join seven other recipients of the Nobel Peace Prize in issuing an appeal to all the governments and parties concerned in the war in Vietnam to take immediate action to achieve a cease-fire and a negotiated settlement of the tragic conflict. Albert Schweitzer's work for world peace may well be considered by future generations to have been his greatest contribution to humanity.

DEVELOPING A MORAL PHILOSOPHY

"The prime ethical postulate—We should take such actions as to preserve & increase the wonder of the universe & to decrease human (and other) suffering."

Notified that he had been selected to receive the Humanist of the Year award given by the American Humanist Association, Pauling got to work on the lecture he would deliver at the honorary event to be held in Cleveland, Ohio, in mid March of 1961. (See pages 165-168.) He prepared the text in advance so that it could be published concurrently in *The Humanist*. He had earlier considered the issue of suffering in his book *No More War!*—for instance, "I believe that one goal that human beings strive for is that of decreasing the amount of suffering in the world." He was also pondering philosophical positions on human morality, and later said that he had found the ethical ideas of the British philosopher John Stuart Mill especially relevant.

An interesting sidelight in this period of Pauling's life is that in January of 1960, a year before giving this talk, Pauling had undergone a severely disturbing experience—spending a long, cold, and lonely night stranded on a cliff high above the Pacific Ocean at his California ranch in the Big Sur area. Doubtless he gave some thought to his own mortality. Though he seemed all right after he was rescued the next day, two days afterwards he suddenly fled from people and stayed home for about a week, apparently suffering from post-traumatic shock. For the rest of his life he refrained from discussing this unsettling episode, indicating an underlying vulnerability in his nature that he had learned as a child to conceal and suppress.

Possibly while preparing the "Humanism and Peace" speech he carefully perused the softcover edition (printed in 1958) of a book on philosophy titled *Existentialism and the Modern Predicament*. Its flyleaves on both ends are covered with Pauling's notations as he read; occasional comments are also in the margins of pages. Here are some of them. They show his impatience over ponderous speculations about existence, as well as his interest in the issues of morality and human suffering.

G reat progress can be made following and built upon moral principles.

Philosophers have devoted too much attention to man, not enough to the world.

500,000 species of animals on Earth—man is one.

Transformation of evil into good—i.e., possibility of decreasing suffering in the world.

We can discover probable principles by analyzing our information about the world as a whole; and then apply these principles to man's problems, in which we have an especially great interest.

My ideas—Consistency not necessary in theory of values of morality or ethics (any more than in chemistry).

"Humanistic universalism," as name for a new philosophy, emphasizes that it encompasses the universe & lays weight on the importance to human beings of their own place in it.

The prime ethical postulate—We should take such actions as to preserve & increase the wonder of the universe & to decrease human (and other) suffering.

Emphasis on human justified. So far as we can be sure, consciousness of the beauty & wonder of the universe is unique to man. Hence we must preserve man. If we were sure that after destruction of mankind another form of sentient being would develop our prime postulate might be different—but we are not.

Not man for himself, but man for the world of all time—future as well as present.

MINIMIZING SUFFERING

"This great organism, humankind, is now master of the Earth, but not yet master of itself."

The first half of Linus Pauling's long speech on "Humanism and Peace," given on the occasion of his receipt of the Humanist of the Year award in 1961, contains Pauling's first significant mention of his important doctrine of the "minimization of suffering." He would refer to this principle for the rest of his life in determining correct decisions for public policy as well as private conduct. (This position was foreshadowed by his remark on "the prime ethical postulate" in the flyleaf of the book noted in the previous passage.) Here, too, Pauling explained his sense of humanism. And he mentioned some difficult ethical issues introduced through increasing genetic research and molecular biology.

Pauling also stressed the importance of the unique communication possible among people as a unit, in a passage whose organic imagery seems to foretell the amazing electronic circuitry now spanning the Earth. The Internet enables rapid and effective information to be relayed among those with access to computer modems. Thus Pauling's hoped-for "mutation" in human genes—maybe adding a capacity for extrasensory perception—instead takes the form of a shortcut created by human invention. Science and technology may in time well serve the cause of world peace, although at present the Internet's potential for this service is only minimally utilized. Pauling's sense of urgency as to the importance of developing rapid and effective communication among all nations and peoples is worthy of special attention.

What have we as human beings, to hope for? We suffer from attacks by the vectors of disease, from accidents, striking with the blind malevolence of chance, from the ills accompanying the deterioration of age; and also, in a sense the most viciously, from man's inhumanity to man, especially as expressed in the evil institution of war.

I believe that we can have hope, and that we can win a great victory not only over the plague of man's natural condition, the physical ills that beset us, but also over the terrible plague of man's oppression by man, over the evil of war.

The world has been changing rapidly during recent decades. This change has involved especially a greater understanding by man of the causes of human suffering. We now know that certain combinations of genes, which in some cases can be predicted to occur with high probability, lead to gross physical or mental defects which cause great suffering for the person who is so afflicted and for his parents and others. We know now that the pool of human germ plasm is continually being changed by gene mutation, and that the natural process of removing deleterious genes from it, in order to preserve its integrity, involves much human suffering.

We are faced with an ethical problem, characteristic of the many that we shall have to face as our knowledge of the nature of human beings and of the world increases. Shall the deleterious genes that exist in the pool of human germ plasm, and that would otherwise continue to increase, be removed by the suffering and death of millions of children, or by a procedure that attempts to recognize them and to prevent the conception of these defective children?

This question is one of ethics, of philosophy, in the sense expressed by Corliss Lamont, that philosophy involves the analysis and clarification of human actions and aims, problems and ideals. Many admirable statements have been made about these matters in the past by great philosophers and teachers.

I believe that there is great value in the philosophy of humanism— that the chief end of human life is to work for the happiness of man upon this Earth (and we might soon have to add the moon and then Venus and other planets).

Humanism, as I understand it, is a rational philosophy. It rejects the mysticism and supernaturalism of the revealed religions. It rejects life after death and the idea that suffering in this world may, for the righteous, be compensated for by the bliss of an afterlife. Included in this rejection of the supernatural is the rejection of a belief in an omniscient, omnipotent, and omnipresent god who watches over and cares for human beings, interfering, sometimes in response to prayer, with the ordered regularity of events as determined by natural laws.

Humanism is a philosophy of service for the good of all humanity, of application of new ideas, of scientific progress, for the benefit of all men—those now living and those still to be born.

Dr. Albert Schweitzer believes that not only man but also other forms of life should be included in the field of our concern. He has expressed this belief in his principle of Reverence for Life. I would like to go further: I advocate the principle of Reverence for the World.

This is a wonderful world in which we live. Yet some of its wonders are being annihilated, destroyed, so that our children's children will never be able to experience them. I do not like to think of the beautiful minerals, beautiful crystals, that are being removed from the ground and destroyed in order to make more copper wire or uranium rods, especially for the useless activities of preparation for war. There will never be a second crop of minerals.

Instead of the principle of maximizing human happiness, I prefer the principle of minimizing the suffering in the world. The difference between maximizing happiness and minimizing suffering requires weighing of the factors involved. On a scale of income, we may select a certain value as standard—one that is just enough for a satisfactory life, different, of course, according to duties and circumstances. An increase of 80 percent in income would give some added happiness—but the suffering caused by a decrease of 80 percent surely deserves a far greater weight, perhaps 10 or 100 times greater.

Man has reached his present state through the process of evolution. The last great step in evolution was the mutational process that doubled the size of the brain, about 700,000 years ago; this led to the origin of man. It is this that permits the inheritance of acquired characteristics of a certain sort—of learning, through communication from one human being to another. Thus abilities that have not yet been incorporated into the germ plasm are not lost until their rediscovery by members of following generations, but instead are handed on from person to person, from generation to generation. Man's great powers of thinking, remembering and communicating are responsible for the evolution of civilization.

Yet a man or woman is not truly an organism, in the sense that a rabbit is, or a lion, or a whale. Instead, he is a part of a greater organism, the whole of mankind, into which he is bound by the means of communication—speaking, writing, telephoning, traveling over long distances, in the way that the cells of a rabbit are interconnected by nerve fibers and hormonal molecular messengers.

This great organism, humankind, is now master of the Earth, but not yet master of itself; it is immature, irrational; it does not act for its own good, but instead often for its own harm.

We must now achieve the mutation that will bring sanity to this great organism that is mankind. Must this be a mutation of some of the genes in the pool of human germ plasm? Perhaps such a genetic mutation, providing, for example, extrasensory perception and instantaneous communication among all human beings, would do the job; but I fear that we do not have time for this mutational process to be effective. The human race may cease to exist in a decade.

We must accordingly hope that the mutation can instead be in the nature of the giant organism, humankind, itself—a mutation in the means of communication, in the nerve fibers of the organization, that will transfer to this whole great organism some of the desirable and admirable attributes that are possessed by the units of which it is composed, the individual human beings. The attributes that must be transferred from the units, human beings, to the great organism, humankind, are sanity (reason), and morality (ethical principles).

I believe that this change will occur. I believe that we are now forced to this change by the development of weapons that could destroy the world, and that will do so unless the nature of the great human organism changes in time.

SQUABBLING AMONG PEACEMAKERS

"We said, 'We support any organization working for world peace.'"

Apart from several peace-connected convocations that they themselves had organized, the Paulings actively participated in a number of national and international meetings. Notable among these were some of the Pugwash Conferences on Science and World Affairs, which periodically gathered together scientists and other concerned professionals from around the world to discuss how peace might be achieved in the nuclear age. (The name Pugwash came from the place of the first meeting, at a town of that name in Nova Scotia. It was the summer home of the meeting's sponsor, wealthy industrialist Cyrus Eaton.)

But not all of the Paulings' experiences with peace groups and peace conferences went well. When reporting on the dismal outcome of the 1963 Oxford Conference of Non-Aligned Peace Organizations, the Paulings gave the following caveat based on their recent observations and experiences. (Their remarks may have wider relevance to a number of worthy endeavors by nonprofit organizations and charitable causes.)

> *It is, we think, dangerous to have organizations represented at such an important meeting only by employed staff members, who may feel restricted by instructions and may not have the freedom of action that would permit them to contribute in a positive rather than a negative way to the discussions and negotiations. . . . This may be the explanation of the unfortunate actions of some of the U.S. delegates that have caused the American peace movement to lose much of the worldwide respect that it had formerly received.*
>
> *Professional peace workers may do harm to the peace movement because of their concern for their own careers and for the interests of their own organizations, rather than of the world as a whole, because of their lack of imagination, and because of their striving for power. These organization men of the peace movement sometimes seem to have lost sight of the great goal of peace and disarmament and to have lost hope that the problem of militarism and nuclear war can be solved.*

Here is what Pauling said when reflecting back upon experiences in the early '60s. The setting was a sustained dialogue (face-to-face in 1989, continued in letters afterward) with the Japanese philosopher Daisaku Ikeda. The dialogue took place three decades after these events. The second example briefly explains why the Paulings wrote the paragraphs quoted above.

For a short time I was a member of the national board of directors of SANE [aka National Committee for a Sane Nuclear Policy]. Then when McCarthy attacked SANE, Norman Cousins—I guess it was he—replied that there was no need for the government to investigate the people associated with SANE, that they would carry out their own investigations and question members of the board of directors about their beliefs. So I sent a note saying I was resigning because I didn't give the chairman of the board of SANE or anybody else the right to question me about my beliefs.

My wife and I argued with two matters in these organizations that we were affiliated with. One, the right of organizations to question individuals; and the other, a policy of keeping Left-wingers out of an organization. We said, "We support any organization working for world peace."

Well, we went to a peace conference in Oxford, England, as representatives of ourselves. We didn't go as representatives of any organization.
And there were representatives of various peace groups that were going to
participate. . . .

The Americans objected to the fact that there were going to be some
people from behind the Iron Curtain attending the peace conference. And
the peace conference was not held. It broke up after the first meeting or
two, when there was a fight as to whether the American policy of throw-
ing out the people from behind the Iron Curtain would be followed or not.

So my wife and I wrote an article about the Oxford Peace Conference
that was published in the journal *The Minority of One*, in which we said
that this hardly seems a sensible policy, to be working for world peace but
not to be talking with people in the other countries who are working for
world peace too. Pretty funny.

NOBEL'S GREAT REWARD FOR PEACE ACTION

*"I remind you that Alfred Nobel wanted to invent 'a substance or a
machine with such terrible power of mass destruction that war would
thereby be made impossible forever.'"*

In 1962 the Nobel Peace Prize Committee reported its inability to agree
in selecting a worthy recipient. A year later, it chose a dramatic day to
announce the delayed choice: October 10, 1963—exactly the date when
the three-way limited nuclear test-ban treaty, signed several months earlier, would go into effect. Linus Pauling was the honoree.

Gunnar Jahn, representing the Nobel Peace Prize Committee, gave
the explanation for the award:

> *No one would suggest that the nuclear test ban is the sole
> work of Linus Pauling. But does anyone believe that the treaty
> would have been reached if there had been no responsible sci-
> entist who, tirelessly, unflinchingly, year in and year out, im-
> pressed on the authorities and on the general public the real
> menace of nuclear tests?*
>
> *Even though the test-ban treaty has been effected, this is only
> the first step toward an agreement for complete disarmament and
> peace. Though the road may be long and difficult, Linus Pauling
> has an unshakable belief that one day humanity will succeed in
> banning war: "I believe that there is a greater power in the world
> than the evil power of military force, of nuclear bombs—there is
> the power of good, or morality, of humanitarianism."*

> *By the enlistment of these forces Pauling believes it will be possible to build a world community in which the actions of all nations will be subject to just supervision and control through the medium of international law and justice.*
>
> *As far as I know, Linus Pauling has not drawn up any concrete plan for the future. But one thing is certain; he has great faith in the role of science, as he demonstrates in his suggestion for the setting up of a World Council for Peace Research, to be affiliated with the United Nations, and representing every branch of science as well as the humanities. . . . (See pages 252-256.)*
>
> *It is Linus Pauling's highly ethical attitude to life—the deepest driving force within him—that drew him into the fight against nuclear weapons. Through his campaigning he has manifested the ethical responsibility that science, in his opinion, bears for the fate of mankind, today and in the future. The scientist's urge to wrest her secrets from nature is one that Linus Pauling could never root out. As long as the world exists, there will be bold, adventurous minds taking up the challenge of nature, and new thrusts will be made, always toward unknown goals.*
>
> *Should Pauling have contributed, if only a little, to restoring to science its ideals, his work will have been of such value that we living today cannot yet appreciate the full extent of the debt we owe him.*

Pauling had well satisfied Alfred Nobel's original instructions, made in 1895. The annual Peace award was to go "to the person who shall have done the most or the best work for fraternity among nations, for the abolition or reduction of standing armies, and for the holding and promotion of peace congresses." These activities were the very ones in which Pauling had earned a sharply divided reputation—as peacemaker or troublemaker.

The news came to Pauling via a telephone call from his daughter Linda to the ranger's station near his ranch home on the central California coast. "It was a great surprise," he would often say later. "At the time, I said my having received it made working for peace respectable."

The only regret he expressed was that the great award had not been given to his wife, Ava Helen Pauling, as well. He almost certainly would never have chosen on his own to take the difficult path toward peace that he began in 1945, nor would he have been able to pursue it consistently ever since. (See pages 85-99.) As it was, she had always been at his side in both spirit and deed, and much of the time in person as well.

In the United States the news of the Nobel Peace Prize inevitably got a mixed reception. *Life* magazine headlined its article about the award as "A Weird Insult from Norway"—itself an insult that Pauling often cited later to exemplify the treatment accorded him for years by the establishment's press, reflecting the mean and defensive attitude of the pronuclear military-industrial partnership encouraged by the U.S. government. (Interestingly, the same periodical in a simple and beautiful eulogy to Linus Pauling following his death in 1994 called him "far and away the century's greatest chemist" and applauded his "sweeping vision.")

New Nobelists are expected to present a lecture to the assembled notables and family members at the ceremony. (The Science and Literature awards are given in Stockholm, Sweden, whereas the Peace award takes place in Oslo, Norway.) Pauling prepared a talk that partly combined and adapted sections of his previous speeches and writings, including the Scientists' Appeal of 1957-58. He also quoted portions of notable documents by others that reflected the history of the antiwar and antinuclear efforts of the past two decades. (Moreover, in future talks around the world—as a Nobel Peace laureate he naturally received frequent invitations—he could conveniently lift parts of his Nobel lecture.)

Here is the beginning of Pauling's Nobel Peace Lecture.

I believe that there will never again be a great world war—a war in which the terrible weapons involving nuclear fission and nuclear fusion would be used. And I believe that it is the discoveries of scientists upon which the development of these terrible weapons was based that are now forcing us to move into a new period in the history of the world, a period of peace and reason, when world problems are not solved by war or by force, but are solved in accordance with world law, in a way that does justice to all nations and that benefits all people.

I remind you that Alfred Nobel wanted to invent "a substance or a machine with such terrible power of mass destruction that war would thereby be made impossible forever." Two-thirds of a century later scientists discovered the explosive substances that Nobel wanted to invent— the fissionable substances uranium and plutonium, with explosive energy 10 million times that of Nobel's favorite explosive, nitroglycerine, and the fusionable substance lithium deuteride, with explosive energy 50 million times that of nitroglycerine.

The first of the terrible machines incorporating these substances, the uranium-235 and plutonium-239 fission bombs, were exploded in 1945, at Alamogordo, Hiroshima, and Nagasaki. Then in 1954, nine years later, the first of the fission-fusion-fission superbombs was exploded, the 20-megaton Bikini bomb, with energy of explosion one thousand times greater than that of a 1945 fission bomb. This one bomb, the 1954 superbomb, contained less than one ton of nuclear explosive. The energy released in its explosion was greater than that of all of the explosives used in all of the wars that have taken place during the entire history of the world, including World War I and World War II.

Thousands of these superbombs have now been fabricated; and today, 18 years after the construction of the first atomic bomb, the nuclear powers have stockpiles of these weapons so great that if they were to be used in a war hundreds of millions of people would be killed, and civilization itself might not survive the catastrophe.

Thus the machines envisaged by Nobel have come into existence, and war has been made impossible forever.

The world has now begun the metamorphosis from its primitive period of history, when disputes among nations were settled by war, to its period of maturity, in which war will be abolished and world law will take its place. The first great stage of this metamorphosis took place only a few months ago—the formulation by the governments of the United States, Great Britain, and the Soviet Union, after years of discussion and negotiation, of a treaty banning the testing of nuclear weapons on the surface of the Earth, in the oceans, and in space, and the ratification and signing of this treaty by nearly all of the nations in the world.

I believe that the historians of the future may well describe the making of this treaty as the most important action ever taken by the governments of nations, in that it is the first of a series of treaties that will lead to the new world, from which war has been abolished forever.

THE FUTURE REIGN OF WORLD LAW

"War and nationalism, together with economic exploitation, have been the great enemies of the individual human being."

In his Nobel Peace Lecture, Pauling stressed the urgent need to work toward disarmament. As he had so often before, he emphasized the crucial importance of ensuring peace among nations by instituting a system of international law that would monitor justice and civil rights all over the planet. It would prevent nations from attacking and invading one another when they were unable to settle disputes in a fair and rational manner, making great armamentaria unnecessary. This overarching legal framework would also guarantee democracy everywhere—the will of the majority of the people residing within any land in selecting their representatives and leaders and in creating or amending the nation's own laws.

It was an idealistic plan, but certainly a sensible goal to strive for. It encouraged admission to the U.N. and full diplomatic status for newly established or reconstructed nations, such as China. And it did, after all, envisage a future time when the monolithic, rigidly authoritarian communist system enforced in the USSR might be compelled by the peoples' actions to accede to democratic processes, as began happening several decades later. Also, as he had often done explicitly in the past, Pauling now implicitly charged his own country with interfering in the political will of the people in another nation—mentioning the problem of Vietnam. (See pages 208-216.)

In this speech, too, Pauling brought up his growing concern that the horrible prospect of using nuclear weapons could be equaled or even surpassed by chemical and biological agents in warfare—research for which was going on in a number of nations.

Why is no progress being made toward disarmament? I think that part of the answer is that there are still many people, some of them powerful people, who have not yet accepted the thesis that the time has now come to abolish war. And another part of the answer is that there exists a great nation that has not been accepted into the world community of nations—the Chinese People's Republic, the most populous nation in the world. I do not believe that the United States and the Soviet Union will carry out any major stage in the process of disarmament unless that potential great nuclear power, the Chinese People's Republic, is a signatory to the disarmament agreement; and the Chinese People's Republic will not be a signatory to such a treaty until she is accepted into the community of nations, under conditions worthy of her stature. To work for the recognition of China is to work for world peace.

We cannot expect the now existing nuclear weapons to be destroyed for several years, perhaps for decades. Moreover, there is the possibility, mentioned by Philip Noel-Baker in his Nobel Lecture in 1959, that some nuclear weapons might be concealed or surreptitiously fabricated, and then used to terrorize and dominate the disarmed world; this possibility might slow down the program of destroying the stockpiles. . . .

Is there no action that we can take immediately to decrease the present great danger of outbreak of nuclear war through some technological or psychological accident or as the result of a series of events such that even the wisest national leaders could not avert the catastrophe?

I believe that there is such an action, and I hope that it will be given consideration by the national governments. My proposal is that there be instituted with the maximum expedition compatible with caution a system of joint national-international control of the stockpiles of nuclear weapons, such that use could be made of the American nuclear armaments only with the approval both of the American government and of the United Nations, and that use could be made of the Soviet nuclear armament only with the approval both of the Soviet government and of the United Nations. A similar system of dual control would of course be instituted for the smaller nuclear powers, if they did not destroy their weapons.

Even a small step in the direction of this proposal, such as the acceptance of United Nations observers in the control stations of the nuclear powers, might decrease significantly the probability of nuclear war.

There is another action that could be taken immediately to decrease the present great hazard to civilization. This action would be to stop, through a firm treaty incorporating a reliable system of inspection, the present great programs of development of biological and chemical methods of waging war.

Four years ago the scientists participating in the Fifth Pugwash Conference concluded that at that time the destructive power of nuclear weapons was far larger than that of biological and chemical weapons, but that biological and chemical weapons have enormous lethal and incapacitating effects on man and could also effect tremendous harm by the destruction of plants and animals. Moreover, there is a vigorous effort being made to develop these weapons to the point where they would become a threat to the human race equal to or greater than that of nuclear weapons. The money expended for research and development of biological and chemical warfare by the United States alone has now reached $100 million a year, an increase of 16-fold in a decade, and similar efforts are probably being exerted in the Soviet Union and other countries.

To illustrate the threat I may mention the plans to use nerve gases that, when they do not kill, produce temporary or permanent insanity, and the plans to use toxins, such as the botulism toxin, viruses, such as the virus of yellow fever, or bacterial spores, such as of anthrax, to kill tens or hundreds of millions of people.

The hazard is especially great in that, once the knowledge is obtained through a large-scale development program such as is now being carried out, it might well spread over the world, and might permit some small group of evil men, perhaps in one of the smaller countries, to launch a devastating attack.

This terrible prospect could be eliminated now by a general agreement to stop research and development of these weapons, to prohibit their use, and to renounce all official secrecy and security controls over microbiological, toxicological, pharmacological, and chemical-biological research. Hundreds of millions of dollars per year are now being spent in the effort to make these malignant cells of knowledge. Now is the time to stop. When once the cancer has developed, and its metastases have spread over the world, it will be too late. . . .

The replacement of war by law must include not only great wars but also small ones. The abolition of insurrectionary and guerrilla warfare, which often is characterized by extreme savagery and a great amount of human suffering, would be a boon to humanity.

There are, however, countries in which the people are subjected to continuing economic exploitation and to oppression by a dictatorial government, which retains its power through force of arms. The only hope for many of these people has been that of revolution, of overthrowing the dictatorial government and replacing it with a reform government, a democratic government that would work for the welfare of the people.

I believe that the time has come for the world as a whole to abolish this evil, through the formulation and acceptance of some appropriate articles of world law. With only limited knowledge of law, I shall not attempt to formulate a proposal that would achieve this end without permitting the possibility of the domination of the small nations by the large nations. I suggest, however, that the end might be achieved by world legislation under which there would be, perhaps once a decade, a referendum, supervised by the United Nations, on the will of the people with respect to their national government, held, separately from the national elections, in every country in the world.

It may take many years to achieve such an addition to the body of world law. In the meantime, much could be done through a change in the policies of the great nations. During recent years insurrections and civil wars in small countries have been instigated and aggravated by the great powers, which have moreover provided weapons and military advisors, increasing the savagery of the wars and the suffering of the people. In four countries during 1963 and several others during preceding years democratically elected governments with policies in the direction of social and economic reform have been overthrown and replaced by military dictatorships, with the approval, if not at the instigation, of one or more of the great powers. These actions of the great powers are associated with policies of militarism and national economic interest that are now antiquated. I hope that the pressure of world opinion will soon cause them to be abandoned, and to be replaced by policies that are compatible with the principles of morality, justice, and world brotherhood.

In working to abolish war we are working also for human freedom, for the rights of individual human beings. War and nationalism, together with economic exploitation, have been the great enemies of the individual human being. I believe that, with war abolished from the world, there will be improvement in the social, political, and economic systems in all nations, to the benefit of the whole of humanity.

Might science come up with a solution to man's inhumanity to man, to nations' continuously lethal strife? Or might peace be accomplished by that variation on religion called humanism—based primarily and firmly on ethics? Pauling really seemed to think that both approaches could solve tough problems—by working together. He wanted to make a science out of morality.

Pauling's receipt of the Nobel Prize validated his social and political activism. There was still much work to be done, and he felt impelled to help do it. Changed circumstances would soon make it possible for him to spend several years in a position that actually encouraged him to speak out for peace.

But the news of this great honor had not pleased a number of the administrators, trustees, and faculty members at Pauling's own institution, the California Institute of Technology. They resented Pauling's giving so much time and energy to his antinuclear and peace-advocating activities, which had gained him notoriety. Some were vehemently opposed to his oft-expressed ideas. Since Pauling was usually introduced or identified as a professor at Caltech, people might get the impression that the Institute's views coincided with his. (This problem continues to bedevil both institutions and their individual faculty members, who may have widely differing opinions. The former are usually conservative and cautious—especially when already part of the government-linked "establishment" or dependent upon its approval and financial support.) The ongoing tension between Caltech's administration and Pauling was among the high costs Pauling incurred as an activist.

Moreover, much of the time during the '50s and early '60s Pauling was either distracted by the pressing work that was neither academic nor research-connected, or else out on the road giving speeches or attending peace conferences. He left much of the chemistry division's business, the supervision and conduct of his many research projects, and his course teaching up to his associates and assistants. How many of the other Caltech people, without a Nobel Prize in science (or even with one) and other kudos to lend prestigious status, could have gotten away with something like this? The Caltech administrators' long-disapproving attitude, then, was scarcely surprising, even though it may have seemed mean or craven to Pauling and his supporters.

In 1958 Caltech President Lee DuBridge induced Linus Pauling to resign from his position as chairman of the Division of Chemistry and Chemical Engineering, which he had held since 1936. His salary then shrank, and a portion of the laboratory space allotted to his numerous research projects was taken away from him. Fortunately, Pauling by now had a sizable supplemental income from royalties on his chemistry textbooks. But he was no longer as content as he had been, from the late '20s to at least the early '50s, as a Caltech professor.

In sharp contrast with his ebullience over the Peace Prize, Pauling's unhappiness over his situation at Caltech became acute when he learned of President's DuBridge's lukewarm, even rather critical remarks to a reporter asking him to comment on Pauling's most recent honor. There was more insult, neglect, and hurt to come. Congratulations from colleagues were often tepid or perfunctory. Pauling couldn't help but compare this time with that of nine years earlier with the first Nobel Prize, when his chemistry department had given a grand party to honor him. Now nothing happened. Finally the biology division, with which Pauling had close connections, hosted a celebration.

Before Pauling left for Oslo for the solemn ceremony in December of 1963, at which he would receive the gold Nobel medal from the King of Norway, he announced his intention of becoming a research fellow at the Center for the Study of Democratic Institutions in Santa Barbara, about a hundred miles northwest of Los Angeles. Unhappy at Caltech for some while now, Pauling had earlier informed Robert M. Hutchins, CSDI's director, of his interest in becoming affiliated with this liberal-tending "think tank" largely supported by the Fund for the Republic, through the Ford Foundation. Pauling saw this move as a step toward fulfilling his vision of creating a World Peace Research Organization, as expressed in *No More War!* five years earlier, and later refined into a proposal made to the United Nations. (See pages 252-256 in Part VI.) A former student of Pauling's who had become wealthy as an inventor came up with funds to create a position for him there.

Pauling was attracted to the prospect of dividing his time between doing the theoretical research he loved—especially developing a new theory about the structure of the atomic nucleus—and applying a scientific approach to solving world problems that were ignored by or eluded the career diplomats, national leaders, and influential political scientists and economists. After all, it was in diligently pursuing the latter endeavor over the past decade and a half that Pauling had incurred the disapproval of Caltech's administrators and colleagues. But now he would actually be employed to do so.

Pauling had a lively correspondence and relationship with British philosopher and mathematician Bertrand Russell, a fellow peace activist. In 1962 Lord Russell sent Pauling a handwritten limerick:

> *There was a great man, Linus Pauling,*
> *who left all the barristers crawling*
> *when he said, "In your shelter*
> *you'll die in the welter*
> *while H-bombs around you are falling."*

(Photo courtesy of Linda Pauling-Kamb)

*Pauling with a photo of Dr. Martin Luther King, Jr. at a memorial service in 1968. The slain black leader epitomized to him the struggle for human rights in America: "He was opposed to violence, to suppression, to the exploitation of man by man. He devoted his life to justice and morality, to achieving true brotherhood of all men, to abolishing the evils of unrestrained selfishness and hate. It is not enough for us to mourn him and to show our respect for him. It is our **duty** to work to achieve the goals that he pointed out." (Photo courtesy of Linda Pauling-Kamb)*

Part V

The Scientist
in Society

After Linus Pauling received the 1962 Nobel Peace Prize—belatedly
awarded in 1963—for having spearheaded the great public protest
against nuclear testing, he acquired instant value as a commentator on
world affairs. It gave him, of course, more legitimate attention in his
peace-promoting work than the Nobel Prize in Chemistry had done—
though he had also put that to good purpose. Requests began pouring
in, more than ever before, for him to speak, write book introductions, contribute articles, sign declarations and petitions, launch new crusades to
protest or further promote the wellbeing of humanity.

Pauling got his best chance to propose solutions to world problems
in the mid 1960s. His approach to practicing social science came from
his accustomed use of the scientific method: he assembled research
data and scrutinized them to seek patterns and relationships. He would
then reach conclusions based on the evidence at hand and posit certain
theories. He believed that the same process could be applied to considering and then resolving problems in human society—including, and
perhaps above all, international disputes.

In his dedication to the principle of applying science and rationalism
to the achievement of world peace, Pauling also continued to urge his
fellow scientists, at home and abroad, to be actively engaged in identifying and resolving serious societal issues. His made his own contribution
by alerting the public, scientists included, to matters that should concern
people; disclosing information that was not widely known or else had
been misreported; and whenever possible, engaging the accepted
authorities in debate.

Pauling in 1967 expressed a few of his thoughts as to why scientists were especially qualified to address important issues in society:

> As scientists, we have not had any special training or experience in settling war; but we do have experience in tackling and solving complicated problems. We have learned that to solve a difficult and complicated problem we must be objective, free from bias.
>
> Scientists have had to learn to accept changes in their picture of the world, revolutionary changes. Newton changed our understanding of the world when he discovered universal gravitation and the laws of motion. Einstein showed that Newton's laws of motion have to be revised. The quantum theory introduced great changes in our ways of thinking about the physical world. Twelve years ago Lee and Yang discovered that parity, a sort of symmetry, is not conserved in certain nuclear reactions. This discovery was a lesson to some other scientists, who could have made the discovery several years earlier if they had been more imaginative and open-minded.
>
> The scientists have learned this lesson—that the world changes and that they must accept the changed world. A physicist who refuses to use relativity and quantum mechanics is not successful in attacking his problems. I hope that the leaders of the governments of the world will learn the lesson, too; the lesson that the existence of nuclear weapons has changed the world, that war must be abolished.

Rather like a naughty boy, Pauling often seemed to delight in upsetting a complacent status quo, leaving it to other scientists to be more patient and forbearing in their negotiations with the powers that be. Fear of censure had never made Pauling quiescent—at least for long. He felt it was important for him to set an example for the scientific community, no matter how much he might be criticized or derided for his outspokenness. He was more populist than diplomat. And though he promoted peaceableness, he could be a pugilist with words—and, increasingly, in legal battles. In the early 1960s Pauling began filing lawsuits in the company of others. The first one was against the U.S. government, to try to force it to refrain from more weapons testing. He then went on his own to sue newspapers and newsmagazines, such as the *St. Louis Globe-Democrat,* the New York *Daily News,* and the *National Review.* He asserted that editorials and articles made statements that maligned his character and sullied his professional reputation. Most of his libel suits, however, if not achieving early out-of-court settlements, eventually were dismissed because of a new U.S. Supreme Court ruling *(New York Times v.*

Sullivan): Public figures, unlike ordinary citizens, could not expect legal protection from such attacks. Since Pauling was decidedly a prominent personage, he might be treated in the same malicious way as politicians often were during campaign frays or when under public scrutiny for a suspected or proven wrongdoing.

Certainly the Center for the Study of Democratic Institutions—or The Center, as Pauling and others called it—was eager to feature its recently acquired, highly visible and vocal Peace Nobelist, once the Paulings moved to Santa Barbara in early 1964. He was encouraged to travel around the nation and the world, discussing serious peace-threatening problems with other concerned notables, and talking to gatherings of people. And so Pauling did, with Ava Helen generally accompanying him. Their four grown children had left home some years earlier to pursue their own lives and interests, so Mrs. Pauling felt free now to travel extensively with her husband, or even on her own. She found herself being sought as a speaker herself, in this period when women's voices were growing stronger and gaining in value, especially to other women and to women's organizations. (See pages 94-97.)

MORALITY AMONG NATIONS

"I do not accept the contention that we do not know what is good and what is evil."

In 1964 Pauling contributed a chapter-essay to a volume being prepared to honor India's recently deceased first prime minister, Jawaharlal Nehru, the great leader who with Mohandas K. Gandhi had crafted India's independence from British colonial rule in 1947. Pauling himself had known Nehru. Nine years earlier, the Paulings had taken a round-the-world tour following his acceptance in Stockholm of the 1954 Nobel Prize for Chemistry. They had gone to India among other countries, and there they met with Nehru. Shortly afterward Pauling had published his summary of that visit.

> *Of the men whom I met on this trip I was most impressed by Premier Nehru of India. My wife and I had dinner with him, and heard him give three public addresses. Although he is the head of a great nation, he did not read his speeches from a manuscript but spoke without notes. It was evident that he had thought deeply about the problem that he was discussing, so deeply that it was not necessary for him to refresh his memory with notes or to use a manuscript in order to express his opinions accurately. He gave me the impression of having great mental powers, excellent*

judgment, and complete sincerity. In my opinion Nehru is one of the greatest men in the world, and I think that future historians may well give him a major share of the credit for avoiding a third world war.

Nehru said that India's approach to peace is a positive, constructive approach, not a passive, negative, neutral approach. He expressed himself as being disturbed by the kind of strong language that statesmen now use. He said that if you seek peace you cannot go far in your search through warlike methods; you must be peaceful in your approach. He said that various countries, including also the Soviet Union, are obviously interested in finding ways out of the tangle of the Formosa [Taiwan] problem and other problems, and in finding some way for a peaceful solution through conferences and diplomatic approaches.

Nehru said that both Britain and India are proud of the way in which the problem of the freedom of India was settled. This peaceful settlement of the problem has changed hostility of the two peoples into friendship. . . .

Nehru feels strongly that Red China should be admitted to the United Nations. He has pointed out that it is very odd for the United Nations not to recognize the existence of this major country, Red China. He has said that it is unreal to have a so-called representative of China in the United Nations who has nothing to do with the real China. The Indian government and people seem to be making great progress in improving conditions in India. I could see how rapid the progress is in science and technology.

The world had changed, and India along with it, in the decade since early 1955 when Pauling first went to India and met Nehru. In 1964, taking up the challenge of memorializing Nehru's vision in some way, Pauling surveyed these changes. The partial test-ban treaty was now in place after four years of difficult, intermittent negotiations in which each side compromised by moving from earlier entrenched positions. Since Stalin's death in 1953, Soviet leaders had proved less tyrannical and obdurate, and on occasion more rational, flexible, and accessible, than their predecessors. Sometimes small faults and failures were even admitted in the history or workings of the world communism they still firmly espoused. At times the Cold War seemed to be losing some of its intensity.

Writing "World Morality and World Peace" gave Pauling the opportunity to publish an assortment of ideas that he had been considering, and also to repeat statements that he had made in the past years, including his Nobel Peace lecture. Here is Pauling's first significant mention of a moral principle that could unite people around the world, with diverse sets of religious beliefs that too often caused conflicts. He found it in the Golden Rule ("Do unto others—") which might be differently expressed in various cultures. For him it became the gold standard for determining one's own behavior and judging that of other people—and nations. It would reappear in various guises in talks and articles for the remainder of his life.

This essay too shows Pauling's continuation of a philosophical position that he first stated in his 1961 talk on "Humanism and Peace" (see pages 165-168): the minimization of suffering, which was linked with the Golden Rule. It had become his basic credo, and he often repeated it over the years. He included it in his popular book *How to Live Longer and Feel Better* (1986), when presenting his ideas on nutritional medicine. Frequently he introduced the theme by quoting from and then paraphrasing a passage from *The Merchant of Venice* in which Shylock protests against Antonio's viewing him as unfeeling—attesting to the universal commonality of human experience.

As for Nehru's earlier comments about Red China, it took longer than he or Pauling expected. In 1964, when the Nehru volume was published, the People's Republic of China still had not been admitted to the U.N. Its entry finally would come in 1971. President Nixon visited China the following year, helping to open diplomatic relations between the U.S. and communist China.

In this essay Pauling criticized the growing American involvement in the conflict within Vietnam, first brought up prominently in his Nobel Peace Prize lecture. It was a major target of his protest activity by the late '60s. (The passage was removed here, but see pages 208-212 and 214-216.) He was also focusing more now on economic factors as precipitators of world and social unrest, which he explored and expounded upon during the rest of the '60s and afterward.

I can think of no more appropriate subject to discuss in an essay in honor of Shri Jawaharlal Nehru than world morality and world peace. Shri Nehru has striven to solve world problems in ways compatible with moral principles, and there exists in the world the continuing hope that India will take a leading part in the now mandatory process of abolishing war.

It is characteristic of the world of today, as of all earlier times, that the principles of morality that apply to the actions of individual human beings do not apply to the actions of nations. There is a tremendous difference between personal morality and national morality. Whereas most men and women, all over the world, accept the principles of ethics and morality that have been formulated and expounded by the great philosophers and religious leaders of the past, and behave in accordance with them, nations act in ways that are determined almost entirely by considerations of selfish national interest.

Commenting on the rejection of ethical principles by governments, Alfred Jay Nock wrote: "A legislature sometimes does a good thing; but it never does it just because it is a good thing."

Aristotle asked: "Can a moral man represent his nation?" and he answered: "No, because nations are immoral; it is considered proper for a strong nation to attack a weak one, if she can benefit herself thereby, irrespective of what the principles of morality have to say about such an action."

The immorality of nations is associated with the retention of the principle of national sovereignty, which is the rejection of world law, the refusal to formulate and accept a set of dispute-settling rules based upon the principles of ethics and morality. Nations have instead depended upon war or the threat of war as the mechanism for the settling of disputes.

I believe that the development of tremendously destructive weapons, based upon nuclear fission and nuclear fusion, now forces the world to abolish the institution of war and to replace it by world law. I believe that we can win a great victory over the evil of war, and at the same time over the plagues of man's condition, over poverty, starvation, and economic exploitation, and over much of the suffering caused by disease.

Instead of the principle of maximizing human happiness, I prefer the principle of minimizing the suffering in the world. . . .

I do not accept the contention that we do not know what is good and what is evil. Even though my relationship to myself is subjective and that to other human beings is objective, I accept the evidence of my senses that I am a man, like other men; I am "fed with the same food, hurt with the same weapons, subject to the same diseases, healed by the same means, warmed and cooled by the same winter and summer"; when I am pricked I bleed, as do other men; when I am tickled, I laugh; when I am poisoned, I die. I cannot contend that it is the result of anything but chance that I am I, that this consciousness of mine is present in this body.

I cannot in good faith argue that I deserve a better fate than other men; and I am forced by this logic to accept as the fundamental ethical principle the Golden Rule. As variously expressed over the ages, it reads: "This is the sum of duty: Do naught unto others which would cause you pain if done to you" (Mahabharata); "What you do not want others to do to you, do not do to others" (Confucius); "We must behave to our friends as we would wish them to behave to us" (Aristotle); "As ye would that men should do to you, do ye also to them likewise" (Luke); "To do as you would be done by, is the plain, sure, and undisputed rule of morality and justice" (Lord Chesterfield); "I must always act in such a way that I can at the same time will that the maxim by which I act should become a universal law" (Immanuel Kant); "To do as one would be done by, and to love one's neighbor as one's self, constitute the ideal perfection of utilitarian morality" (J. S. Mill).

I have made a modern formulation of the Golden Rule: "Do unto others 20 percent better than you would be done by—the 20 percent is to correct for subjective error."

But what is the Golden Rule of *nations* in their mutual intercourse? It seems to be: "Do unto others as evilly as you can find an excuse for."...

I believe that the time has now come for the nations of the world to cooperate in the solution of world problems, and to work together for the welfare of the whole of humanity. I do not believe that either capitalism or communism will succeed in ridding the world of the other—instead, each of these systems will continue to develop and to improve, during the period of coexistence that has now begun, and in the course of time they will grow toward one another, with the acceptance of those attributes of each system that are good and the elimination of those that are bad.

But in the meantime the national governments continue for the most part along the path of immorality and national selfishness. The diplomats and national leaders for the most part still retain the policy that it is just as important to do harm to other nations and peoples as to do good for one's own nation and people.

In discussing the immorality of nations, I shall refer most often to my own nation, the United States of America—not because other nations, such as the Soviet Union, are significantly less immoral, but because I have both greater knowledge about the actions of the United States than of other nations and greater interest in its morality....

It is the concept of "economic systems" that is responsible for the Cold War and the "hot wars" of the last two decades.... The record of the United States over a long period of years has been one of rejection of moral principles and of democracy in favor of support of capitalism.

THREE MODERN REVOLUTIONS

"Most scientists and technologists in the world today are working to make the rich richer and the poor poorer, or are working on the development and fabrication of terrible engines of mass destruction and death."

At the Center for the Study of Democratic Institutions, Pauling could spend part of his time on scientific interests, particularly theoretical work that required thinking, a calculator, and writing tools—not the laboratories and research assistants which weren't available to him. But as the Nobel Peace laureate staff member, he was asked to contemplate, and discuss with others, important peace issues— including world law, disarmament, international problem-solving, and long-range societal planning.

Contributing a chapter to the anthology memorializing Jawaharlal Nehru (see previous selection) also enabled him to incorporate summaries of certain provocative statements made by other people—or reports on discussions in which he had participated with others. For instance, he considered the future-anticipating document "The Triple Revolution." His introductory paragraph about it contains themes that often recurred in other writings and talks, perhaps especially during his several years at The Center. As for the three revolutions: the first, weaponry, was already well known by 1964. The second, cybernetics—basically the electronic age brought on by transistors, robotics, computers, and other high-technology inventions—had yet to undergo the rapid development and widespread availability that would transform science, business, industry, and personal lives in ways not yet predicted or fathomed. And the third, the human and civil rights movement, was just beginning, inspired by the leadership of Dr. Martin Luther King, Jr., and accelerated by mounting public concern and fierce protests against the growing conflict in Vietnam (especially among young people), protests that would reach their apogee by the decade's end. (See pages 213-216.)

O ur system of personal morality, as expressed in the operating social and economic structures as well as in law, is full of imperfections, and these imperfections have been accentuated during recent decades by the changes in the nature of the world that have been brought about by science and technology. There is great misery caused by the abject poverty of about half of the world's people; yet most scientists and technologists in the world today are working to make the rich richer and the poor poorer, or are working on the development and fabrication of terrible engines of mass destruction and death whose use might end our civilization and exterminate the human race.

A few months ago, in March 1964, a group of 32 people (all citizens of the United States except one, the Swedish economist Gunnar Myrdal) issued a statement entitled "The Triple Revolution: An Appraisal of the Major United States Crises and Proposals for Action." This statement, which is directed mainly to problems in the United States, is in fact pertinent to the greater problem of world morality and world peace to an extent such as to justify my summarizing and discussing it.

In their statement the members of the Ad Hoc Committee on the Triple Revolution point out that recent changes in the nature of the world, resulting especially from the discoveries of scientists, demand a fundamental reexamination of existing values and institutions. Three separate and mutually reinforcing revolutions are now taking place: the weaponry revolution, the cybernation revolution, and the human rights revolution.

The weaponry revolution has involved the development of explosives with several million times the explosive power of those used in earlier wars, and the building up by the two great nuclear powers, the United States and the Soviet Union, of stockpiles of nuclear weapons with total explosive power about 50,000 times as great as that of all of the explosives used during the whole of the Second World War. It is almost certain that if these weapons were to be used in an all-out nuclear war the United States and the Soviet Union would cease to exist, and the people of these countries would all be killed; great damage would also be done to other countries and to the people in them.

The cybernation revolution involves the use of computers and automated self-regulated machines in developing a system of almost unlimited productive capacity that requires a smaller and smaller amount of human labor. Under an economic system in which economic resources are distributed on the basis of contributions to production, the development of cybernation has been leading to the withholding of purchasing power from a larger and larger fraction of the American people. The consequence is that there are about 10 million unemployed people in the United States at the present time (about 5 million unemployed and looking for employment, and another 5 million who have quit looking for work and are not included in the unemployment statistics of the U.S. Department of Labor).

The moral question arises as to whether or not all people are entitled to benefit from the resources of the earth and the products of industry. In the United States today, the major economic problem is not how to increase production, but rather how to distribute the abundance that is provided by cybernation. It is recommended by the Committee that "society, through its appropriate legal and governmental institutions, undertake an unqualified commitment to provide every individual and every family with an adequate income as a matter of right." This recommendation is made for the United States; but I believe that it should be extended to the whole world.

The third revolution now under way is the human rights revolution. All over the world there can be found the increasing conviction that oppression of human beings must be abolished, and that social, political and economic systems must be developed in which every human being will be of value and will feel valued.

THE COMBAT BETWEEN TWO ECONOMIC SYSTEMS

"During most of the Cold War the United States has led in militarism, and the Soviet Union has followed our lead."

By moving away from the familiar academic routine of teaching, oversee-ing graduate students' work, and giving close attention to research progress in his Caltech laboratories, Pauling could give more undivided time to current events and historical studies. For several years he was busy at the Center for the Study of Democratic Institutions in this new pursuit, involving reading, talking with colleagues, traveling, lecturing, and publishing. He also made time for some theoretical work in nuclear physics, and still took interest in brain chemistry.

In 1964 he published a paper that he often cited later: "The Role of Unilateral Action." It summarized his observations and reasoning regard-ing U.S. and Soviet relations for the last two decades. He hoped he had made it clear that he did not subscribe to a pacifism that would capitu-late to communism or any other system that tried to impose itself upon the United States from the outside (as he had often been accused of agreeing to do). Nor did he expect the USSR to capitulate militarily either. He started out by announcing:

> *I have never advocated unilateral disarmament by the United States or by the Soviet Union. I fear that the militarists in the other country would take advantage of the opportunity provided by such an action. But the United States and the Soviet Union have in fact taken many unilateral actions, and these actions have dur-ing the past 15 years been largely in the direction of increased militarism.*

Pauling always regarded the long feud between the two main play-ers in the Cold War not only as grossly wasteful of natural resources and human effort, but also needlessly destructive of human health and life. The enmity contained much of the underlying irrationality of a conflict between two religions—for it involved two separate world views that essentially had become fiercely opposed dogmas, to be fought to the death if necessary, to prove that the winning side held the Truth.

In 1967 Pauling stated his own economic orientation in this way:

> *I dislike imperialism, military colonialism, and economic colonialism, the exploitation of the poor people, whether they live in the developed countries or the underdeveloped countries. I dislike the capitalist system when it operates in an unbridled way. I believe in free enterprise, but not so free and unrestrained as to introduce gross inequities.*

He often expressed admiration for the form of moderate socialism achieved by the Scandinavian countries, where government support of social, economic, and educational programs that benefited the citizenry was balanced by personal responsibility, political freedom, and regulated free enterprise.

Thirty years after writing the critique below of the Cold War's costly arms race, a crazed competition producing nuclear weapons with an "overkill" factor that could destroy the world and all its people many times over, Linus Pauling would get no satisfaction from beholding the seeming triumph of the West's system of free enterprise and capitalism over the crumbling social and economic bulwark of the USSR and its satellites, whose cohesion had long been rigidly held together by force and fear.

Pauling knew that at the times of great transitional upheavals in governments and economies, it was usually the ordinary people who experienced the worst suffering—especially the ethical ones, those with compassion and a conscience. This misery and chaos, too, would be the dismal legacy of the Cold War. Furthermore, when the USSR collapsed, its far-flung network of nuclear defenses in missiles, submarines, and bombs would no longer have a strong central control or sufficient economic support. The breakdown of totalitarian command, commendable though it might be in other ways, greatly increased the probability of black-market sales of weapons and fissionable materials, as well as chemical and biological warfare agents, to unstable or renegade nations and terrorist groups—thus underscoring the Paulings' earlier warnings about the spread of nuclear weapons.

In 1964, the same year that he was considering the role of unilateral actions on the part of nations, Pauling wrote an introduction to a book by Sidney Lens entitled *The Futile Crusade: American Anti-Communism as American Credo*. The piece dealt briefly with unilateral decisions in the Cold War, and described some notable consequences of the fervent rivalry between the United States and the Soviet Union. It ended with a summarizing invocation characteristic of many Pauling speeches and articles over the years.

T he last 15 years have seen greater waste of the natural resources of the Earth and of the results of man's labor than the whole of previous history. During this decade and a half the great nations, in the course of the Cold War, have expended nearly a thousand billion dollars on militarism. The United States and the Soviet Union have built up stockpiles of nuclear weapons and vehicles for delivering them such that each nation could, in a great nuclear war, completely destroy the other, and neither could prevent its own destruction.

I have estimated that the nuclear weapons now in existence total 320,000 megatons. The Second World War involved the use of six megatons of weapons, over a period of six years. The present nuclear stockpile would permit a six-megaton war, equivalent to the Second World War, to be fought every day, day after day, for 146 years.

For several years the United States (and the Soviet Union) have lived under the shadow of the possibility of complete destruction. We are still in great danger—tomorrow, or the day after tomorrow—that the psychological or technological accident might occur that would initiate a nuclear war that might mean the end of civilization.

It is hard to understand how the American people, who are sensible human beings, and the Russian people, who are sensible human beings, could have been led to permit the wasteful expenditure of a large fraction of their national income to achieve a goal that is itself irrational and almost inconceivably perilous. One factor that has operated is that the danger that a nuclear war would be initiated by design has been thought to be smaller if the destructive power of the Soviet Union and that of the United States were approximately equal, than if one nation were to fall far behind the other.

During most of the Cold War the United States has led in militarism, and the Soviet Union has followed our lead. We made and exploded the first atomic bombs and built up the first atomic stockpile. Three years later the Soviet Union followed our example. We made and exploded the first modern bomb, with explosive energy enough to destroy any city on Earth; the Soviet Union was one year behind. We built up the first nuclear stockpile great enough to achieve the annihilation of an enemy country. The Soviet Union followed.

Only in the pollution of the atmosphere with radioactive materials has the Soviet Union taken the lead. By testing a large number of nuclear weapons during the year beginning in September 1961, including a 60-megaton bomb, the Soviet Union assumed the onus of responsibility for two-thirds of the radioactive pollution, and for two-thirds of the millions of genetically damaged children who are the sacrifices of future generations to the nuclear militarism of our generation.

Why did our national leaders decide upon this policy of increased nuclear militarism? I do not know the answer, but I surmise that some arguments relating to the control of communism were involved. And why did the sensible American people permit it to be done? Why did the scientists, who during the years immediately following the use of atomic bombs to destroy Hiroshima and Nagasaki were, by the hundreds, active all over the United States in informing their fellow American citizens about the nature of nuclear weapons and nuclear war and the possibilities of devastation unless war were abolished and replaced by international law, not continue their vigorous campaign for peace and reason in the world?

I hope that very many Americans will [think about] the plight of the world today, and the need to continue the move toward the abolition of war that was initiated in 1963 by the test-ban treaty. In his address to the United Nations General Assembly in September 1961 our late President John F. Kennedy said, "The goal [of disarmament] is no longer a dream. It is a practical matter of life or death. The risks inherent in disarmament pale in comparison to the risks inherent in an unlimited arms race."

I believe that we need to understand the important aspects of our recent history—in order that we may be helped in the effort to achieve the goal of the abolition of war and its replacement by world law. I am confident that the intelligence and good sense of the human race are equal to this task, and that we shall be able in the course of time to build a world characterized by economic, political, and social justice for all human beings, and a culture worthy of man's intelligence.

THE RIGHT TO A GOOD LIFE

"Modern means of waging war seem to be more easily available to the underdeveloped countries than drugs, food, and machines for increasing the production of goods."

In February of 1965 the Center for the Study of Democratic Institutions hosted a three-day international conference in New York City. At the *Pacem in Terris*—Peace on Earth meeting notable scholars, thinkers, and diplomats discussed issues presented in a powerful and influential papal encyclical letter issued by Pope John XXIII before his death in 1963. Linus Pauling gave an impassioned talk in which he clearly agreed with that widely beloved, liberal, ecumenical pope.

Pauling characteristically pieced together ideas he had expressed earlier in passages written for *No More War!* (1958), the "Humanism and Peace" talk (1961), the Nobel Peace Lecture (1963), and the chapter contributed to the Nehru memorial volume (1964). His recycling of words did not make them any less genuine and moving.

Pauling had found his own operative humanistic philosophy. Here, sometimes almost in a biblical cadence, this declared agnostic or atheist gave respectful and even reverential attention to the teachings of the former leader of Roman Catholic Christendom, including—surprisingly— joining in a final prayer. (Note that in this speech Pauling once again warned against the immoral American involvement in Vietnam. The reference to the war would grow longer and more vehement in tone as the '60s went on, as it would throughout a nation convulsed by this unpopular, expensive, and bloody involvement in Southeast Asia.)

For thousands of years, throughout the entire period for which we have historical knowledge, war has been one of the principal causes of human suffering.

I believe that we have now reached the time in the course of the evolution of civilization when war will be abolished from the world, and will be replaced by a system of world law based upon the principles of justice and morality.

In his encyclical letter *Pacem in Terris* Pope John XXIII said:

> *Men are becoming more and more convinced that disputes that arise between States should be resolved not by recourse to arms, but rather by negotiation.*
>
> *It is true that on historical grounds this conviction is based chiefly on the terrible destructive force of modern arms; and it is nourished by the horror aroused in the mind by the very thought of the cruel destruction and the immense suffering that the use of those armaments would bring to the human family. For this reason it is hardly possible to imagine that in the atomic era war could be used as an instrument of justice.*
>
> *Nevertheless, unfortunately, the law of fear still reigns among peoples, and it forces them to spend fabulous sums for armaments: not for aggression, they affirm—and there is no reason for not believing them—but to dissuade others from aggression.*
>
> *There is reason to hope, however, that, by meeting and negotiating, men may come to discover better the bonds that unite them together, deriving from the human nature that they have in*

common; and that they may also come to discover that one of the most profound requirements of their common nature is this: that between them and their respective peoples it is not fear that should reign but love, a love that tends to express itself in a collaboration that is loyal, manifold in form, and productive of many benefits.

Let us consider the significance of war as a cause of human suffering, in comparison with other causes. . . .

We suffer from accidents, from natural catastrophes, from disease, from the ills accompanying the deterioration of age, and also, in a sense the most viciously, from man's inhumanity to man, as expressed in economic exploitation, the maldistribution of the world's wealth, and especially the evil institution of war.

Man has reached his present state through the process of evolution. The last great step in evolution was the mutational process that doubled the size of the brain, about one million years ago; this led to the origin of man. It is this change in the brain that permits the inheritance of acquired characteristics of a certain sort—the inheritance of knowledge, of learning, through communication from one human being to another.

Thus abilities that have not yet been incorporated into the molecules of deoxyribonucleic acid that constitute the pool of human genetic material are not lost until their rediscovery by members of following generations, but instead are handed on from person to person, from generation to generation. Man's great powers of thinking, remembering, and communicating are responsible for the evolution of civilization.

During year after year, decade after decade, century after century, the world has been changed by the discoveries made by scientists and by their precursors—by those brilliant, original, imaginative men and women of prehistoric times and of more recent times who learned how to control fire, to cook food, to grow crops, to domesticate animals, and then to build wheeled vehicles, steam engines, electric generators and motors, and nuclear fission power plants. And, of course, in the early days, the scientists were the theologians, the religious leaders, too. Sometimes the thought occurs to me that the world will not be saved unless we return to this condition.

I remember the Pugwash conferences on science and world affairs, where scientists from many countries—20 countries—have come together 13 times to discuss important problems. I remember how the scientists of the East and West are, so far as I can see, very much like one another. They resemble one another not only in their knowledge of science but also in their acceptance of moral principles. It seems to me when

I compare scientists with diplomats—with other people—that the scientists of the whole world are more closely related to one another than scientists are to other people in their own country. There is a better understanding among them than with other people. This understanding must spread. The discoveries that scientists have made provide now the possibility of abolishing starvation and malnutrition, and improving the wellbeing, and enriching the lives of all of the world's people.

The effect of the discoveries of scientists in decreasing the amount of human suffering is illustrated by the control that has been achieved over the infectious diseases. In many parts of the world it is now rare for women to die of puerperal infection, for infants to die of diphtheria or scarlet fever, for people to die of diseases such as smallpox or bubonic plague. Cancer remains a cause of great human suffering not yet brought under control; but we may hope that this terrible disease will also succumb in the next few decades to the attack on it that is being made by scientists.

The results of medical discoveries and technological developments have not yet been made available to all of the world's people. Modern means of waging war seem to be more easily available to the underdeveloped countries than drugs, food, and machines for increasing the production of goods. . . .

The already enormous disparity in the standards of living of different peoples has been increasing, rather than decreasing, in recent years. The use of a large part of the world's wealth, $120 billion per year, for the support of militarism and the failure to stop the increase in the amount of human suffering due to poverty are causing a deterioration in morality, especially among young people.

I believe that it is a violation of natural law for half of the people of the world to live in misery, in abject poverty, without hope for the future, while the affluent nations spend on militarism a sum of money equal to the entire income of this miserable half of the world's people.

Pope John in his great encyclical letter said that every human being is a person, that every man has the right to life, to bodily integrity, to food, clothing, shelter, rest, medical care, and social services, to security in case of sickness, inability to work, widowhood, old age, unemployment, or deprival otherwise of the means of subsistence through no fault of his own; the right to respect for his person, to his good reputation; the right to freedom in searching for truth and in expressing and communicating his opinions; the right to be informed truthfully about public events; the right to share in the benefits of culture; the right to a basic education and to suitable technical and professional training; the right to free initiative in the economic field and the right to work under good working conditions, with a proper, just, and sufficient wage; the right to private property, with its accompanying social duties; the rights of residence and of freedom of movement, of membership in the human family and membership in the world community.

Most human beings are now denied these rights. It is our duty to work to achieve them for everyone.

In the words of Pope John: "It is not enough . . . to acknowledge and respect every man's right to the means of subsistence: one must also strive to attain that he actually has enough . . . food and nourishment."

One of the most evil aspects of human suffering is the absence of any justice or meaning in its distribution. Accidents, natural disasters, and excruciatingly painful diseases strike with the blind malevolence of chance. I am asked by a friend, "Why should my mother, who was a good and gentle person all of her life, have had to suffer so terribly while she was dying of cancer?"; and by another friend, "What have we done that our two children should have suffered from cystic fibrosis during their few years on Earth, and then have died, while other children are healthy and happy?"

There is little consolation in the knowledge that through pure chance the defective children had inherited a mutated gene, a molecule that had been damaged by a single quantum of high-energy radiation or a single ionizing particle passing through the reproductive organs of a parent or grandparent. But we may hope that preventive or palliative measures will be discovered that will permit most of these injustices of nature to be eliminated.

War has become increasingly unjust and immoral both in the magnitude and in the distribution of the suffering that it causes. Great nations claim the right to sacrifice human lives and to take human lives. Instead of being citizens who volunteer to protect their families and their country, soldiers often have been forced into military service, sometimes with execution as the alternative. It is chance that determines whether or not the soldier will be killed, and also whether the civilian will be killed. Instead of Hiroshima, another Japanese city might have been destroyed by the first atomic bomb used in war; instead of the hundreds of thousands of human beings in Hiroshima who were killed or were injured by the blast, fire, and high-energy radiation, other hundreds of thousands, in another Japanese city, might have suffered this fate. It is impossible to support the contention that there was justice in this terrible concentration of suffering on the people of Hiroshima.

The injustice and immorality of the great wars of the past would be far transcended by a great war in the nuclear age, a war in which the devastating weapons involving nuclear fission and fusion that now exist were used. Instead of tens of millions, hundreds or even thousands of millions of human beings might be killed. Great nations might be exterminated. Civilization might come to an end. There is even the possibility that the human race would not survive the catastrophe.

As rational and moral beings, we are forced now to find a rational and moral alternative to war. . . .

Now the time has come to obey the exhortation of Pope John: the exhortation to cease military aggression, to bring this evil war [Vietnam] to an end, to meet and negotiate and make a great practical application of the principles of morality and justice.

FACTS VS. WORDS

"This is what they must do—not just use words that they don't define and carry on vague discussions, but try to make their concepts more precise, to have ideas that can be closely related to fact."

Connected with the Center for the Study of Democratic Institutions, Pauling was often in the company of social scientists. He expected them to give the same precise attention to societal problems as physical and life scientists gave to finding answers to nature's perplexities. The disciplines of cultural anthropology, sociology, psychology, economics, and political science increasingly utilized the standard techniques of the scientific method, including statistical measurements in attaining results or reaching conclusions. From these conclusions pragmatic new public policies could originate.

However, Pauling was becoming frustrated with all the high-flown talk at the Center that too often seemed ungrounded in fact, in reality. To him it seemed self-indulgent, and it rarely got anywhere toward making a difference in the world. He was still at CSDI when he gave a talk to a 1966 meeting of science educators. In it he expressed indirectly some of his growing dissatisfaction with his tenancy at a place where many of his associates, either there or in conferences he attended elsewhere, used "Words, words, words." He was already feeling ready to move on. In his conclusion he also reiterated his belief in the value to everybody of at least some educational exposure to science and the scientific method. (Pauling's own sort of rigorous examination of facts can be seen in the selection after this one, when he analyzed India's problems by using official statistics.)

S cientists . . . have the duty to help educate those of their fellow citizens who represent what C. P. Snow called "the other culture." If I remember correctly, Lord Snow divided the two cultures in this way: the scientists, the people who understand the world, including our scientific knowledge of it, constitute one culture, and the nonscientists, who understand only those parts of the world that we describe as nonscientific, constitute the other culture. Not long ago Professor Denis Gabor of the Imperial College in London participated in a symposium in the Center for the Study of Democratic Institutions. After this experience with a large group of social scientists, he suggested that the division is not really between the scientist and the nonscientist, but between those people interested in facts and ideas on the one hand, and those interested in words on the other.

This seems harsh, but I think that there is something to it. I recall a series of discussions at the Center about the presidency, in which presidents of the United States were categorized as Washingtonian, or Jeffersonian, or Hamiltonian. Finally I asked, "Have you laid down some attributes of the actions or decisions of the presidents and assigned to them their percentage weights of Washingtonianism, Jeffersonianism, and Hamiltonianism, and then analyzed the actions and decisions of the various presidents to find out what the quantitative conclusions are? Have you done this, or have you done anything such as to lead you to think that two different people who classified the presidents among your three categories would reach the same conclusions about them?" The answer was that this sounded interesting but had not been done. Yet, this is what they must do—not just use words that they don't define and carry on vague discussions, but try to make their concepts more precise, to have ideas that can be closely related to fact.

In the class of people who are interested in facts and ideas, we have, of course, most scientists, and also a good number of nonscientists who think along the same lines even though they don't have scientific training. In the other class—those interested in words—we have some scientists and some philosophers, and many nonscientists. I remember reading a book on philosophy in which the author went on, page after page, on the question: If there is a leaf on a tree and you see that it is green in the springtime and red in fall, is that the same leaf or is it a different leaf? Is the essence of leafness still in it? Words, words, words, but "chlorophyll" and "xanthophyll"—which are sensible in this connection of what has happened to that leaf—just don't appear at all. Admittedly, we have some people who are called scientists who are in the category of those who talk about words rather than facts and ideas.

What is the solution going to be? I believe that the ultimate solution will be that *everyone* will have a knowledge of science, but it will take a generation, two generations, for us to reach this goal, even in the United States. I believe that we *shall* reach this goal if the world is not destroyed. I believe that reason will win out and that the world will continue to improve.

A SCIENTIST LOOKS AT INDIA'S PROBLEMS

"We are all brothers, we, human beings, we, the men, women, and children of the world, and we must join together in solving the great world problems."

In 1967 Pauling was invited to give two major lectures in India: the two-day Azad Memorial Lecture in New Delhi and the Chettyar Memorial Lecture in Madras. He planned these lectures carefully because he wished to give close attention to India's special problems as a nation. This year was the 20th anniversary of Indian independence. He regarded these lectures also as opportunities to present his deep concerns about American foreign policy—the Vietnam War in particular. (See pages 214-222.)

Both lectures were published in India later that year as small books: *Science and World Peace* and *Foreign Policies and Disarmament*. (A few copies found their way to the United States.) He said many of the same things in both of them, but the Azad lecture, twice as long, was more ambitious. In later years Pauling would note its importance in propelling him into considering the great problem of overpopulation, not just in India but in his own nation, the world at large, and the world of the future. Several selections from the lecture, given here, show the investigative acumen that Pauling brought as a scientist to the problems of nations and communities—human societies.

"I believe that the time has come when the methods of science can and should be applied to all of the great world problems," Pauling declared in the first Azad lecture.

> *The problems of the world have become so great that we must use all of our wisdom in attacking them.*
> *I believe that the scientist has a special responsibility, the responsibility of helping his fellow citizens to understand the great problems, of helping in the solution of these problems, all of which are closely connected to science; and, in addition, the responsibility also of helping to awaken the public conscience about these problems.*

In his two Azad lectures, Pauling tackled some specific current problems in India. He scolded some leaders for unconscionable expenditures in building its military might, including conducting research for acquiring nuclear weapons capability. (See pages 257-260.) He made many of his points by using statistics. By now Pauling was well practiced in using demographic data and governmental fiscal reports. When he began giving public lectures and writing extensively about the frightening prospect of nuclear weapons development and warfare, he proved his points by scrutinizing, comparing, correlating, and interpreting figures for population, military budget, income level, and mortality. When applying for grants in medical research, he would cite demographic and health statistics to demonstrate the need for pursuing the cause and possible remedy for some disease.

Thus Pauling, when readying himself to visiting India again to deliver several provocative lectures about its current societal status, consulted some basic sources of recent and comparative statistics. His message about achieving peace on Earth was, expectably, intermixed with certain recommendations for his own nation as well as India. Inevitably, he found telling connections between a nation's military budget, inflationary trends, diminishing per-capita income, and a poor living standard for people with the lowest income, whose number was expanding despite their inability to adequately feed their children and themselves.

India exemplified for Pauling the predicament of many nations and of the world itself. Warfare, whether preparing for it or conducting it, ended up by robbing Earth of scarce resources that would either be wasted by disuse or, worse, result in death and devastation. Money and human effort that could have gone into reducing widespread poverty and misery—attempting to eliminate hunger and malnutrition, finding solutions to serious infectious and degenerative diseases—instead was diverted into the so-called defense industry. The militant global mentality, nourished by the Cold War, contributed to making the rich richer and the poor poorer.

Although the threat of nuclear and other forms of warfare continued to concern him, Pauling by the mid 1960s was widening his area of concern to encompass several problems that had begun to seem monumental in their consequences. These can be grouped in two main categories: environmental degradation and overpopulation. His alarmist opinions coincided with those of new or reenergized environmental organizations such as Greenpeace and the Sierra Club, and population-limiting movements like Zero Population Growth. In the remaining three decades of his life he often featured these two areas when he spoke or wrote on peace issues.

One cannot help but feel discouraged when confronting, less than 40 years after this lecture of warning by Pauling, the fact that by the end of the 20th century India's population is likely to have doubled, to reach one billion persons, with comparable increases in many other lands. Meanwhile, of course, the natural environment continues to be exploited and further ravaged by humankind—collectively oblivious to the long-term consequences to the wellbeing and survival of most living creatures on the planet.

The world needs peace, not militarism. Militarism is the cause of human suffering in two ways: directly, through the savagery of the war itself, and indirectly, through the waste of the resources of the world, and the consequent increase in suffering caused by poverty and disease.

The world needs India as a leader in the fight for peace and world cooperation and in the fight against poverty and disease. There is great misery caused by the abject poverty of about one half of the world's people. . . . Even in the United States, the richest country in the world, the poor people are becoming poorer. During recent years the national income of the United States increased by about six percent per year. This increase would suggest that the people are getting richer, but in fact the increase has not brought prosperity to the poor people, the ordinary people.

First, there has been an increase in population of between one and two percent per year; second, there has been inflation, decrease in the purchasing power of the dollar, by about two percent per year; and third, there has been, during the last eight years, an increase in the profits from investments from 8 percent of the invested money per year to 14 percent per year, on the average, and also an increase in the amount of invested money greater than the increase in the national income, leading to an increase in the fraction of the national income that is paid to the investors, rich people, and the corresponding decrease in the fraction that goes to the ordinary people, the poor people.

Militarism is the explanation of the inflation, the decrease in the purchasing power of the dollar. There would not have been inflation in the United States except for the great military budget. As to the increase from 8 percent to 14 percent in the average profits from investments, this unbridled economic exploitation that is now operating in the United States will lead to catastrophe if it is continued.

We do not have completely free enterprise in the United States. There are government regulations of various sorts, which are planned to operate to control monopolies and to achieve a proper distribution of the national income among the various classes of people. These regulations, however, have not been operating effectively during the recent years.

I believe that we should work toward a goal of having in every country in the world a social, political, and economic system that permits the maximum freedom of choice to every person, compatible with the rights of other persons. By allowing the freedom of choice to persons—choice of vocation, choice of place of residence and living conditions, choice as to the division of time between work and recreation (with in general an accompanying decrease in income associated with a decrease in amount of work done), choice of association with other persons in personal relationships. A system based upon individual freedom permits a great increase in the happiness of human beings with no significant decrease in the happiness of others.

I have observed that bureaucracy may operate in such a way as to cause much human suffering with no corresponding benefit to any human beings or to society. . . .

I believe that freedom of enterprise should not, however, permit a person or small group of persons to obtain ownership of great natural resources, or ownership of corporations providing public services, which are essentially monopolistic. I believe that the state should carry on many activities, providing services to the people as a whole and preventing the exploitation by monopolistic private corporations that operate in a way that does damage to the people as a whole. It is my opinion that the socialist governments of the Scandinavian countries provide the best approximation to the ideal at the present time.

In the world of today we see processes operating that can lead to serious economic exploitation and neo-colonialism in the near future. India should be warned by the example of Chile and other Latin American countries, where a small initial investment of money by foreign capitalists, such as the investment 100 years to 50 years ago in the nitrate and copper mines of Chile, has led to the continued bleeding out of larger and larger amounts of money from the country. The natural riches of the country itself have largely gone to benefit people in foreign countries.

The ideal economic policy at the present tine is that of the four Scandinavian countries: Sweden, Norway, Denmark, and Finland. These countries have laws forbidding any foreigner to own any part of industry or any property within the country. Even a citizen who moves outside the country and becomes a permanent resident of some other country must give up his ownership of stock and property in the country. This is a way of preventing the disaster of continued economic exploitation of the resources of the country by foreigners.

An underdeveloped country, such as India, may have such need for capital to permit industrialization that such a policy could not be adopted. For such a country I advocate that the policy be to obtain loans and to permit [foreign] investments only during a limited period of time.

I have made an effort to analyze the economy of India, with use mainly of the *India Pocketbook of Economic Information* (Department of Economic Affairs, Ministry of Finance, 1966), as the source of facts. My analysis has led me to the conclusion that during the past 18 years the people of India have been getting poorer.

The per capita income in India was Rs. [rupees] 250 average per year in 1948, and Rs. 500 in 1966. The average income, measured in rupees, has accordingly doubled during this period. The purchasing power of the rupee, however, has decreased: 100 rupees in 1966 had the purchasing power, for food and other essential commodities, of only 42 rupees in 1948. The average per capita income for 1966, Rs. 500, has purchasing power equal to that of Rs. 210 in 1948. This amount, Rs. 210, is less than the 1948 average income of Rs. 250, and accordingly I am led to the conclusion, stated above, that the people of India as a whole have been getting poorer, rather than more prosperous.

In attempting to find the cause of this trend toward poverty and away from prosperity, I may ask first as to the cause of the inflation of the currency.

From one of the tables of the *India Pocketbook of Economic Information* we learn that the rupee decreased in purchasing power by an average of 3.4 percent per year during 14 years from 1948 to 1962. From the tables in this *Pocketbook*, supplemented for the last year by the *Quarterly Bulletin of the Eastern Economist for 1966*, I find that inflation has increased to 10 percent per year during the four years from 1962 to 1966. During the four years since 1962 inflation of the rupee has caused a decrease in the purchasing power of the people's money by 64,000 million rupees, an average of 16,000 million rupees per year.

In the year 1963 the military budget of India was more than doubled, so that it reached the amount 4.7 percent of the national income, which was 340,000 million rupees; that is, the military budget reached the amount 16,000 million rupees in 1963. This sum of money, the military budget, is just equal to the decrease in the purchasing power of the income of the people of India that has been caused for the average year since 1962 by inflation of the rupee. This comparison indicates that the purchasing power of the people's income would not have decreased if these great expenditures for militarism had not taken place....

Earlier in these lectures I mentioned that the national income of the United States does not in itself constitute a measure of the wellbeing of the people of the country, and that increase in population is one factor that must also be taken into consideration. The population of the United States is now increasing by somewhat less than 1.5 percent per year, as the result of immigration and of natural increase (excess of birth rate over death rate). The rate of natural increase of population for the United States in a representative recent year, 1963, is given as 1.2 percent (birth rate 2.12 percent, death rate 0.94 percent) by Roger Revelle, Director of the Harvard Center for Population Studies, in his article on population and food supplies, published in the *Proceedings of the National Academy of Sciences* of the United States of America for August 1966.

The average rate of population increase for the countries that might be described as developed countries (large amount of industrialization, per capita income of more than $1,000 per year) was 1.2 percent in 1963, ranging from 0.3 percent for Hungary to 1.6 percent for Canada, and is probably less now. Increase by 1-2 percent per year leads to a doubling in the population in 60 years. The underdeveloped countries, with a gross national product of less than $400 per capita per year, have a rate of natural increase of more than 3 percent per year, which leads to a doubling in the population in 24 years, a quadrupling in 47 years.

The problem of increasing production of food and other commodities to provide for such an increased population is a tremendous one, which the underdeveloped countries have not been able to solve. This problem has for many countries become serious only during the last decade or two. One hundred years ago the death rate in many countries was equal to the birth rate, and there was no natural increase in population.

A great change in the conditions of health and the causes of death has taken place in many parts of the world during the 20th century. In former centuries the principal causes of death were the diseases of childhood that result from a combination of infection and malnutrition. This combination of infection and malnutrition as a cause of death is still the most important in many of the underdeveloped countries, but in the developed countries infant mortality is low, for most developed countries ranging from 0.10 to 0.25 percent (death before one year of age), childhood deaths are rare, most people live at least to middle age, and cardiovascular disease and cancer are the principal causes of death. The control of infectious diseases has been largely responsible for this change.

In India the birth rate in 1951 was 4 percent per year (40 births per thousand population per year) and the death rate was 2.7 percent, corresponding to a rate of natural increase of 1.3 percent per year. The birth rate now is four percent per year, but the death rate has decreased rapidly, because of control of infectious diseases, and is only about 1.5 percent per year, leading to a natural increase in the population by 2.5 percent per year.

Let us consider the effect that the decrease in the death rate has had on India. During the 16 years between 1951 and 1967 the birth rate has continued essentially unchanged, at 4 percent per year. The death rate was 2.7 percent per year in 1951. It has decreased steadily, and was 1.8 percent per year in 1961. The rate of natural increase in population had changed from 1.3 percent per year in 1951 to 2.2 percent per year in 1961, an extra 0.9 percent per year.

During the last 16 years the population of India has increased from 365 million to 500 million. This increase has been to a considerable extent the result of the decrease in the death rate from 2.7 percent in 1951 to 1.8 percent in 1961 and then to 1.5 percent at present, with no significant decrease in the birth rate, and with corresponding increases in the rate of natural increase in population, from 1.3 percent in 1951 to 2.2 percent per year in 1961.

Let us ask how many people there would be in India at the present time if the birth rate had decreased from year to year by the sane amount as the death rate, so that the rate of natural increase had remained at 1.3 percent per year. A rate of natural increase of 1.3 percent per year leads to an increase in population by 23 percent in 16 years; that is, the population would have increased from 365 million to 450 million by 1967, rather than to 500 million, There are 50 million more people in India now than there would have been if the birth rate had been decreased by an amount sufficient to make up for the decrease in the death rate,

This extra 50 million people is 10 percent of the present population. Fifty million extra people to be fed constitutes a most serious added economic burden, which is in part responsible for the increasing poverty of the people of India

A rapid increase in the population does not lead to security, nor to power, nor to wealth. It leads to poverty and to misery.

Methods of controlling the population by preventing conception are now available. The cheapest and most certain are vasectomy and salpingectomy [tubectomy].

The government of India has adopted an enlightened policy of responsibility for control of the population. In the past, it has not, however, applied this policy in an effective way. It is essential that the birth rate be decreased to correct for the decrease in the death rate, and indeed, even somewhat more, to bring the increase in population to a stop, to achieve the elimination of poverty, to increase the wellbeing of all the people, to move toward the goal of national prosperity and greatness.

This path should have been taken 15 years ago, in 1951, when the great decrease in the death rate became definitely known in the census. It is absolutely essential that it be taken now. . . .

And what should be the [population] goal for India? I have pointed out that during recent years the people of India have been becoming poorer and poorer, that the decrease in purchasing power of the money earned by the average person in India has been especially great during the past few years, and that the economic decline, which can be attributed in part to the military expenditures by the government, is also in large part the consequence of the very rapid increase in population.

I think that the people of India may well be less happy than they were five thousand years ago, during the Stone Age. In Kerala a few days ago I watched the fishermen who were diving and fishing from sunrise until sunset, getting only a meager catch, diving into the ocean for mussels all day long in the hope of making enough money to live or getting enough food to keep them alive. I watched the workers beating coir, little boys, men, and women working from early morning until late at night to earn enough money to keep alive, living in huts like those in which men lived at the dawn of civilization; living lives not greatly different from those of Stone Age man.

However, some thousands of years ago the people living in that region had purer water flowing in their rivers and streams. The number of people was not so great as to contaminate their water supply. The food available could be gathered without the extreme competition that exists now. Stone Age man did not have books to read, he could not go to the cinema for recreation. But approximately 72 percent of the people of India now are illiterate; to these 72 percent of the people the intellectual satisfaction of reading is still denied. Many do not have enough money to go to the cinema. . . . A large fraction of the people of India are under-nourished, half-starved.

I suggest that, in order that the people of India may be healthy and happy, may lead lives with greater intellectual and philosophical satisfaction, the government and people of India should adopt the proposal made by Sir Joseph Hutchinson for the United Kingdom in his British Association address. The suggestion by Sir Joseph Hutchinson that there should be 40 million people in the United Kingdom, instead of 50 million, may be translated for India as a proposal that there should be 400 million people in India rather than 500 million. The effort should be made, over a period of a few generations, to reach this goal of a population of 400 million. It may be that a revision of the goal would be made before even one generation has gone by; perhaps the revision would be in the direction of a still further reduction.

The policy should, I believe, be one that permits every family to have one or two or three children. I believe that one of the greatest sources of human happiness is that of having children, of knowing that of the complement of 100,000 molecules of deoxyribonucleic acid that constitutes the genes you yourself have received from your forebears and that have determined your nature, one half, 50,000, have combined with 50,000 molecules of deoxyribonucleic acid contributed by your wife or husband to determine the character and the nature of the new human being who represents a sort of fusion of you and your spouse, a sort of reincarnation of you and your spouse, and of your parents and your wife's parents. But then let there be every pressure, every incentive, every aid available to bring the family's increment to the population to a stop. I repeat that this is the path to the elimination of poverty, to the increase in the wellbeing of all the people, to national prosperity and greatness. It is essential that this path be taken, that this policy be adopted and prosecuted vigorously by the nation as a whole. It is already late. The burden of the extra 50 million people has already made itself evident in such a way as to suggest the impending catastrophe.

With a smaller number of people India would be able to contribute more actively than now to the solution of the great world problems. We are all brothers, we, human beings, we, the men, women, and children of the world, and we must join together in solving the great world problems, in preventing catastrophes, in cutting down the amount of human suffering and misery that is due to the maldistribution of the world's wealth and to the ravages of war.

I believe that if we work together we can abolish war, abolish economic exploitation, abolish the misery that results from ignorance, poverty, and disease, and that we shall in the course of time achieve a world full of happy people, a world with economic, political, and social justice for all human beings and with a culture worthy of man's intelligence.

THE IMMORAL WAR IN VIETNAM

"This is an immoral activity—the strafing and burning of villages is immoral. I do not like my great nation to be involved in this activity."

In the United States by the mid '60s there were troubling signs of societal discord: violence and terrorism, whether random or conspiratorial acts by individuals and groups, such as the assassinations of President John F. Kennedy in 1963 and of Robert F. Kennedy and Dr. Martin Luther King, Jr. in 1968. Corruption and chaos broke out in developing countries in Asia and Africa that had long been colonies of European nations, and in unstable Latin America. As countries' leaders and parties veered toward either communism or capitalism, they attracted the supportive attentions of the USSR and China, or of the U.S. This would come in the form of "advisors" and the infusion of armaments to back up an existing regime or support the opposition that perhaps aimed for revolution. The weapons industry also found this political strategy profitable.

In the early 1960s Vietnam had become just such a hot spot. Discussing Vietnam in his 1964 contribution to the Nehru Memorial volume, Pauling had warned of the growing peril of a much larger war, should other nations—such as Red China to the north—enter directly into the fray.

An excerpt from the Chettyar Memorial Lecture that Pauling gave in Madras, India, in 1967 provides Pauling's summary of the historical background to the current and expanding Vietnam War—much as he was doing elsewhere during the 1960s. The passage below expresses Pauling's intense compassion for both the Vietnamese civilians and the youthful American warriors, drafted often against their will and placed in combat in a land not properly theirs to defend. It also exemplifies his bitter criticism of the war's conduct by American forces and his angry frustration over the Johnson administration's failure to negotiate an end to the war.

The war in Vietnam is dangerous because of the possibility that it will escalate into a nuclear war. I hope that it will soon come to an end. It is an immoral war. I cannot see any justification for the human suffering that is involved in this war. Here, thousands of young men from the United States are being killed far away from home in a country about which they know essentially nothing and care nothing; they are drafted, most of them—this is contrary to the principle of free enterprise that is supposed to operate in the United States.

Tens of thousands, hundreds of thousands of people in Vietnam are being killed and injured; caused to die of starvation, burnt to death by phosphorus bombs dropped by jet bombers; burnt by flame-throwers when they are trapped in caves; killed by razor-sharp pieces of steel that are sent shooting out by the thousands from an exploding lazy-dog weapon; subjected to starvation by crop destruction by chemicals.

You know, when there is starvation in a region, it is not the young men in the army who die of starvation; it is the old and the sick, the women and children and babies who die of starvation. This is an immoral activity—the strafing and burning of villages is immoral. I do not like my great nation to be involved in this activity. As I think of it, I am reminded, through my contacts with medicine, of the battered child syndrome—the small child or baby who is brought to the hospital with its arms and legs and ribs broken, perhaps a fractured skull; black and blue, perhaps burns all over his body—the result of ill-treatment by some irrational parent.

Here is my great nation, the United States, the greatest nation in the world, on the one side, and the other side the few millions of people in a poor country, people who believe that they are fighting against the foreign aggressor, fighting for their freedom.

What are the facts about Vietnam? This country for a long time had some relationship with China. For about a thousand years, there was a sort of governor-general from China who lived in Vietnam, but it was run pretty much by the Vietnamese. They considered themselves a nation and they did not suffer very much under this sort of a Chinese rule.

Then the French ruled for 80 years. Vietnam was a colonial country under the French. And then the Japanese were their rulers for five years. In 1945 the Vietnamese felt that at last they would be free and independent; but the French did not agree. They came back, and so there occurred a revolutionary war, with, on the one side, the Vietnamese peoples' forces and, on the other side, the so-called French Vietnamese Forces including General Ky and most of his present staff. This war ended in 1954 in the Geneva Accord Agreement on the Cessation of Hostilities in Vietnam.

I have the Geneva Accord, here; it is a long and complicated document, as is necessary when a cease-fire is brought about and it becomes necessary to settle problems arising from the war. There are demilitarized zones—the regions where the two forces were fighting—a zone at the 17th Parallel, and a zone around Hanoi, which was in French possession, a zone around Haiphong and another small zone. There are articles about exchanging prisoners of war, articles about people being allowed to move from one region to the other; various articles of this sort. And there is an article about an election to be held in 1956 under international auspices. The governments that signed the treaty agreed—the two governments of the Vietnamese Peoples' forces and the French Vietnamese Forces, essentially governments of the North and South regions at that time of the civil war.

There is also a clause saying, "This treaty shall be binding upon all successor governments to the signatories of the treaty," and there is a statement that the demilitarized zone at the 17th Parallel is not to be considered a political boundary dividing Vietnam into two parts. The United States refused to sign the document; but we issued a statement about it, that "We support the idea that Vietnam should be a single nation." And then the Diem government that came into power as a successor government refused to go ahead with the preparations for the elections and refused to allow the elections to be held. This was a great blow at democracy, a repudiation of democracy in this region.

We can ask why the United States refused. I think the answer is economic. President Eisenhower, in his memoirs, said: "If Indochina goes, the tin and tungsten and other products that we so greatly value would cease coming"; and of course there was a sort of anticommunism involved in it too. What happened? The Diem government became more and more oppressive and dictatorial, the rich became richer, the poor became poorer, and there developed a revolution. This revolution became more and more successful, and we know how the American advisors then became a small American military force and then a larger American military force, now over 400,000. Senator Fulbright has said that he is convinced that the fight against the Diem dictatorship began as a true revolt of the South Vietnamese people against their dictatorial government, and not as a subversive activity of North Vietnam. Later the United States began bombing North Vietnam, and now we are at the present situation where this horrible war continues.

President Johnson has said, over and over again: "We will talk with any government, at any time, any place about peace in Vietnam," but there is a joker in this statement. I wrote to him, asking: "Are you willing to talk with the National Liberation Front of South Vietnam?" He did not answer the letter; he has not answered any of my letters. But I received a letter from the Under-Secretary of State Mr. George W. Ball saying: "The position of the United States Government is clear. We do not recognize the National Liberation Front as having any status under international law." And so this savage, immoral war goes on.

I have had the argument advanced to me that we are justified in prosecuting this war, even under the principle of minimizing the suffering of human beings, because we are making the sacrifice now of the lives of human beings, Americans and Vietnamese, in order to prevent a greater suffering in the future—the great suffering that would occur if there were to be a generation or two or more generations of Vietnamese people suffering under a despotic, communistic dictatorship. I reject this. After I have thought it out, I have decided that this argument does not have validity. First. we cannot predict the future well enough to say that the amount of suffering under the Ho Chi Minh government would be as great as the amount of suffering that has been inflicted upon the people of Vietnam and the young men of the United States by this war. Second, I think that there is reason to believe that the amount of suffering under Ho Chi Minh would not have been very great.

You know, I can quote these words—"All men are created equal; they are endowed by their Creator with certain inalienable rights. Among these rights are life, liberty, and the pursuit of happiness"—the opening words of the United States Declaration of Independence, and also the opening words of the Vietnam Declaration of Independence written by Ho Chi Minh in 1945. He was an admirer of the United States. He thought at that time that the United States would support him in the efforts to free his country from the foreign oppressors. And I believe that if the United States had done this, or if, in 1954, the United States had supported the Geneva Agreement that brought the French Vietnam war to an end, then there would have been in that country, Vietnam, a government and people friendly to the United States and other countries in the way that the government of Yugoslavia, the Tito government, is friendly to the United States and the other countries, even though it is a communistic form of government.

I AM SICK OF THIS WAR!

"Another way to impress the rulers of this country, to hit them where it hurts—in the pocketbook—is to go on a buyer's strike."

Ahead of most of his fellow Americans, Linus Pauling in the early 1960s had spotted the probable consequences of U.S. involvement in the quagmire of Vietnamese political struggles. By the late 1960s the U.S. became convulsed by this dismal faraway combat. Especially vehement were rebellious young people, the generation asked to fight in this no-win war that took heavy casualties on both sides.

The year of his India lectures was also the year of Expo 67 in Montreal, Canada, when Pauling gave a major public address on the subject of scientific solutions to human problems, "Science and the World of the Future." And 1967 also marked his final year at the Center for the Study of Democratic Institutions. Impatient with the tendency there to talk rather than take action, and also deeply missing his connection with experimental science, Pauling accepted a visiting professorship at the University of California, San Diego. By fall of 1969 he had moved on to Stanford University, near San Francisco. Although intensely involved with biomedical and nutritional research, particularly with his new interest in what he called "orthomolecular medicine," he often took time out to talk to gatherings of people—usually students—about the need for the U.S. to end the Vietnam War.

This war was something that Pauling could not let go of. It had not as yet elicited the use of nuclear weapons—probably in part because the USSR did not directly involve itself in the warfare. But there was always the chance that they might be used by the U.S. forces. American military leaders were embarrassed by their inability to win this war with a rustic, ill-equipped, but clever and persistent foe, causing the frustrating combat to drag on year after year.

To Pauling it was, from the start of his concern, an immoral and unwinnable war. The most inflammatory speeches he ever gave were about Vietnam, and they reached a fever pitch by 1970. Not even nuclear testing had aroused such vehemence and rancor in him. At the same time, he identified with the young Americans who rebelled against the U.S. government, the police, the military-industrial establishment, and the polite society that permitted racial intolerance, war profiteering, and blatant injustices. Propelled by youth, the '60s were a time of revolution on many fronts, including civil and human rights.

Pauling's political and social activism over the years may have served a useful function in giving him an emotional outlet. He passionately pursued many perplexities and unknowns in a wide variety of scientific fields, but rarely presented his quests, speculations, and findings with the intense feelings he showed when he talked about war and peace. The formal scientific papers themselves were, of course, dispassionate and impersonal; his readers and audiences were mostly scientists. Eloquent passages in some of his lectures or writings on science were temperate and well built, and on some grand occasions, such as award ceremonies, allowed for more eloquent displays.

But when Pauling broke out of the sphere of science, especially the "pure" science of structural and physical chemistry that dealt with atoms and molecules, ions and isotopes, and took on subjects concerned with human society as a whole and human behavior in particular, a change often took place—almost with the transformational power of a tornado or earthquake. He wanted to induce his listeners or readers to gain insights into the actual situation; to shape their views or alter entrenched opinions based on the establishment's news media; or to take some specific, concerted action to affect public policy.

Pauling had earned a reputation for "showmanship" as a lecturer in freshman chemistry. He had studied and practiced oratory while in college, and had acquired some tricks, or else knew instinctively how to draw and hold people's attention—in part by gauging the level of their understanding and not talking far beyond it. As a public speaker in his activist role he outdid his scientist self, sometimes also allowing himself an emotional tone that he would not have normally used in his personal life. He lambasted unmercifully public figures whose policies and actions he opposed, such as Presidents Johnson and Nixon, and physicist Edward Teller. He became by turns empathic, visionary, ridiculing, furious, caustic—and as condemnatory as any fire-and-brimstone preacher. (It is curious how a number of irreligious persons get caught up in their own dogmas, create their own catechisms and rituals, and become as rigid in their opinions and judgmental about others as their polar opposites in matters pertaining to the human sphere.)

A number of similar handwritten manuscripts survive from this '60s protest period, when Pauling joined the Peace and Freedom Party, supported the concepts of Black Power and the Free Speech movement, and spoke with the revolutionary zeal of the notorious SDS (Students for a Democratic Society). Needless to say, many university administrators, trustees, and tenured faculty members, who might expect and tolerate radical behavior in the young, found Pauling's noisy stumping unseemly and unacceptable in a man of his age (mid to late 60s) and stature. But he could not restrain his fury over the Vietnam War, which epitomized so many other things wrong with unchecked American capitalism. Feeling freer to risk disapproval, he proudly accepted the Lenin Peace Prize in 1970, the first non-Soviet to receive it. (The Paulings had made the first of several trips to the Soviet Union in 1957.) He gave an acceptance speech at the Soviet Embassy in Washington, D.C., in which he congratulated both the USSR and the U.S.—"We Have Survived This Decade!" In the same period he delivered a sermon at Glide Memorial Methodist Church in San Francisco that praised V.I. Lenin's analytical abilities, so much like a scientist's. At times he did tend to get carried away.

Here are some of his notations for a speech Pauling was preparing to give in the San Francisco Peninsula area in 1970. As usual in his later years, his manuscripts were written with wide black felt-tip marker pens. His political speeches in this period were scrawled, filled with capitalized words and phrases, underlinings, and stabbing exclamation marks. He might glue or tape on clippings from current newspapers. Although this talk was hot-tempered, it was not as flammable as some other speeches of that period. He always kept in view, too, the need to emphasize the Garrison-Tolstoi-Gandhian principle (and tactic) of nonviolent protest, which had been so effectively used by civil rights leader Dr. Martin Luther King, Jr., until his assassination in 1968.

I believe that now it is the duty of every person to oppose the continuation of the war in Southeast Asia, by every means that seems to him to be reasonable and likely to be of some effect.

I do not advocate that you lose your jobs. That is Nixon's policy—to increase unemployment, cut down on the amount of money going to the ordinary people, to make them pay for the war, while the rich get richer.

I am sick of this war. I am sick of the lies, the chicanery, the double dealing.

I am sick of an administration that (Sec. of State Rogers) tells Congress (House Appropriations Committee) on 23 April that no American troops will be sent to Cambodia, and then five days later (night of April 27-28) invades with U.S. advisors and aircraft, April 30 with thousands of U.S. ground troops.

I am sick of this war, of this administration.

I am sure that you are sick of it.

I remember the end of the First World War.

Millions sick with a great epidemic, the flu.

Now is the time . . . now is the time for another epidemic, for a week, when everyone is sick, the work stops, the economy is slowed down.

If there is such an epidemic here, during the next week, it might spread to the whole Bay region, and then over the whole country!

Let our slogan be "We're sick of the war."

Another way to impress the rulers of this country, to hit them where it hurts—in the pocketbook—is to go on a buyer's strike.

Your money isn't worth much now—inflation, caused by diversion of production from consumer goods to military.

What can we do?

Help other people to understand what the war is doing:
* its immorality
* its wastefulness
* decrease in consumer goods
* inflation
* unemployment

Take action:
* Turn in U.S. gov't bonds.
* Slow down military activities—"I'm sick of this war."

Save your money till the war is over. Don't buy any goods.

Save your money, don't spend it.

Save it until prices go down, when the war is ended and the Pentagon budget is cut.

Save it, and hurt the economy, until they learn the lesson and end the war!

Don't buy a new automobile.

Don't buy a new TV set, new clothes, anything.

Get along with what you have, and save your money for a new day.
Don't fly across the continent. Make only essential trips. Cut down on
gasoline purchases.

Do not be violent!

Do not destroy property!

There is enough violence in the world—too much—the violence, the
killings, the suffering in Southeast Asia, caused by the government, by
the policy of militarism, reliance on military might, the violence of the
police, the National Guard, the trigger-happy weekend soldiers with live
ammunition in their guns and orders to use it at their own discretion.

Do not destroy property. The people of the world need the wealth of
the world. There is too much privation, malnutrition now, too much
wealth, property, destroyed by the Pentagon, the military.

We must preserve, conserve the wealth of the world, distribute it
properly to the people.

HEALTH CONSIDERATIONS FOR THE WORLD

*"Both the physical and mental wellbeing of nearly everyone in the world
could be improved by an improvement in the quality of his nutrition."*

Beginning in the mid 1950s, for over a decade Pauling spent considerable time researching the causes and possible remedies for mental
problems, including retardation, schizophrenia, and senile dementia. He
often associated with psychiatrists and other physicians who specialized
in mental disorders. He was especially influenced by the medical
researchers who believed that defective brain chemistry, perhaps
genetic or diet-linked in origin, were more likely the causes of most mental and emotional problems than purely environmental or family-based
issues. These were routinely treated through psychotherapy, even
lengthy and costly psychoanalysis—but too often unsuccessfully. (At that
time there were few prescription drugs specifically designed to amelio-
rate particular conditions such as chronic depression, bipolar illness,
and obsessive compulsive disorder.)

Pauling maintained that intelligence was partly determined by nutritional factors, positive or negative, during the rapid formation of the brain
tissue and interconnecting neurons during fetal and early childhood
development. Thus any nation concerned about the wellbeing of its
future citizenry—and he especially targeted his own United States—had
a responsibility toward its low-income families and others ill-educated
about good nutrition. On the much larger world scale, the effects of
chronic malnutrition or famine-caused starvation would destroy the

promise of an entire class of people in a Third World country or a land deeply engaged in warfare, including civil strife. Also, as Pauling had expressed earlier in *No More War!* and his India-based Azad lectures, overpopulation contributed to these problems.

He often asserted such opinions, as in this 1969 talk to a gathering of psychiatrists. And of course he couldn't resist hammering away at the health-damaging habit of smoking—at a time before it began to be regarded as a public health problem. He must have noticed that a number of physicians in his audience showed signs of this addiction.

The poor people of the world get a bad start in life. Fetal and child-hood starvation and malnutrition lead to poor bodies and poor minds. Most of the people in the word suffer from a decreased mental ability because of early malnutrition. With a present total of 3.5 billion people we are straining the resources of the Earth. I believe that we have passed the optimal population, not only for the world as a whole, but for nearly every nation. In every nation, and in the world as a whole, governments should set up commissions to study the question of what numbers of people would be optimal, would lead to the smallest amount of human suffering and the greatest amount of wellbeing.

Studies should also be made of the relations of environmental factors and habits to wellbeing. Over a century ago an Englishman named Gompertz discovered that the age-specific death rates are an exponential function of the age. A doubling of the death rate, and also of the rate of incidence of various diseases, is found for each eight and one-half years' increase in age. The curves for different populations are similar in shapes, but may be shifted along the age axis. The Gompertz curve for a population of one-pack-per-day cigarette smokers is shifted by eight years from that for nonsmokers, and the curve for two-pack-a day smokers is shifted by 16 years. On the average, the one-pack smokers die eight years earlier than nonsmokers, and the two-pack smokers die 16 years earlier. At a given age the one-pack smokers have twice the incidence of illness of nonsmokers, and the two-pack smokers have four times.

I have no doubt that the relation of the incidence of mental illness to cigarette smoking is similar, and that this great drug addiction is accordingly of importance to social psychiatry. I may say that I am disturbed whenever I see a cigarette between the lips or the fingers of some important person, upon whose intelligence and judgment the welfare of the world in part depends.

Let me return to the matter of malnutrition. Most of the people in the world are half-starved; they do not have enough to eat. Their food supply does not contain enough protein to permit the optimal development of their bodies, including the brain, nor enough fat and carbohydrate to provide the energy for their optimal physical and mental functioning. It is imperative that the rate of change of the population and the distribution of wealth be regulated in such a way as to give every person the possibility of leading a good life, unhampered by the debility and misery of semi-starvation.

Moreover, both the physical and mental wellbeing of nearly everyone in the world could be improved by an improvement in the quality of his nutrition. In particular, I have reached the conclusion that the usually recommended amounts of certain vital substances, especially some of the vitamins, are far less than the optimal amounts. . . .

What would be the consequences for the world if the national leaders and the people as a whole were to think more clearly, even only 10 percent more clearly? Surely we could then move rapidly toward the goal of a rational and just society, toward a world from which the evil of war had been abolished, toward a world of justice and morality, in which all human beings cooperate to keep the amount of human suffering to a minimum.

Pauling entered his 70s along with the 20th century. Persons moving into old age are often inclined to conserve their energy and focus their diminishing supply of time on projects with good prospects of completion. And, if they have been productive, they will reflect back on a lifetime's succession of endeavors and accomplishments.

Linus Pauling certainly did these things. But he was not yet ready for a sideline seat in a rocking chair. He took up new concerns, causes, and combats, often quite vigorously. A number of them inevitably concerned war, peace, human wellbeing, and the survival of the planet.

Let us follow him now in these aspects of his work to the end of his days.

The Paulings outside their cabin at Deer Flat Ranch, a 165-acre property on the central California coast purchased with the cash award from the 1954 Nobel Prize in Chemistry. The 1962 Nobel Peace Prize later enabled them to build a large new home on the property, where they spent much of their time. It was here that Pauling died in 1994. (Photo courtesy of Björn Larsson)

*An elderly but ever dauntless Pauling sailed through the U.S. blockade
of Nicaragua with several other Nobel Peace laureates and activists in
1984, to bring emergency food and medical supplies and hold a protest
(shown here) in front of the U.S. Embassy in Managua. (Photo courtesy
of Linda Pauling-Kamb)*

Part VI

Future Prophecies

Even in his younger years, Linus Pauling was often regarded as a futurist or visionary—someone who could anticipate significant changes and warn against possible catastrophes. His opinions were sought especially in science, of course. But because of his long, committed involvement in social issues, people looked to him for other insights into the future as well.

Although he would continue to contribute to peace efforts at home and abroad, Pauling's final crusade—spanning two decades—lay more in the area of health. This interest extended to environmental health, including problems caused by overpopulation, pollution, and the misuse of natural resources. This led him to a concern with the wide and growing disparity between the wealth and power of the well-to-do, who had access to good food, health care, and quality education; and the sparse resources of the powerless poor. This disparity was prevalent in the U.S. as well as in developing or Third World countries. Pauling asserted that these crucial issues had to be solved in all lands in order to achieve a lasting world peace.

Just as Pauling sought comprehensive explanations for particular phenomena in the natural world, he looked for swift, rational solutions to problems in human society. By 1970 he believed he had found the best way to guarantee health and a long, productive life to the greatest number of individuals: good nutrition. Pauling turned his crusading spirit and educating impulse toward publicizing the concept of orthomolecular medicine—the provision of substances like vitamins and minerals needed in the body's biochemical processes involving growth, cell repair, and metabolism. He wanted to further both research and medical practice in this area. Though not directly connected to his involvement in peace issues, Pauling's focus on health reflected his overarching commitment to human survival and the "minimization of suffering."

Pauling's activism noticeably slowed down after the U.S. pulled out of the Vietnam War in 1973. He periodically lent his name and presence to causes he approved of: the 1983 peace rally in New York City; the Nuclear Freeze campaign; the four Nobel Peace laureates' journey to Nicaragua in 1984, taking food and emergency medical supplies in symbolic protest against the American embargo of Daniel Ortega's communist regime.

Above all, the decrease in Pauling's peace-connected work was due to a great loss in his life, one he could never fully overcome: the death of his wife, Ava Helen Pauling, in 1981.

NOW IS THE TIME FOR CHANGE

"We now ask ourselves how much progress the world has made toward a world of morality, a world of brotherhood, a world of reason, a world from which war has been eliminated. . . . The answer is that we have made shockingly little progress."

After the publication of his best-selling book *Vitamin C and the Common Cold* in 1970 (which caused sales of this vitamin to skyrocket), Pauling was sought more by the public for his nutritional advice than his antiwar and antinuclear messages. His peace activism especially diminished after the formation of the Linus Pauling Institute of Science and Medicine near San Francisco in 1973. His research, writing, educational, and fundraising work centered at the Institute, which occupied much of his time from 1973 until his death.

In September 1975 the centennial anniversary of Albert Schweitzer's birth was celebrated in two Japanese cities, Tokyo and Hiroshima. Linus and Ava Helen Pauling were invited to provide some words for the event. The Paulings had been special friends of the Japanese people ever since their first visit to Japan in 1955, when their strong antinuclear stance became well known. They participated several times in solemn memorial events conducted at Hiroshima.

By now Pauling had enlarged his view of dominant world problems beyond the nuclear threat to issues of economic disparity, environmental concerns, and overpopulation. The tone of this piece (taken from his draft script) is largely pessimistic, as it increasingly tended to be. Only in the final paragraphs did he regain his inherent optimism.

It is now just 50 years since Albert Schweitzer formulated his philosophy of "Reverence for Life." Gunnar Jahn, in the presentation address for Schweitzer for the Nobel Peace Prize in Oslo on 10 December 1953, described the discovery of the idea that solved Schweitzer's effort over most of his first 40 years to find a philosophy and a world-view that enshrine life. Jahn said:

> One day in 1915—Dr. Schweitzer was 40 years old at the time—while traveling on a river in Africa, he saw the rays of the sun shimmering on the water, the tropical forest all around, and a herd of hippopotamuses basking on the banks of the river. At that moment there came to him, as if by revelation, the phrase that precisely expressed his thought: Reverence for Life. . . . On this thought Schweitzer builds his universal ethic, and through it he believes mankind comes into spiritual communion with the eternal. . . . If altruism, reverence for life, and the idea of brotherhood can become living realities in the hearts of men, we shall have laid the very foundations of a lasting peace between individuals, nations, and races.

Schweitzer himself, in his Nobel lecture, delivered in Oslo a year later (4 November 1954), said:

> It is my profound conviction that the solution [of the problem of peace] lies in our rejecting war for an ethical reason; namely, that war makes us guilty of the crime of inhumanity. . . . May the men who hold the destiny of peoples in their hands studiously avoid anything that might cause the present situation to deteriorate and become even more dangerous. May they take to heart the words of the Apostle Paul: "If it be possible, as much as lieth in you, live peaceably with all men." These words are valid not only for individuals, but for nations as well. May these nations, in their efforts to maintain peace, do their utmost to give the spirit time to grow and to act.

Twenty-one years have gone by since Schweitzer gave his Nobel lecture, 17 years since he made his warning to the world that a great nuclear war might take place that would mean the end of civilization and perhaps the end of the human race. It is appropriate that we now ask ourselves how much progress the world has made toward a world of morality, a world of brotherhood, a world of reason, a world from which war has been eliminated, from which the yoke of militarism has been thrown off, in which every human being is enabled to lead a good life, with good food, clothing, shelter, education to the extent from which he can profit, work that is satisfying to him and that permits him to do his share for humanity, and leisure and a suitable income to permit him to enjoy the wonders of the world.

The answer is that we have made shockingly little progress. Although the threat of complete nuclear destruction prevents the great powers from embarking upon an all-destructive world war, we still have wars—the war in Korea, the war in Vietnam, the Israel-Arab war. We are saddled with an increasing burden of armaments and other forms of militarism. Exploitism of peoples continues—the rich people get richer and the poor get poorer, the rich nations get richer and the poor nations get poorer. Uncontrolled technology and industry continue to wreak devastating damage on the environment and on the health of human beings.

The quality of life deteriorates as the number of people continues to grow further and further beyond the number for which the Earth can possibly provide a good life. The specter of increasing malnutrition and mass starvation looms ahead, and the leaders of governments make only futile and ineffectual efforts to cope with the problems of inflation, unemployment, collapse of the economic system, decreased production, the suppression of democracy in many countries.

The task that faces us at this Schweitzer Commemoration Symposium is that of analyzing the problems, assessing the situation, and discussing the steps that should be taken to achieve the sort of world that Schweitzer dreamed of and that we all have been hoping for. . . .

We are witnessing the breakdown of the system of unrestricted free enterprise, depending on immediate profits, without consideration of damage to the environment, the exhaustion of the resources of the earth, and the needs of future generations.

In the United States we have a shortage of civilian goods, inflation, and ever increasing prices, and at the same time 10 million people out of work. This is an irrational and intolerable situation, but our government seems to be unable to act to rectify it, because it is shackled by the free-enterprise system.

Let me quote some sentences about poverty from the document, Progressio Populorum, issued by Pope Paul VI on 25 March 1967:

Rich peoples enjoy rapid growth whereas the poor develop slowly. The imbalance is on the increase. . . . There are certainly situations whose injustice cries to heaven. When whole populations destitute of necessities live in a state of dependence barring them from all initiative and responsibility, and all opportunity to advance culturally and share in social and political life, recourse to violence, as a means to right these wrongs to human dignity, is a grave temptation. . . .

We want to be clearly understood: the present situation must be faced with courage and the injustices linked with it must be fought against and overcome. . . . Urgent reforms should be undertaken without delay. . . . Individual initiative alone and the mere free play of competition could never assure successful development.

Unless we apply the method of science—discover the facts, and analyze them, change our course, abolish war, and work to achieve a rational and moral system through peaceful evolution—there will inevitably be a great worldwide bloody and violent revolution, which may end in the nuclear holocaust.

During the past hundred years there have been astounding developments in science and technology, developments that have completely changed the nature of the world in which we live. But the conduct of international affairs has changed very little. The time has come now for this aspect of the world to change. The risk associated with this change is small compared with the risk of complete and irreversible damage to society that we can foresee as the consequence of our present course.

Now is the time for us to change from our immoral course, from our dedication to the archaic institution of war, to a policy of peace and rationality and morality. We must follow the teachings of Albert Schweitzer, and bend all our efforts toward achieving the goal of a world of justice and morality, a world in which the resources of the Earth and the fruits of man's labor are used for the benefit of human beings, permitting each one to lead a good and full life, a world of freedom and dignity, a world in which our idealistic young people will be glad to take part.

I believe that we can achieve that goal.

GOALS AHEAD FOR THE U.S.

"It is our moral duty to take such actions as will leave the world in a condition such that future generations of human beings are able to lead good and full lives, with the minimum of suffering."

A nation's milestone anniversaries tend to be treated with special honors. Prognosticators come forth to render visions of the future. The bicentennial year of 1976, commemorating the founding of the United States of America, was one such time.

The Senate Committee on Government Operations gave hearings on "Our Third Century: Directions," and invited Linus Pauling to appear on February 6 to offer his recommendations for steering America's course in the coming years. He emphasized many of the same issues brought up a year before in Japan, while also harking back to his lectures in India a decade earlier and reiterating his credo, "minimize suffering."

I believe that the goal that we should strive to reach during the third century of the United States of America is that of constructing a country in which every person has the possibility of leading a good life.

I believe that we should in all our actions and decisions conform to a basic principle of morality. The principle that seems to me to be the most reasonable is the principle of the minimization of suffering: decisions among alternative courses of action should be made in such ways as to minimize the predicted amounts of human suffering. This principle is not new—there are essentially equivalent principles in all the major religions and in the ethical systems of almost all philosophers, among whom I may mention especially John Stuart Mill and Henry Sidgwick.

Suffering and happiness are closely correlated. The basic ethical principle might be expressed as making decisions in such a way as to maximize happiness. I feel, however, that there is so much suffering in the world, much of it unnecessary and avoidable, that it is better to place the emphasis on minimizing suffering.

To minimize suffering we must provide every person not only with adequate food, clothing, and shelter, but also with education to the extent that he can benefit from it, with the opportunity to develop himself to the fullest extent, to exercise his creativity, and to express his personality. Freedom of choice in personal actions is essential; also the preservation of different cultures, which enrich the world, and the preservation of the world's natural wonders, the redwood forests, the wildernesses, the mountains, the lakes, which should not be sacrificed to the advancing technology.

Every person should have suitable employment, such as to give him the satisfaction of knowing that he is making his contribution to running the world, and he should have leisure for recreation, for travel, for developing his own interests, and for enjoying the world's wonders.

Unemployment: About 10 million people in the United States are unemployed. Most of them would like to work, and are made miserable by not being able to find work. The existence of this great body of unemployed persons shows that there is something wrong with the economic system and with the government. The problem of unemployment should be attacked and solved, in such a way that every person with the ability to do part of the world's work is provided with a job suitable to his ability. Solution of this problem would eliminate a great amount of suffering for millions of individual human beings.

It is not true that full employment would require a sacrifice by our nation as a whole. On the contrary, it would enrich our nation. Our wealth comes from our natural resources and from labor, the work done by our people. If the unemployed were to be put back to work their labor would increase our wealth. For every year during which we have millions of people unemployed our nation loses billions of dollars, the value of the products their labor could have produced if they had been employed.

The Congress and the administration should take immediate action toward the solution of the problem of unemployment. On the basis of my own observations, I advocate the immediate revival of the Civilian Conservation Corps and the Work Projects Administration. I remember the many improvements made in our parks and forests by the CCC. I remember the WPA guidebooks for the various regions and the works of art produced by WPA artists. I remember the contributions to scientific research made by helpers provided to researchers in our universities by the WPA. Some of the work may not have been very efficiently done, but it was productive—something was got for the money, and the artists, writers, park and forest workers and others were spared the misery and unhappiness caused by the idleness of unemployment.

In addition, the Congress and the administration should ask the economists, scientists, and other experts to analyze the problem of unemployment and to search for a way to eliminate it. I am sure that this problem can be solved. Its solution would not only decrease the amount of human suffering but would also enrich our country through the products of the labor of the increased labor force.

Our Responsibility to Future Generations: I believe that it is our moral duty to take such actions as will leave the world in a condition such that future generations of human beings are able to lead good and full lives, with the minimum of suffering. We cannot, of course, be sure about the future, but we should strive to predict the probable course of mankind and the world, and then make our decisions in such a way as seems most likely to minimize the suffering not only of people now living and their immediate descendents but also of future generations, even those in the distant future, with, of course, smaller weight given to the future because of the uncertainty in our predictions.

One of the sources of happiness for many people is the enjoyment of the forests, wildernesses, deserts, lakes, and other natural wonders, and the many different kinds of animals and plants. We should not deprive the people of future generations of this source of happiness, and we should accordingly conserve these wonders, and not permit them to be sacrificed to the advance of agriculture and technology.

Future generations should also not be deprived of their share of the world's natural resources. Some of these resources are inexhaustible. An example is sunlight. We may convert some of the energy of sunlight into electric power, which, after doing useful work, is finally converted to heat and warms the Earth, as it would have done if it had not been converted to electric power. The sun will continue to shine for future generations, whether we use it for electric power or not. Solar energy, like energy obtained from the winds or tides, does not rob future generations.

Coal and oil, however, are present on Earth in finite amounts, and when they are burned the supply is decreased. These are valuable substances, not only as fuels but also as the raw materials for making drugs, textiles, and many other compounds of carbon. But we are depleting their stocks at such a rate that they may be exhausted in a few generations.

Use of nuclear fission for generation of power is not the solution, because there is only a limited supply of fissionable elements, and our extensive development of fission power plants would soon exhaust the nuclear fuel, leaving little or none for future generations. A thorough study of the energy problem, with consideration of our obligations to future generations, would probably lead to the conclusions that great efforts should be made to obtain energy from the inexhaustible sources, and also that the amount of energy used should be kept as small as possible. There is no doubt that in past decades an increase in the amount of energy available has led to an improvement in the quality of life for many people, but there also is no doubt that a large fraction of the energy used is now wasted. Many common devices, such as air conditioners, are now built to operate inefficiently, using much more power than necessary.

Population: The problem presented by the continued increase in the world's population needs to be attacked vigorously. Education and the provision of incentives for limiting the number of progeny are needed. It is inevitable that the population will during the next century reach a limit. This limit may be very large, perhaps 15 billion, reached when the maximum exploitation of the Earth's capability for producing food, achieved by sacrificing forest lands and other natural resources that should be conserved, becomes insufficient to prevent the death by starvation of millions of people. An alternative that we should strive to achieve is to limit the population to the value that would permit every person, including those of future generations, to lead a good life and to experience a minimum of suffering.

In my Azad Memorial Lectures, given in New Delhi in 1967, I discussed this problem. I mentioned that Sir Joseph Hutchinson, Professor of Agriculture in Cambridge University and President of the British Association for the Advancement of Science, had pointed out that Britain was overcrowded to such an extent that the people did not have good water to drink, good food to eat, good air to breathe, nor proper opportunities for recreation and the enjoyment of full lives. He said that there should be only 40 million people in the United Kingdom (now nearly 60 million), and that the government should adopt the policy of achieving this goal over the next few generations, by the control of population by procedures, formulated through thorough and careful discussion of the problem, such as to involve only such interference as is necessary in the private affairs of individual human beings.

I pointed out that during recent decades the people of India had been getting poorer and poorer, in part because of large expenditures by the government of India [on military equipment] and in part because of the rapid increase in the population, which had reached 500 million in 1967. I urged that India, with a large fraction of her people half starved and unable to lead good lives, strive to reduce her population and achieve the goal of 400 million, with a corresponding increase in the quality of life. Instead, the population has now reached 600 million, and the quality of life has decreased to a still lower level, such that tragedy certainly looms ahead.

I also asked a question about my own country: What number of people living in the United States would permit those individual human beings to lead the best lives, the fullest lives, the richest lives, with the greatest freedom from the suffering that is caused by poverty, malnutrition, and disease, and with the greatest satisfaction of their intellectual curiosity, of their cultural needs, and of their love of nature?

The people in the United States do not have the happiness that comes from drinking good natural water; instead they drink diluted sewage containing chlorine and organic and industrial contaminants. They breathe air contaminated with oxides of nitrogen and sulfur, with hydrocarbons and aldehydes, with lead and carbon monoxide and soot. There is increasing encroachment on the national parks, the great forests, and the wilderness regions, and increasing damage to the wild life. The quality of the food continues to deteriorate. I believe that we should have in the United States such a number of people that every person could lead a full and rich life and such as would lead to the preservations of the beauties and wonders of the world for the enjoyment of future generations.

My analysis led me to the estimate 150 million for this optimum population of the United States. I urge that the Congress arrange that a continuing study of this question be made, that the value of the optimum population be agreed on, and that steps be taken to achieve this goal.

The Distribution of Wealth: The wealth is not distributed uniformly. In the United States 5 percent of the national income goes to less than one percent of the people, and another 5 percent to 20 percent of the people (the poor). In general, wellbeing increases as income increases, but this relation probably does not apply in the region of very large incomes—it is unlikely that the very rich lead happier lives than the well-to-do.

The moderate redistribution of the nation's wealth would surely lead to a considerable decrease in the amount of human suffering. The rich people would remain happy, to the extent that happiness is determined by having a rather large amount of money, and the misery of the poor people (20 percent of the total) would be somewhat alleviated by the doubling of their incomes, to half the national average rather than one quarter. To be effective, the increase in their income should be achieved not by an increased dole but rather by suitable employment or subsidy.

Many young people would now like to lead simple lives, in the country, devoting themselves to farming in the old-fashioned way, to handicrafts, or to some form of art or creative writing or similar individual activity. The system of welfare payments and unemployment insurance should, I suggest, be revised in such a way as to encourage these people, instead of to hamper them, and I recommend that a thorough study be made of this problem.

War and Militarism: An additional great amelioration of the misery of the poor and improvement in the quality of their lives as well as of those of other people would result from the allocation to these ends of the resources that are now wasted on war and militarism. Of all of the follies of modern man, the waste of one-tenth of the world's wealth, year after year, on war and militarism is the greatest, and the successful attack on this problem will lead to the greatest benefit to mankind.

In 1946 Albert Einstein said that "Today the atomic bomb has altered profoundly the nature of the world as we know it, and the human race consequently finds itself in a new habitat to which it must adapt its thinking. . . . Now with rockets and atomic bombs no center of population on the Earth's surface is secure from surprise destruction in a single attack. . . . There is no defense in science against the weapon that can destroy civilization. Our defense is not in armaments, nor in science, nor in going underground. Our defense is in law and order. . . . Future thinking must prevent wars." . . .

War between the United States and the Soviet Union is unthinkable. There is no doubt that these nations could destroy one another.

War is one of the greatest causes of human suffering. It destroys all human values. Alfred Nobel described war as "the horror of horrors and the greatest of all crimes."

Nevertheless, we continue to spend hundreds of billions of dollars on arms and militarism and the refinement of nuclear weapons. I cannot find any justification, rational or moral, for this policy.

In his Nobel Peace Prize lecture on 12 December 1974 Sean MacBride said that:

> *Peace, then, has to be the DESPERATE IMPERATIVE of humanity. Many imperatives flow from this only too obvious conclusion. These imperatives would be comparatively easier of achievement if those in authority throughout the world were imbued with an ethic that made world peace the primary objective and if they were inspired by a moral sense of social responsibility. . . .*
>
> *The practical imperatives for peace are many and far reaching, But there is no shortcut and each must be tackled energetically. They are:*
>
> 1. *General and complete disarmament, including nuclear weapons.*
> 2. *The glorification of peace and not of war.*
> 3. *The effective protection of human rights and minorities at national and international levels.*
> 4. *Automatic and depoliticized mechanisms for the settlement of international and noninternational disputes that may endanger peace or that are causing injustices.*
> 5. *An international order that will ensure a fair distribution of all essential products.*
> 6. *An International Court of Justice and legal system with full automatic jurisdiction to rectify injustice or abuse of power.*

7. *An international peace-keeping force and police force with limited function.*
8. *Ultimately, a world parliament and government.*

I believe that the Congress of the United States of America, with the support of the people, can change the policy that our government has been following, can break the stranglehold that the Pentagon and the defense contractors have on us, and can set the world on the right track—the track that in fact we are forced to follow because of the development of weapons that if used would destroy the world, the track that will lead to the goal of world peace, the goal of a world of morality, of cooperation, in which our resources and the products of our labor are used for the benefit of human beings and not for death and destruction.

The Congress could move swiftly to decrease the burden of the military expenditures, with, I believe, an increase, rather than a decrease, in our national security. The elimination of war from the whole world will require much study and will take time, but if the United States adopts world peace as a goal it can, I think, be reached before the end of our third century as a nation.

A DARK VISION

"I am forced, as I think about what has happened in the world during my lifetime . . . to conclude that the coming century is probably going to be one in which the amount of suffering reaches its maximum."

Several months after his Senate committee appearance (previous selection) in 1976, Pauling was invited to deliver a keynote address to the American Chemical Society, which he had served as president during a somewhat stormy tenure during 1949. This was a significant honor because the occasion was the centennial year of the organization as well as the nation's 200th birthday.

Auspicious though the year 1976 was, it proved a difficult time for the Paulings. Ava Helen was diagnosed with stomach cancer. The tumor was removed. Pauling was already convinced that high-dose vitamin C often reduced the suffering of cancer patients and prolonged lives, sometimes even reversing the disease. Certainly he expected this precious person in his life to respond favorably to this regimen. He could not imagine inhabiting the world without her.

In "What Can We Expect for Chemistry in the Next 100 Years?"* Pauling mentioned several honored ACS speakers in past eras who similarly gazed into the crystal ball and guessed at what the future held. Some of their visions had been astute, others went unfulfilled.

After going over much of the same ground as his Senate testimony, Pauling presented a deeply troubling scenario. Doomsday was sandwiched between two relatively bland periods—the present time and the world a century hence. A large reduction in population would force people to belatedly learn some terrible lessons—ones that he and his peace-advocating associates had been vainly trying to teach the world for 30 years.

I am an optimist, and I think that by the year 2076 war will have been almost entirely eliminated from the world, and replaced by a system of world law. The expenditures on militarism will be much less than at the present time. The social and economic systems will have changed . . . in such a way that in the U.S., the Soviet Union, and other countries systems will have been developed that incorporate the good points of the present systems and eliminate some of their bad points; for example, great unemployment that now causes so much suffering will have been eliminated. More use will be made of man's labor, and less use of energy, in doing the world's work. . . .

The population of the world will have become stable a century from now. I am not able to predict its value. We have just reached 4 billion people, and it is likely that there will be 8 billion people in the world by the year 2010. My estimate of the optimum population for the world is 1 billion. By 2076 we may well be approaching that limit, from above. . . .

During the coming century chemists and other investigators will, I believe, succeed in finding the regimens, nutritional and environmental, that would lead in a decreased rate of aging and increased life expectancy. If civilization survives, there will be, I predict, an increase by 25 years (to about age 100) in the life expectancy, with a corresponding increase in the length of the period of wellbeing, before the deterioration that culminates in death.

But what is actually going to happen during the next century? We see that the leaders of the nations and the government in general, as well as the people, concentrate on the immediate problems. It is unusual for a country to develop a five-year plan, and unheard of to have a 100-year

* Excerpted with permission from *Chemical Engineering News*, April 19, 1976 54(17), pp. 33-36. Copyright © 1976 American Chemical Society.

plan. Only when a crisis arises, when a catastrophe occurs do governments take action.

I am afraid that within 25 or 50 years there will occur the greatest
catastrophe in the history of the world. It might well result from a world
war, which could destroy civilization and might well be the end of the
human race, but civilization might end because of the collapse of the systems upon which it depends. Paul Ehrlich has pointed out that the collapse
could take many forms, [such as] the complete loss of oceanic fisheries
through overfishing, marine pollution, and the destruction of estuaries,
which could lead to global famine. Or the end of civilization might result
from weather changes induced by governments to improve the yield of
crops; or it might end by the rapid destruction of the ozone layer, or by the
accumulation of poisonous wastes that would make the air unbreathable
and water unpotable.

I am forced, as I think about what has happened in the world during
my lifetime and as I observe governments in their processes of making
decisions, to conclude that the coming century is probably going to be one
in which the amount of suffering reaches its maximum. Unless we are
wiser than we have shown ourselves to be in the past, we chemists and we
citizens, we advisors of the government and we government officials,
there will be a catastrophe during the coming century, perhaps a series of
catastrophes. The human race might survive.

By 2076, we shall, I hope, have solved these problems, and from then
on we may have a world in which every person who is born will have the
opportunity to lead a good life.

THE GOAL IS STILL PEACE

*"If we do have a nuclear war, there will be some little animal that
survives and 64 million years in the future the Earth will perhaps again
be occupied by intelligent beings. In the case that this happens we can
hope they are more intelligent than human beings!"*

The early 1980s were a painful time for Linus Pauling. His wife's cancer
returned within five years—and this time it was inoperable. Ava Helen
died at the end of 1981. For a time, after so many years of close reliance
on her companionship, Pauling went into near seclusion at their ranch on
the California coast. After he made a trip on his own to Oregon, to visit
places of his childhood and to return to the Paulings' alma mater and
meeting place—now Oregon State University—he took up his usual pur-
suits. Since Ava Helen had been his primary motivator in peace and

humanitarian causes, he pulled back further from a once-steady vigilance. However, authors still wanted him to write introductions to their books, interviewers still wanted to talk with him about world events, and invitations still came for peace conferences.

Since the early 1970s, the name, face, and voice of Linus Pauling had become familiar again to the public not because of his Nobel-winning scientific work or peace activism, but because of his promotion of the amazing virtues of vitamin C. He was revered by many as a vitamin guru, despite his lack of professional training as a nutritionist or medical practitioner. In 1979 he coauthored, with physician Ewan Cameron, the controversial book *Cancer and Vitamin C*. In 1986 his book *How to Live Longer and Feel Better* would repeat the success of *Vitamin C and the Common Cold*; it has enjoyed perennial popularity.

Though now without Ava Helen, in 1983 Pauling had almost gotten back to his old fighting form on behalf of peace. He was alarmed at the increased militancy toward the Soviet Union and excessive military expenditures by the new Reagan administration. One of his activities was literary: he prepared addenda and additional appendices for a new, expanded edition of *No More War!* to commemorate its 25th anniversary.

That same year he was invited to deliver an address to a peace convention whose attendees were mostly medical practitioners. "The Prevention of Nuclear War" conference was held in Canada. Pauling's recorded keynote address (transcribed for publication) was "The Path to World Peace." First, he introduced himself amiably to his listeners. Then he launched into a horrific vision of a future nuclear apocalypse. Pauling gave the audience a glimpse at what the world would be like following the outbreak of a nuclear war. In that saber-rattling time, resembling previous periods of high tension between the Soviet Union and the United States, such a scenario did not seem wholly farfetched.

I love this world. I have had a good life. . . . I have been fortunate in many ways, and have been able to see many of the wonders of the world. I like everything about the world. I like the mesons and the hadrons, and the electrons and the protons and the neutrons; and the atoms, the molecules, the self-replicating molecules; the microorganisms, the plants and animals; the minerals—the zunyite and cuprite, and pyrite and marcasite and andalusite, and all of the other minerals; the oceans and the mountains, and the forests; the stars and the nebulae and the "black holes" out there; the "Big Bang" 18 billion years ago. I like all of it!

I like satisfying my intellectual curiosity. As a scientist, I have been fortunate to have been aware of what has been done during the last [century]. Every month I read about something new and interesting about the universe that some scientist has discovered, such as what it was that caused the extinction of the dinosaurs 64 million years ago. It is really wonderful, the world, and one wonderful part about it is that there are sentient beings here who are able to appreciate the wonders of the world, to understand them!

So I feel that we have a duty to try and prevent the nuclear war, to reverse this situation. I believe that it can be done. Otherwise I wouldn't be here. Why should I waste my time if the effort is not going to be successful? I might as well be enjoying myself, making some quantum mechanical calculations! . . .

The only solution is to have peace in the world, continued perpetual peace. It will take a long time to achieve this goal, but we have to be starting on it now. You must not think that individuals are unimportant. Each individual human being can contribute something. Of course, enough individuals can have a great effect. . . . People as a whole, especially the young people, can get the government to change its policy. You know how to do it, to demonstrate, to vote whenever there is a possibility of voting. I do not advocate taking violent action of any sort. I am not in favor of harming people or destroying property. As for civil disobedience, I do not advise people one way or the other. If someone feels strongly enough to be willing to go to jail because of his ethical principles, then he might want to commit civil disobedience. After all, Bertrand Russell went to jail as a young man protesting against the First World War and he went to jail as an old man protesting against nuclear weapons. . . .

In a nuclear war in which, let us say, 30,000 megatons were used, [the] yield would amount to 300 billion deaths. That is 75 times the population of the Earth. . . . So sometimes I say that we have a 75-fold "overkill" capability, [though] really we have a 150-fold overkill capability.

Of course, conditions would not be the same everywhere. Some people live out in the country and might escape death, but the results of studies are much the same as one performed back in 1959 by Hugh Everett III and George E. Pugh of the Institute of Defense Analysis in Washington. In testimony before a Senate hearing, they described the effect of a 10,000 megaton attack on the United States and a similar attack on the Soviet Union. Sixty days after the attack, of 800 million people in the United States and Europe (including the European part of the Soviet Union) 720 million would be dead, 60 million severely injured, and 20 million more not yet dying but waiting to die. They would have to deal with the disorganization of society, disruption of communications, extinction of livestock, genetic damage, the slow development of radiation poisoning from the ingestion of radioactive materials, and many other problems. In the rest of the world, fallout would cause a tremendous amount of damage to hundreds of millions of people.

Other problems of a great nuclear war only recently have been subjected to careful analysis, as additional scientific information has been obtained about chemical reactions involved in the production and destruction of ozone molecules and the stratospheric ozone layer. A 5,000 megaton war might destroy 70 percent of the ozone layer. By extrapolation, a 20,000 megaton war might destroy 90 percent. With even a 70 percent destruction of the ozone layer, so much ultraviolet light would get through that human beings might not be able to survive. The ozone layer would take many years to heal.

A nuclear war would start fires over much of the Northern Hemisphere, and the Southern Hemisphere also, to the extent that nuclear bombs were exploded there. Almost all forests, houses, and other combustible materials would burn. The amount of smoke and dust thrown up from ground bursts might be enough to prevent sunlight from getting to the surface of the Earth for months. We know that species of animals and plants die out under this condition.

There was an earlier great extinction for which human beings were not responsible. It occurred 64 million years ago, whereas human beings separated from the anthropoid apes only four million years ago. Sixty-four million years ago a very interesting phenomenon occurred. The paleontologists studying layers of rock find that there is a series of layers containing a great many fossils deposited over millions of years. Above these are more layers deposited over millions of years but nearly free of fossils. There is a much smaller number of fossils, representing a lesser variety of animals.

These rocks are observed all over the world. The explanation of this fact is that 64 million years ago an asteroid 11 kilometers in diameter hit the surface of the Earth. It is believed that it did not hit the continent mass but landed in the ocean, because it would have left a visible crater, had it hit a continent. When the asteroid hit the rocks at the bottom of the ocean, it was vaporized by the energy of the impact, and it vaporized also 10 times its mass of rock. Once up in the atmosphere, this vapor condensed to dust, and it is thought that for a year or two sunlight did not get to the surface of the Earth. Plants stopped growing, plankton in the ocean stopped growing, many species of plants died, and many animals also died. More than half of the existing species of plants and animals died out in this great extinction, including all 18 species of dinosaur, which had been the predominant life form for 150 million years.

We know that this happened because of a very interesting geological structure discovered by Professor Luis Alvarez and his son, Walter. All over the Earth one finds these strata separated by a layer of clay two centimeters thick. This layer of clay is found even in cores obtained from the ocean bottom. This is the dust created by the impact of the asteroid, which settled down in a few years to the surface of the Earth. There is 100 times as much iridium in this clay as there is in terrestrial rocks in the layers above and below. In meteorites, iridium is 1,000 times more concentrated than in ordinary rocks. The idea that the asteroid vaporized 10 times its own mass of rock is suggested by the observation that there is only 9 percent as much iridium in the clay as there is in meteorites. In other words, the asteroid was diluted 10-fold.

So this great extinction occurred, and a little animal, perhaps a mole or something like that, survived and began evolving into different lines. A little horse preceded the big horses and other animals evolved including cows, mice, rats, and so on. Later, there were primates, Rhesus monkeys, and ultimately four million years ago, human beings. So perhaps if we do have a nuclear war, there will be some little animal that survives and 64 million years in the future the Earth will perhaps again be occupied by intelligent beings. In the case that this happens we can hope they are more intelligent than human beings! I do not want this to happen.

I do not want the second great extinction to occur on Earth because of man's inability to control himself.

ORGANIZING THE PEACE EFFORTS

"Scientists have an important role to play in the creation of conditions for a secure and peaceful world, but I do not believe that scientists alone can achieve the goal."

In 1983, Pauling added a final addendum to the special 25th Anniversary Edition of *No More War!* that commented on the continuing emphasis on militarism in both communist and capitalist nations, especially the Soviet Union and the United States. This was during the Reagan administration, which regarded the constant saber-rattling and strengthening of the military establishment as having benefits that outweighed the high costs: it guaranteed America's ability to launch devastating first or retaliatory strikes, and forced the Soviet Union to spend much of its resources in competing with the U.S.

As he had often done in the past, Pauling used a forceful document to emphasize and validate the message he wanted to convey. He ended by paraphrasing George Kistiakowsky, a chemist friend who worked on developing the atom bomb in World War II and later became a prominent pacifist. Kistiakowsky had recently died, just after writing an eloquent warning about the continuing peril of nuclear warfare that was published in the *Bulletin of the Atomic Scientists.* (See also pages 242-243.)

A lthough there are now many peace research organizations, both those supported by governments and those independent of government, they are rather small, and their impact has not been great. In the words of the 33 scientists from 22 countries who participated in a symposium on Scientists, the Arms Race, and Disarmament in Ajaccio, France, from 19 to 23 February 1982, organized jointly by UNESCO and the Pugwash Conferences on Science and World Affairs:

> *About half a million scientists and technologists—a high proportion of the total scientific manpower—are directly employed on military research and development. They are continually devising new means of destruction, making the existence of the human species on this planet ever more precarious. . . . This role of scientists is contrary to their traditional calling. The objectives of scientific endeavor should be a service to mankind, helping to better the fate of man and raise material and cultural standards. The basic unmet needs of a majority of the people in the world present a challenge great enough to warrant a huge and sustained effort by scientists. For an enormous effort of scientists to be instead directed toward wholesale destruction, to a return to a state of primitive savagery among the survivors of a nuclear war is an unforgivable perversion of science. . . .*
> *There is an urgent task for all scientists to help in stopping and reversing the arms race, and to work for genuine disarmament measures, ultimately leading to general and complete disarmament. Scientists have already demonstrated that their efforts in these directions can be fruitful and effective. Movements of scientists—such as the Pugwash Conferences on Science and World Affairs, which provide a forum for objective and informative debate between scientists from East and West, North and South—have made valuable contributions to the international negotiations on arms control. These negotiations have led to a few agreements, but without them the arms race might have acquired even more catastrophic dimensions. The work of institutes of peace research*

provides factual information of great value to those concerned with the implementation of disarmament measures. This urgent task can no longer be left to the small number of scientists actively involved in the effort to stem the arms race. It should be the duty of all scientists to acquaint themselves with these issues. There is tremendous scope for scientists to counteract the arms race and seek means to reduce the threat of nuclear war.*

Among the detailed suggestions made at the Ajaccio Conference are that UNESCO should intensify efforts to promote goals and means of disarmament education, in the most effective manner, and should mobilize the world's scientific community to make its contribution to the scholarly study of the problems of the arms race and of disarmament in both developed and developing states, and to ensure the wide distribution of the results of such study.

The Ajaccio statement ends with the following paragraph:

The continuing arms race with no prospect for its reversal in sight, and the ensuing threat of a nuclear holocaust, produce fear, frustration, and a feeling of helplessness and hopelessness among people, particularly in the younger generation. They also lead to apathy and pessimism in the ranks of the scientific community. But a formulation of specific tasks may hearten and activate scientists to do something worthwhile and enable them to return science back to its true calling. We believe that the above recommendation, including those addressed to the United Nations and UNESCO, if implemented, would provide the much needed optimism that it is still possible to prevent catastrophe; and the hope— indeed the conviction—that scientists have an important role to play in the creation of conditions for a secure and peaceful world.

I, too, believe that scientists have an important role to play in the creation of conditions for a secure and peaceful world, but I do not believe that scientists alone can achieve the goal. As George Kistiakowsky pointed out, our only hope is that a mass movement will arise, a mass movement for peace such as there has never been before. We are facing the unprecedented threat of extinction of the human race in a nuclear war,

---

* Reported in *Scientists, the Arms Race, and Disarmament,* ed. Joseph Rotblat, Paris: UNESCO, 1982.

and we must all join in taking unprecedented action to prevent this annihilation and to achieve the goal of the abolition of war.

LOOKING AHEAD

"The greatest of all questions now is whether or not the world will have a future—whether there will be a tomorrow."

As mentioned above, George Kistiakowsky was a particular hero of Pauling's. His death at the end of 1982 possibly reawakened Pauling's fighting spirit in 1983. That year, among other public appearances, Pauling gave a stirring talk on the occasion of the 250th anniversary of the birth of minister-chemist-activist Joseph Priestley—an appropriate forerunner of his receipt the following year of the Priestley Medal, the American Chemical Society's highest award. Assigned the customary lecture for the honorary occasion on April 9, 1984, he wrote a speech that was sent in advance for publication in ACS's monthly journal, *Chemical and Engineering News*. It is excerpted below.

It is important to note, however, that Pauling did not actually deliver this lecture on "Chemistry and the World of Tomorrow" at that event. As on other occasions, he strayed from his prepared text and gave a very different talk from what was expected. Professor Derek Davenport (who had initially proposed Pauling for the award) recently told the story of how Pauling instead declaimed a succession of inflammatory remarks, including lambasting the Reagan administration. Within the audience were a number of appalled chemist colleagues who had somehow expected that this old firebrand (now 83) would have mellowed over time and given up scolding them for their social inactivism and conservative or reactionary political positions.

I t is a source of satisfaction to me to know that the three chemists who nominated me for the medal said that I have some similarity to Priestley, in that the interests of both Priestley and me have included not only science but also morality. I may point out, however, that there is a difference between us. With me, it was science that came first; I then, several decades ago, formulated a basic ethical principle through what I have contended is essentially a scientific derivation. With Priestley, it was morality that came first. . . .

One of Priestley's biographers, Gibbs, has asked, "How was it that, in this difficult and obscure field [of the existence and nature of different kinds of gases] he was able to make advances that had eluded so many men of science? He himself put it down to his habit of searching into dark and mysterious corners, and of following a scent wherever it might lead, without any preconceived ideas. Almost alone among scientists then living, he was honest enough to credit part, at least, of his success to enthusiasm and a sense of adventure. If he was looking at a piece of mint standing in an upturned jar over a bowl of water, or at a mouse in an inverted beer glass, great issues were at stake. He was watching carefully for any hint that might lead to means for enhancing the welfare and happiness of mankind. And behind it all he was convinced that the rapid progress of knowledge would 'be the means, under God, of putting an end to all undue and usurped authority in the business of religion, as well as of science.'"

We ourselves have seen the rapid progress of science during recent decades. Right now . . . it is likely that the discoveries that are being made will have a pronounced effect on the nature of the world of the future. A few decades ago a new science, molecular biology, was developed as a result of the interest of structural chemists in the question of the nature of living organisms. The consequences of this development can be seen about us now, in the effort that is being spent on genetic engineering and related fields.

Most important of all, with respect to science and the world of the future, is the existence of nuclear weapons, based upon the processes of nuclear fission and nuclear fusion that were discovered by physicists and chemists half a century ago. The greatest of all questions now is whether or not the world will have a future—whether there will be a tomorrow. It is with respect to this question that chemists have their primary obligation as citizens.

Many of us remember an outstanding physical chemist, George Kistiakowsky, who died a year and a half ago at age 82. He had been an officer in the White Russian army at age 21 and a manual laborer in the Balkans, and then he studied chemistry in Berlin and came to the U.S. I worked with him in the explosives division of the National Defense Research Committee, and in 1944 he became head of the explosives division at Los Alamos. From 1959 to 1961 he was science advisor to President Eisenhower. During the last 12 years of his life he devoted himself to working for world peace. His last article, published Dec. 2, 1982, in the *Bulletin of the Atomic Scientists*, was on world peace. In it he described the development of nuclear weapons, and wrote:

> *The Soviets, of course, kept up with us in most respects. And*
> *so here we are, possessors of some 50,000 nuclear warheads:*

*more than enough to produce a holocaust that will not only de-
stroy industrial civilization but is likely to spread over the Earth—
environmental effects from which recovery is by no means certain.*

*As one who has tried to change these trends, working both
through official channels and, for the last dozen years, from outside, I tell you, as my parting words, forget the channels!*

There is simply not time enough before the world explodes.

*Concentrate instead on organizing a mass movement for
peace such as there has not been before.*

The threat of annihilation is unprecedented.

And so, Kisty said, we must now take unprecedented action to save
the world.

We, as chemists, can contribute to developing a better world. Our primary duty now is to work to help educate our fellow citizens. We are facing the unprecedented threat of extinction of the human race in a nuclear
war, and we must all join in taking unprecedented actions to prevent this
annihilation and to achieve the goal of the abolition of war. We must do
our part to see to it that there is a world of tomorrow.

SAVING THE PLANET

*"We have to live with diversity in a manner that does not threaten the
security and prosperity of all people."*

Whenever and wherever Linus Pauling went among scientists, he got
involved in discussions about the future of the planet—even when the
meeting was held for quite another purpose. Attending a 1988 conference on structural chemistry in Cavtat, Yugoslavia, Pauling took an
active part in composing "The Cavtat Declaration," which was then
widely circulated.

The world predicament that so deeply concerned the author-signers
of this document would soon emerge in the microcosm of intolerant bru-
tality that broke out in the "ethnic cleansing" following the disintegration
of Yugoslavia.

M embers of the human race have never been so united by a common
destiny as they are today. Humanity is threatened both by the risk
of total destruction, which would result from nuclear war, and by a growing danger of worldwide economic collapse, brought about by the arms

race and the ruthless exploitation of natural resources. On top of these dangers there is now, for the first time in history, the threat of global eco-logical disaster that could engulf all of us. Our forests are dying, our riv-ers are poisoned, the seas are dying. The climate itself is being modified; the ozone layer, which for millions of years has maintained the equilib-rium of the biosphere, is being destroyed. As scientists, who must bear some share of responsibility for this situation, we plead for a hearing from governments and statesmen, and all those who hold power—and the future of civilization—in their hands.

As members first and foremost of the human race, we neither expect nor desire that one single political or social system should prevail on the whole Earth. A disappearance of cultural differences would make our world poorer. But we have to live with diversity in a manner that does not threaten the security and prosperity of all people This requires above all tolerance and respect for human life, freedom from political, economic, or religious oppression, and the will to remove present injustices in the global distribution of the resources necessary to ensure an acceptable standard of living for everyone. For millions, the basic needs of food, clothing, shelter, health, freedom, education, and opportunities for cul-tural development and leisure time remain unsatisfied. In many parts of the world starvation and disease are commonplace; and the exponential growth of populations aggravates such problems to the point at which mortality, and particularly infant mortality, is the only control.

Against this background, which offers a very gloomy prognosis for the future, we see that the misuse of scientific progress is leading to global catastrophe. The scientific revolution witnessed in this century provides immense possibilities for progress, but requires for their realiza-tion a radical change in the politico-economic systems and in the aggres-sive ideologies, which have so far left us with only an arms race, lethal pollution of air, water, and soil, poverty, injustice, and the prospect of international bankruptcy. To ensure that the use of science and technol-ogy not be perverted in this way, every citizen of the world should be aware of the issues at stake and should challenge the prejudice, vanity, ignorance, and greed which have certainly contributed to our present dilemma.

We believe that a United Nations organization still offers the best hope for the future of humanity, but that its present Charter may need modification: the new need is for a structure based on the fundamental principle of human solidarity, whose primary goal is to serve the basic needs of the human race. The role of sovereign states should be balanced by an increasing emphasis on specialized international agencies with the authority and capability of protecting member states not only from military threats, but also from monetary and economic insecurity and exploitation. Such agencies should prevent the indiscriminate flow of armaments of all kinds; they could also be charged with the formulation and implementation of recommendations for combating the degradation of the ecosystem on a global scale.

We plead for a substantial decrease in military expenditures accompanied by increased investments in science, education, and development. Programs designed to promote social and economic goals must guard against environmental destruction. Particular emphasis should be placed on the development of clean sources of energy and ecologically responsible methods of food production. A portion of all military budgets should be diverted into the improvement of social conditions and health programs. Last but not least, effective population control is a necessity because our planet is simply becoming too small. It is obvious that only concerted actions on a worldwide scale have any chance of success. We therefore call upon our fellow scientists, and upon national, religious, and business leaders to creatively promote these goals and to support vigorous enforcement of effective programs once they have been agreed upon. There is no alternative to international cooperation if global catastrophe is to be avoided and life on Earth is to be saved.

THIS EXTRAORDINARY AGE

"There's no reason why people all over the world should not cooperate with one another and get rid, to the extent that we can, of the evils that have existed in the world for a long time now."

In 1988 Linus Pauling met Daisaku Ikeda, the president of the Buddhist organization Soka Gakkai International. SGI promotes culture, education, and peace through a variety of programs in different nations, including the United States. Pauling's ongoing dialogue with SGI's highly educated, well-traveled, and perceptive leader resulted in *A Lifelong Quest for Peace*, an eloquent book that contains both men's beliefs, feelings, and experiences.

At almost 90, Pauling was asked to deliver a lecture at the Los Angeles campus of Soka University at the Second Pacific Basin Symposium in 1990. The lengthy title of his talk was "Prospects for Global Environmental Protection and World Peace As We Approach the 21st Century."

As the end of the 20th century approached, the world witnessed the rapid dismantling of the Soviet Union's postwar stranglehold on Eastern

Europe. Then came the implosion of the Union of Soviet Socialist Republics itself in 1991. The process had begun with Mikhail Gorbachev's desire, both idealistic and pragmatic, to achieve more openness in society through *glasnost* and the restructuring of the nation's political and economic systems in *perestroika*. He focused on finding rational ways to defuse conflicts within the huge communist bloc, and on establishing a climate of new accord and trust with Western nations. The USSR could no longer keep denying political freedom and the economic incentives of free enterprise to its people. During the six years of Gorbachev's presidency there was considerable progress in arms control negotiations and treaties.

American politicians and financiers inevitably claimed the dissolution of Soviet-style communism as a great victory for the capitalistic economic system. Pauling, however, considered how much deprivation and suffering the competition between the two superpowers had caused ordinary people on both sides of the conflict, with long-lasting consequences in diminished quality of life and a ravaged environment. Few of the large, long-range problems of humankind had been addressed, let alone solved, during the Cold War.

In this brief excerpt from the transcribed and published talk, at times discursive and extemporaneous, Pauling showed his inclination to identify religious, cultural, and ethnic intolerance as the cause of many vicious and irrational wars. Perhaps, as he suggested obliquely, improvements in communication skills and systems could eventually resolve many misunderstandings and problems.

I still read the Bible. . . . I'm horrified at the tales that I find in the Bible about the Israelites overcoming Jericho or someplace like that and killing all the men, women, and children. War was terrible in those days and still is terrible.

And why is the Middle East, for example, such a warlike place? Part of the reason, of course, is religion. Religious sects fight each other because of these religious beliefs that the members of the religions have. It's fine that there are religions that emphasize world peace instead of the sanctity of their own particular brand of religions: God saying thou shalt have no other gods before me, you know, in the Bible.

Another reason is language. People have grown up learning one language and 50 miles away perhaps there are people who have grown up learning another language and they don't understand each other too well when they get together and they tend to fight with one another. Their parents fought and their grandparents fought, they want to revenge something that happened to their grandparents or great-grandparents. I don't know how to solve problems of that sort, but I have confidence enough in human beings to believe that ultimately they could be stopped. But not by sending battleships and tens of thousands of soldiers in and threatening war. . . .

There's no reason why people all over the world should not cooperate with one another and get rid, to the extent that we can, of the evils that have existed in the world for a long time now. Bias and dogmas: it's going to be pretty hard to eliminate the biases of different kinds and dogmatic beliefs. But we can hope that in the course of time they all will be eliminated.

From time to time, I've used essentially the words that I've used now. Now we are forced to eliminate from the world forever the vestige of prehistoric barbarism, this curse of the human race, war. We, you and I, are privileged to live at a time in the world's history, this remarkable extraordinary age, the unique epoch in this history of the world, the epoch of demarcation between the past millennia of war and suffering and the future, the great future of peace, justice, morality, and human wellbeing. We are privileged, right now, to have the opportunity of contributing to the achievement of the goal of the abolition of war and its replacement by world law.

I am confident that we shall succeed in this great task. The world community will thereby be freed, not only from the suffering caused by war, but also from hunger, disease, and fear through the better use of the Earth's resources, the discoveries made by scientists, and the efforts of human beings through their work. And I am confident that we shall, in the course of time, build a world characterized by economic, political, and social justice for all persons and a culture worthy of man's intelligence.

AND STILL THE WARS GO ON

"This wasn't a war. This you could call a massacre or slaughter, perhaps even murder."

In 1991 the directors of the Nuclear Age Peace Foundation in Santa Barbara, California, informed Linus Pauling of their wish to honor him with a special peace award. When the 90-year-old scientist prepared the talk he would give for this occasion, he focused on the news that had been on his mind and that of many other Americans: the Persian Gulf War. He was particularly concerned about the civilian casualties of the American-led U.N. campaign to oust Saddam Hussein's invading troops from Kuwait. Pauling had compassion for the casualties of this and all wars. He was also still quite capable of scolding U.S. presidents when he felt they deserved it.

Pauling and the Dalai Lama, happy in each other's peace-promoting company, at the Nuclear Age Peace Foundation in Santa Barbara. In 1991 the 90-year-old Pauling received a special award from the Foundation. He gave a talk about the recent Persian Gulf War and its toll on the civilian Iraqi population. (Photo courtesy of Linda Pauling-Kamb)

On the 8th of January, I bought a quarter page in the *New York Times* and published an advertisement, "STOP THE RUSH TO WAR!" Instead of going to war, the advertisement argued, let's continue applying pressures—economic pressures and other pressures on Iraq—rather than to go ahead and wage a war that would cause a great amount of human suffering. I didn't expect it to be effective, but I felt that it was my duty to do what I could. So I did by publishing that advertisement.

On the 18th of January, after the war had started, I published another advertisement. I didn't have money enough to buy another quarter page in the *New York Times*, but for a third of the money I got a quarter page in a Washington, D.C., paper. Another paper published the advertisement and charged me only one dollar. It was an open letter to President Bush. It started out, "To kill and maim people is immoral. War kills and maims people. War is immoral. Stop the war. Resort instead to continuing to apply pressures of various sorts. Cancel the ultimatums. Begin discussions, not only of Kuwait but of the great world problems in general."

One of my complaints about President Bush was that he said that he refused absolutely to discuss any other questions than just withdrawal from Kuwait, and that one of the ultimatums was that the rich Arab family that used to own the country was to be restored to ownership of the country. He had given up saying anything about democracy because he knew that Kuwait wasn't a democratic country, with only a few percent of the people in Kuwait having the right to vote. Also, our policy had been to refuse to enter into discussions of the Palestinian problem—which, of course, was one of the points that Saddam Hussein was raising. It's a disgrace that the Palestinian problem should remain unresolved so many decades after it arose, and it has become exacerbated.

So the war went on. My open letter to President Bush probably didn't make any difference at all. I was thinking, What is going to happen now? I wasn't very smart. Part of the reason was that I had stopped working on military explosives when the Second World War came to an end, and I hadn't kept up with the developments that had been occurring in this field. That's the excuse I had for not having foreseen what was going to happen.

The war went on. In the first days we pretty well destroyed the aviation facilities of Iraq. We continued to bombard Iraq and, after some weeks, the war stopped without any extensive ground war having been undertaken. It was almost an entirely aerial war with only 150 Americans killed. I was glad about that. Four hundred thousand Americans were killed in the Second World War and, of course, millions of other combatants—some 50 million people died as a direct result of the war.

I was reading about an event that took place 47 years ago on the 6th of June—the landing in Normandy when the American, British, and Canadian forces, with a few Free French forces, landed on the coast of Normandy. Tens of thousands of young soldiers were killed in that landing. One unfortunate regiment suffered 25 percent casualties on the first day, the 6th of June. The average age of the American soldiers there was 19. The average age of the German soldiers was 17. They had been fighting a long time and were having trouble finding anybody to fight on the front. These young people who had not yet had a chance to enjoy and experience life were sent off to die—by the old people who decide that there will be a war.

In the Korean War, 54,000 Americans were killed. In the war in Vietnam, 58,000 Americans were killed and some hundreds of thousands were wounded and millions of the enemy were killed. We withdrew and negotiations ultimately began after that much loss of life.

This Wasn't a War: So, I was thinking that we're going to have a ground war and perhaps after 50,000 Americans have died, we'll begin negotiating, talking about the problems. That didn't happen, and the reason that it didn't happen was something that I should have been able to foresee, but didn't foresee. There were 150,000 aerial sorties against Iraq, so great damage was done by our Air Force and some by shells shot over from the battleships.

There wasn't much response. Why wasn't there much response? We had sold maybe a billion dollars worth of machines of war—planes and tanks and missiles of various sorts—to the Iraqis during the Iran-Iraq conflict when we were supporting Iraq and opposing Iran. In the meantime, another trillion dollars was spent by President Reagan on changing our military machine. Great effort and great amounts of money were expended. So they had in Iraq, and we knew that they had, the old military machines, and we had new ones against which the old ones wouldn't be very effective. That's what happened. As I say, I should have been smart enough to realize that that was going to happen.

I am sure that President Bush and the people in the Pentagon and the top consultants and advisors in Washington knew that this was the situation. They knew about how superior our weapons of warfare, especially aerial warfare, were and that this was going to be the outcome. What did it result in? One hundred fifty Americans killed. How many Iraqi people—soldiers and civilians, old people, young people, children, babies—died? The one piece of evidence that I have is the 150,000 aerial sorties. During the Second World War in these aerial sorties the average weight of bombs carried and dropped was 2.3 tons per sortie, and three million tons of high explosives were dropped and there were three million people killed. One person was killed per ton of high explosive bomb dropped. That probably is about right for the attack against Iraq.

I don't have much information. You remember there was one Scud missile which carried a little less than a quarter of a ton of high explosives that killed 27 Americans when it exploded. So that was much higher, a hundred times as high as the average of one death per ton of high explosive. That means that some 300,000 Iraqis were killed. Iraq hasn't been willing to state what the number of their deaths was, and at present the United States hasn't released any of our estimates of the number killed. In the earlier wars, we were releasing a statement every day about how many of the enemy were killed.

Three hundred thousand killed. What does that mean? Three hundred thousand. One hundred fifty Americans were killed—2,000 Iraqis were killed per one American killed. That means that this wasn't a war. In a war you have opposing forces that fight and there are deaths on both sides and finally one side wins. In the old days perhaps this was a demonstration of the democratic process—the side with the biggest number of fighters won. This wasn't a war. This you could call a massacre or slaughter, perhaps even murder.

What Does the Future Hold? I am depressed about the fact that the United States carried out this action. Though it's been done, and perhaps it will be done again, what is the future going to hold? There are two things that might happen. First, it may be that the situation with respect to weapons will be sort of frozen. A second possibility is that the weapons that we've brought over there will not be brought back to the United States, but will be sold to the highest bidders—another source of income. And we'll perhaps spend another trillion dollars to develop the next generation of smart weapons so that we would still be ahead in the way that we were ahead in the fight with Iraq.

Whichever way it happens, we have to recognize that now the United States is the one strong power on Earth and President Bush has talked about the new order that we're going to have. There are two possibilities about the new order. One is that we'll have a continuation of the policy that if there is some country that behaves in a way that we don't like, we'll go in and kill a good number of the people there, perhaps 300,000 if it's a good-sized country with some 20 million inhabitants like Iraq. We'll do it in such a way that we have practically no losses and we'll get the sort of government put in that we like, as we did in Grenada or Panama. Grenada had very little in the way of a military machine, and there weren't very many casualties. In Panama there were some thousands of people killed. So that's one possibility—a rule by terrorism in the world.

I looked up terrorist in the dictionary. I'm a sort of dictionary buff. . . . It was in 1931 that reporters started asking me what my hobbies were and I said, "Well, I collect dictionaries and encyclopedias." I've been doing that now for 60 years. Terrorists are people who make an ultimatum, a demand of some sort in the form of an ultimatum threatening to kill hostages or other people if the demand is not met. What did President Bush do? He issued some ultimatums that were absolute that by a certain date the Iraqis would have to withdraw from Kuwait, or else. And "or else" consisted in our killing 300,000 Iraqis, 2,000 to one. It seems to me that our country has become a terrorist country on a very large scale.

Toward a Future Worthy of Man's Intelligence: What is the alternative? The alternative, I think, has been expressed in my statement that war is immoral, to kill and maim people is immoral. The alternative would be for the United States to say, "We are a moral country." We dominate the Earth, and are the greatest country on Earth—although not the one in which the health of the people is the greatest, or the infant mortality is the least, or the distribution of wealth is the best. At any rate, we can contend that we are the greatest power on Earth now and we are a moral country.

We are going to apply pressures to the extent that we can on any other country in the world that behaves in an immoral way. These pressures would not be terrorist threats to attack and kill a certain fraction of the population. Rather, they would be pressures of a different sort, some of which, of course, tend to border on the immoral such as interfering with food coming into the countries so that people begin to starve in the country against which there is an embargo. This is not nearly so immoral as killing large numbers of people.

I hope that the Nuclear Age Peace Foundation will work in the effort to make the United States into a moral country that could lead the world into a future of morality, a future worthy of man's intelligence.

RESEARCH ON THE SCIENCE OF PEACE

"I propose that the great world problems be solved in the way that other problems are solved—by working hard to find their solution—by carrying on research for peace."

By the 1990s, world peace was as urgent yet elusive as ever. In addition to occasional nuclear threats (including some by the U.S.), both the chemical and biological substances that Pauling also dreaded were known or suspected to have been used on several occasions. Iraq wasn't the only nation guilty of this transgression.

Might science come up with a solution to man's inhumanity to man, to nations' continuously lethal strife? Pauling the scientist thought it could—by systematizing the research of well-supported experts in an organization he believed should operate under the auspices of the United Nations.

He had proposed just such a mechanism in the last chapter of *No More War!* in 1958. Here are excerpts describing what he had in mind. The chapter's final passage, which was also Pauling's original conclusion for the entire book, is just as relevant now, on the eve of the 21st century.

How is peace in the world to be achieved? How are the great world problems to be solved, without resort to war, war that would now lead to catastrophe, to world suicide?

I propose that the great world problems be solved in the way that other problems are solved—by working hard to find their solution—by carrying on research for peace.

Research consists in striving in every possible way to discover what the facts are, to learn more and more about the nature of the world, and to use all information that can be obtained in the effort to find the solution to difficult problems.

As the world has become more and more complex in recent centuries and decades there has developed a greater and greater reliance upon specialists to carry on research and to make discoveries.

Much research in science and in other fields of knowledge is carried out by professors in the universities of the world, together with their students and associates. Much of the research done in the universities is fundamental research, not designed to lead directly to the solution of a particular practical problem. It has often turned out, however, that discoveries made in the course of fundamental research have had an immediate practical application. Still more often, these discoveries have formed the foundation for later discoveries that were put to use in the solution of important practical problems. . . .

The world progresses through research.

Research for War: During recent decades greater and greater use has been made of research and of the services of scientists and other scholars in the conduct of war and the preparation for war.

The Second World War was fought almost entirely with weapons and by methods developed by scientists.

Armaments of the great nations of the world are now much different from those upon which they relied during the Second World War. The changes—the development of nuclear weapons, of jet planes, of guided missiles, of ballistic missiles, of improved radar and other methods of detection—have resulted from scientific research, both fundamental and applied.

Even the tactical and strategic techniques are now developed through research. During the Second World War the admirals and generals came to rely more and more upon advice from scientists and other specialists constituting their operations analysis groups. These groups of mathematicians, physicists, chemists, and other specialists are able to develop a far deeper understanding of modern warfare than the admirals and generals, to analyze the problems involved, and to give advice as to how war should be conducted that is far better than the conclusions that the admirals and generals themselves could reach.

These specialists devote years to the attack on the problem of how best to wage war. They make use of giant electronic computers to assist them in their attack. It may well be that some of these able men have found some imaginative and unexpected solutions to some of the military problems.

Great sums of money, hundreds of millions of dollars per year, are now being spent on research for war, and many thousands of scientists and other specialists are involved in this work. . . .

Also, special projects relating to research on methods of defense and methods of waging war are set up under the auspices of universities and technical schools. These projects may cost many millions of dollars, and many able scientists in the world may be attracted into taking part in them.

Research for Peace: The time has now come for the greatest of all problems facing the world, the problem of peace, to be attacked in an effective way.

I propose that there be set up a great research organization, the World Peace Research Organization, within the structure of the United Nations.

The duty of the World Peace Research Organization would be to attack the problem of preserving the peace, to carry out research on preserving peace in the world, to carry out research on peace. This would mean, of course, carrying out research on how to solve great world problems, problems of the kind that have in the past led to war. It would also involve attacking the problem of how to prevent the outbreak of a nuclear war by design or by accident.

The World Peace Research Organization, if it existed today, could make a thorough analysis of the problems involved in an international agreement to stop all testing of nuclear weapons. It could, after making its study, propose a system that, in the opinion of the Organization, would have the greatest safety, the smallest chance of violation by any nation, would be of the maximum benefit to all of the nations and all of the people of the world. Such a proposal would without doubt be given serious consideration by the nations of the world.

The World Peace Research Organization should be a large one. It should include many scientists, representing all fields of science, and many other specialists—economists, geographers, specialists in all fields of knowledge.

In order that these important problems might be attacked with the aid of the advice and help of some of the most able men in the world, satisfactory conditions for work would have to be provided for these men. This means that the facilities and environment would have to be similar to those in the great universities, and the outstanding authorities in various fields would have to be allowed to prosecute their studies in a fundamental and thorough way. They would, however, be at hand to help with special projects, attacks on special problems, when needed.

The multiplicity of the fields of human knowledge pertinent to the problem of peace and the complexity of the problem itself are such that the Organization should have thousands of specialists on its staff. . . .

The appointment of specialists to the World Peace Research Organization of the United Nations should be on essentially the same basis as appointment to professorial positions in the leading universities. The senior men should be given appointments with tenure comparable to academic tenure in universities and to civil service in government service.

We cannot expect that the great problems in the modern world can be solved in an easy way by government officials who have many duties and who cannot devote to the problems the long and careful thought that they require for their solution. These problems need to be attacked in the way that other problems are attacked in the modern world—by research, carried out by people who think about the problems year after year.

There are great possibilities of progress in this way. If thousands of outstandingly able investigators are attacking the world problems by imaginative and original methods, working on these problems year after year, many of these problems should be solved.

It is possible that some great discoveries may be made, discoveries that would so change the world as to make the danger of outbreak of a nuclear war far less than it is at present.

The cost of supporting the World Peace Research Organization within the United Nations on the scale described, with at first 2,000 specialists and many auxiliary members of the staff, increasing to 10,000 specialists in 10 years, would be of the order of magnitude of $25 million per year at the beginning and $100 million per year ultimately.

This cost is very small in comparison with the sums expended for military purposes. . . . Also, the damage that would be done to the world by a nuclear war is inestimable. . . . The World Peace Research Organization would be a cheap insurance policy. . . .

I have no doubt that the World Peace Research Organization would pay for itself in a short while.

The cost of preserving peace in the world would not, of course, be limited to the $100 million per year for support of the World Peace Research Organization. Many of the international agreements that will be made in the future in connection with the solution of world problems by peaceful means will involve the expenditure of considerable sums of money. These sums for the United States might be of the order of magnitude of the four billion dollars per year now expended on foreign aid (including military as well as nonmilitary aid). It may well be that, as the military budget is decreased by several billion dollars a year below its present figure of $40 billion a year in the United States, a significant fraction of the decrease would be allocated to uses connected with the peaceful solution of world problems.

We may, however, anticipate that the world would benefit from these expenditures, and that the United States would benefit. We may expect that the standards of living in the world as a whole and in the United States in particular could be raised significantly. The military budgets of the countries of the world do not contribute to raising the standards of living. They represent almost entirely a waste of world resources, an expenditure of money without any corresponding return in the form of useful goods. A change in policy that leads to a reduction of the military budgets, with increased safety for the nations of the world, can only result in benefit to the people.

President Eisenhower in his address on 17 April 1958 pointed out that great things might be done with the sums of money now being spent on armaments. He mentioned that if the U.S. had spent only $50 billion on defense during the five years 1953 to 1958 rather than the $200 billion that was spent, we could have constructed the entire nationwide interstate system of highways that has been planned, built every worthwhile hydroelectric power project in America, built all the hospitals needed for the next 10 years and all the schools needed for the next 10 years, and have been able also to reduce the national debt by $50 billion.

The World Peace Research Organization should be a research organization, which makes analyses of world problems, makes discoveries, and makes proposals. It should not be a policy-making organization.

One of the greatest of the problems facing the world, closely connected with the problem of war or peace, is the population problem. In eight years the United States has increased in population by over 12 percent, from 151 million in 1950 to an estimated 175 million in 1958. The population of the whole world is increasing at nearly the same rate. Much of the increase has been due to medical progress, in decreasing the infant and childhood mortality, and lengthening the life span.

As the population pressure becomes greater in some countries in the world, the danger of the outbreak of war becomes greater. The population problem is one that should be attacked by the World Peace Research Organization.

Every great nation should also have its own peace research organization. Careful analyses would have to be made by the nations of the proposals made by the World Peace Research Organization. These analyses could be made only by similar groups of specialists. In the United States, for example, a Peace Research Organization might be set up under the Science Advisor to the President. . . .

Another possibility is that it be incorporated within the Department of Peace, in case that a Secretary for Peace is added to the Cabinet. In either case, the Peace Research Organization of the United States should not be an operating organization or a policy-making organization, but a research organization.

The World Peace Research Organization should have its own buildings, located not in a city but in some rural or semi-rural community, suitable to its activities of slow, thoughtful attack on great problems, suitable to the search for the truth. I believe that there would be no difficulty in obtaining the services in the World Peace Research Organization of many of the most able scientists and scholars in the world.

There is no doubt that many of the specialists who would be most effective in this work would also have the strongest emotional attraction to it. An added attraction would be that of association with the many other outstanding scientists and scholars of the world who would constitute its staff. In its intellectual environment the Organization should be comparable to the greatest universities in the world.

NEW NUCLEAR NATIONS

"It is immoral for the rich and highly developed nations of the world to give and sell these weapons of destruction to other nations."

Were he alive in 1998, over 30 years after giving his Azad Lectures, Pauling would have been dismayed and horrified by the resurgence of another nuclear arms race. India's decision to conduct a series of nuclear bomb tests was the very thing Pauling had sought to dissuade its government from doing: expending human and economic resources on developing nuclear technology to make a military statement to China, Pakistan, and the world.

It often appears that there is no reasoning with nationalistic human nature. If there is a chance to acquire sophisticated weaponry, citizens and leaders are tempted to go for it despite the economic penalties and risks involved. India is a nation that cannot adequately feed, employ, or provide minimal health services for the majority of its own people. Its population has almost doubled in the three decades since Pauling's speech—approaching one billion by the close of the 20th century. Nevertheless, its leaders determined to create a nuclear arsenal and then display it before the world, thereby becoming eligible for membership among the nuclear nations. In a matter of days, Pakistan joined, too. The fiercely hostile neighbors have now qualified themselves as nuclear nations, and it is widely feared that a nuclear war may erupt between them in this historically volatile and violent relationship. Also, Pakistan's pride as the first Muslim nation with nuclear weapons has implications for the powder keg that is the Middle East.

They are following the Cold War model: expressing their competition in a grandiose but wasteful accumulation of nuclear devices that could destroy the whole planet many times over. Can any of the Cold War nations now claim that people as a whole benefited from this fixation on weaponry?

How much better it would be, Pauling always maintained, if all nations worked together to solve the innumerable problems that plague all humankind. Instead, nations focus on strategies to enable one economic system to "bury" the other. These unsolved problems, cumulative and mostly irreversible, have blighted the future—imperiling Earth and humankind in less dramatic, slower ways than outright nuclear warfare, but perhaps ultimately as destructive and deadly.

Here is what Pauling told his Indian listeners in 1967.

I have read in the Indian newspapers an argument to the effect that if there is a danger that Pakistan would obtain nuclear weapons, then India needs a stockpile of these weapons. Also, the argument that China has exploded some atomic bombs and that to protect herself India should develop nuclear weapons has been advanced.

As an exponent of morality and peace, I cannot refrain from expressing my disappointment in the action of India in 1962, when the military expenditures of the country were increased from 2.1 percent of the national income to 4.7 percent. I hope that India will again, before long, become the leader of the world in morality and sanity. There is no possibility of India's becoming a world leader in militarism.

I must express my opposition to the proposal that India develop nuclear weapons. I have read that India is now manufacturing weapons-grade plutonium, at Trombay, and, according to a statement made by Dr. Homi J. Bhabha, could fabricate an atomic bomb within 12 months. I cannot think of a greater act of folly than for India to follow such a course. Even the United States, the richest nation in the world, is sacrificing the health and wellbeing of her people to her unfortunate decision to follow a course of militarism, which is now costing $75,000 million per year ($30,000 million per year for the Vietnam War alone). This sum, $75,000 million per year, is equal to 560,000 million rupees per year, twice the annual income of the whole of India, wasted on militarism.

I hope that the government and people of India will reject the recommendations of persons such as Mr. M. Ramamurti, of the General Electro Research Institute, who wrote: "Why should not India get a stockpile of nuclear weapons? As the second largest country in the world, this would transform her flabby image and give teeth to her power status. The second most populous nation in the world cannot afford to take a back seat just because the late Prime Minister made a commitment that India will not go in for the manufacture of nuclear weapons."

In my lecture tomorrow I shall discuss my ideas about how India can transform her "flabby image," to use Mr. Ramamurti's phrase—and not by wasting money on militarism and atomic bombs.

I must say now that the resurgence of militarism in India cannot be blamed entirely on the Indian government and people. The United States is also in part responsible. Last week a, columnist, Mr. T.V. Parasuraman, mentioned in his column in the Indian papers the feeling that but for the United States gift of 1,500 million dollars worth of sophisticated military equipment to Pakistan, Pakistan would long ago have reconciled herself to living within her borders.

Last year I was shocked to read that Mr. Henry Kuss, Jr., Assistant Secretary of Defense in the United States, had received the United States Department of Defense Meritorious Civil Service Medal for his imaginative leadership in the military export sales program. He was given this medal because he had succeeded in selling to the developing countries of the world 1,500 million dollars worth of sophisticated weapons, jet bombers, tanks, machine guns, and other equipment, in one year. In his speech of acceptance he said that "with the proper amount of energy, imagination, and vigor, we should by 1971 be selling 15,000 million dollars worth of sophisticated military equipment to the developing countries." Last week the United States Senate Foreign Relations Committee expressed its concern about the sale of sophisticated weapons to countries of the world that cannot really afford them, with mention of the sale of American Phantom jet fighters to Jordan, Hawker Hunter Sets to Chile, and so on. The principal countries involved in this are the United States, the Soviet

Union, France, Great Britain, West Germany, Czechoslovakia, and Sweden.

I believe that it is immoral for the rich and highly developed nations of the world to give and sell these weapons of destruction to other nations. I believe that we need to make a treaty among the great powers and other nations to forbid the giving or selling of sophisticated weapons to the underdeveloped nations of the world.

As a citizen of the United States, I am, of course, a revolutionary: I subscribe to the Declaration of Independence. I believe that the people have a right to overthrow an oppressive and dictatorial government. In recent years there have been the beginnings of revolution against oppressive and dictatorial governments in 40 countries, but in many countries there has been the violent suppression of the revolutionary movements.

I do not think that it is right to destroy all the hope of a people who are suffering from the oppression of a dictatorship. The development of modern weapons has, however, made it harder and harder for a popular uprising to be successful.

Nuclear bombs can be built by using the uranium in reactors for producing plutonium instead of energy. India was known to possess atomic bombs by 1974, made possible by utilizing nuclear reactors supplied by Canada for converting uranium to plutonium. Pakistan's subsequent acquisition came through reactors and technological information furnished by China, which has had its own standoff with India over Tibet. Other nations, such as Iraq, have had the same reactor-converting capability.

Although there is great energy-generating potential in nuclear fission and fusion reactors, the "anti-nuke" effort to ban reactors has a wider and deeper concern than local health and safety issues. The close surveillance of all nuclear facilities by United Nations teams of experts would appear to be essential to ensure that energy resources are not used to develop weapons.

Another wild card is the nuclear arsenal (and reactors) of the former Soviet Union. Though this arsenal is now under the control of Russia, the continuing economic crises and political turmoil in that large, poorly monitored region inevitably invite the covert sales of radioactive materials.

At the close of the 20th century, other chilling possibilities supplement Pauling's concern over high-tech nuclear weaponry. As he indicated in his Nobel Peace Prize lecture, top-secret research programs in biological warfare have gone on for years in both West and East. Germs and chemicals have been developed that would destroy only humans, not the valuable material infrastructure of their societies. Supplies of deadly or seriously disabling biological or chemical agents have been shipped through black-market arrangements, or devised by scientists working for dictators. They have even occasionally been used in warfare. Chemical and biological weapons might someday be employed by renegade nations or terrorist groups, whatever their political, economic, or religious orientation, to exterminate whole populations of people with different sets of beliefs and practices. (See Pauling's cryptic warning about the 21st century on pages 233-234.)

Perhaps the widespread concern and outrage over the new presence of nuclear weapons in the South Asian subcontinent will finally force the leaders of the world's nations to address seriously the issue of achieving total worldwide disarmament.

Linus Pauling died on August 19, 1994, at his ranch home on the central California coast. The need for abiding world peace is as urgent as it ever was during his lifetime.

Linus Pauling at home and at ease, 1977. (Photo courtesy of Robert Richter)

In the late 1930s the Paulings built this home in the foothills above Pasadena. The house and its two-acre grounds made a memorable setting for entertaining colleagues and younger generations of scientists. Daughter Linda has lived there with her own family since the mid 1960s.

Postlude

Make Your Voice
and Vote Count!

Over the years Linus Pauling often addressed the graduating classes of institutions of higher learning and advanced professional training. On the evidence of commencement talks that were printed afterward or which survive in typescripts or handwritten notes, many were perfunctory in construction and depended on Pauling's excellent memory and his ability to speak winningly wherever the route of discourse took him. Other speeches, rather "boilerplate" in their motivational messages, might be efficiently used with alterations, again and again.

This practiced and much-traveled orator usually spoke extemporaneously about subjects of current interest to him, which he wanted to share with young people just before they were officially sent off with diplomas into the world beyond the walls of academe. Not infrequently, listeners were treated to polemical tirades on political subjects or given advice about what vitamins to take—or both.

For many years, whenever faculty members and administrators were informed that Linus Pauling was the prospective commencement speaker for the radical new graduates of a liberal-arts college, the Nobelist-admiring students of an institute of science, or an establishment-flouting class of a law or medical school, they suspected well enough what they might soon be hearing. The famous but outspoken scientist would say whatever he wanted to say and did not hesitate to rattle the beliefs of the more conservative listeners—whether his oration involved world law, outlawing nuclear-weapons testing, supporting professors' right to an academic freedom that included the privacy of political beliefs, the immediate termination of the Vietnam War, the desirability

263

of impeaching the current U.S. president, or the benefits of megadosing vitamin C.

In his later years Pauling often became more avuncular in tone, even grandfatherly, as when he counseled graduates to "Eat breakfast. Don't eat between meals. Don't smoke. No more than 4 drinks at one time. Exercise regularly. Don't become overweight. Sleep 7 or 8 hours a night." He also sometimes advised them to do as he did: choose a profession that would enable them to work at something that they felt truly passionate about; and to search for a good companion, marry young . . . and stay married.

But above all, again and again, over the years Pauling appealed to youth to save the world from the deadly double consequences of human ingenuity and sheer folly.

The theme that resounded in Pauling's talks at graduation exercises was the need for young citizens—indeed, for all citizens—to take an appropriate and active part in the society around them. To him this did not mean just in the immediate civic community, but for the whole planet, and everything on it. Here in this excerpt, though essentially addressing graduates of a college specializing in science (as reflected in the physics metaphor), Pauling championed political involvement. He never let up on his insistence that scientists, more than any other profession, should honor this responsibility to society.

Pauling was 82 when he gave the talk from which this portion was selected. "The Duties of a Graduate" contains much of the essence of the elder Pauling. It also reflects back, consistently and rather winningly, on the message he gave his classmates at his own graduation from Oregon Agricultural College in 1922, when he had just turned 21—voting age. (See pages 24-28.) In those days, however, the world was not yet facing nuclear annihilation. The nuclear threat gave Pauling's newer messages extra urgency. Nor had Pauling yet begun promoting the virtues of vitamin C—as he did in this speech, but in a portion not included here.

Pauling had often stressed the importance of participating in the government of a democracy, not just by voting, but through other actions: shaping public opinion through speaking out; communicating with legislators and officials; informing oneself and then other people about issues; and lodging public protests, such as petition drives, sit-ins, or strikes. "It doesn't take much," he sometimes observed, "to change the world."

Pauling himself challenged and changed the world, through both science and political action. But the latter came at a considerable price to his scientific accomplishments and his personal reputation. Yet it was work he felt compelled to do, as a scientist and as a human being.

You young men and women are now graduates. As graduates you have, because of your training, reached a position in the world that imposes duties upon you.

One of these duties is to be a good citizen. The first step toward being a good citizen is to take an interest in community affairs, regional and national affairs, and world affairs. Making use of the training that you have now received, you can form opinions about the various problems that need to be solved and express your opinions, both by voting and by discussing the problems with other people.

I believe that every graduate, in addition to carrying out his own work in the world, as determined by his profession, has the obligation to help educate his fellow citizens, to the extent that he can. This obligation is an especially important one for graduates who have studied science. Nearly every problem in the world is to some extent a scientific problem. Scientists are better able to understand these problems than other people, and they may to some extent be somewhat more able to form reliable opinions about them. Accordingly, a scientist should not only strive to give information to his fellow citizens, based upon his special ability to understand the scientific aspects of problems, but should also give his fellow citizens the benefit of his own conclusions and opinions about the problems. . . .

You must not think that your contribution toward solving the problems of the world will be so small as to be unimportant. We have seen that throughout history and especially during recent years public opinion has exerted a great effect on the world. Public opinion is your opinion and the opinion of others like you, which can be expressed in many different ways—by voting, by making statements at meetings or in letters or articles, by taking part in demonstrations, and in other ways.

I am reminded of an analogy. We have learned in our courses in physics that the pressure exerted on the end of the piston in the engine of an automobile is the result of bombardment by the trillions of trillions of molecules in the hot gas. The contribution of each molecule is very small, relative to the total pressure exerted, but if each molecule were to decide that it was unimportant the engine would not operate. In the same way the success of a mass movement depends upon the participation of the individual human beings in exerting pressure toward the goal.

There are many great problems in the world today—encroachment on the environment, the population explosion, the maldistribution of the world's wealth, malnutrition and starvation, contamination of the environment by toxic substances, and especially the misery caused by war and the possibility of the extermination of the human race in a great nuclear catastrophe. These problems and others need to be attacked. . . .

This is a beautiful world. We must all work to save it. Each of you, as a graduate, has a duty to the human race.

Each of you must take what action he can to save the world, and also take action to contribute to the development of a better world, a world worthy of man's intelligence. I repeat: Do not think that you are unimportant. You are an important part of the world.

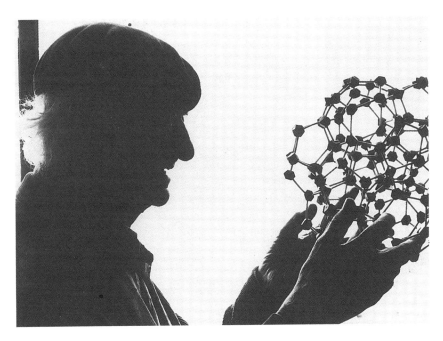

LINUS PAULING 1901-1994

Acknowledgments

The editors would like to thank the following persons and organizations for their assistance and cooperation during the preparation of this book:

Linus Pauling, Jr., M.D., Linus Pauling's eldest son and namesake, not only for writing the eloquent Introduction, but also, as the Pauling Estate's executor, for enabling us to print previously unpublished manuscripts (archived at Oregon State University) and published texts (such as *No More War!*) now in the Estate's domain. He encouraged this project from its initiation as an idea—basically to amplify the peace-activism themes previously presented in the book *Linus Pauling in His Own Words* (1995). He also read the manuscript in a close-to-final form.

Linda Pauling-Kamb, Linus Pauling's daughter, for helping to select and then providing most of the photographs that appear in the book. She is the photo curator of the Pauling family, as well as the president of LCProgeny, which controls the usage rights to the name and image of Linus Pauling. She, too, read the manuscript in a near-finished stage of its evolution, as did her husband, *Professor Barclay Kamb,* of the California Institute of Technology.

Dorothy Bruce Munro, the highly capable and much-respected secretary-assistant of Linus Pauling, who for 21 years was his primary appointment "gate-keeper" at the Linus Pauling Institute of Science and Medicine, as well as communication conveyor, publication developer, archive maintainer, and schedule maker. She helped to select, edit, and proofread the texts in this book.

Zelek S. Herman, Ph.D., Linus Pauling's research assistant for many years, who with Dorothy B. Munro compiled the master list of Linus Pauling's publications—over 1,000 in all.

Karyle Butcher, Deputy Associate Provost for Information Services, and *Clifford Mead,* Head of Special Collections at the Valley Library, Oregon State University, for providing materials and information for the project.

John F. (Frank) Catchpool, M.D., of Sausalito, California, for allowing us to publish the profile of Albert Schweitzer that he wrote with Linus Pauling in 1965, which until now was printed only in German and Spanish translations.

Robert Richter of Richter Productions, Inc. (New York), for letting us use selections from the full transcriptions of his in-depth interviews of Linus and Ava Helen Pauling in 1977, which had provided the core of the soundtrack for his Nova program shown on PBS-TV, "Linus Pauling—Crusading Scientist."

The Linus Pauling Institute, formerly located in Palo Alto, California, and now permanently situated at Oregon State University. LPI initially furnished copies of the majority of documents selected for this book, when Barbara Marinacci was gathering materials in 1994-95 for *Linus Pauling in His Own Words.* Because this first anthology covered all major fields of Pauling's endeavors, only a quarter of the book could be devoted to his peace activities—which was the book he said that he particularly hoped would be done.

Oregon State University, which holds the *Ava Helen and Linus Pauling Papers.* The archives are within Special Collections of the Valley Library at Oregon State University, Corvallis. (OSU originated as Oregon Agricultural College, the alma mater of both Ava Helen and Linus Pauling.)

The admirable *Santa Clara County Public Library* system, most particularly its branches in Saratoga and Cupertino, which came up with all the background reference books we requested—often through their online catalog system or on interlibrary loan.

Soka Gakkai International and its California-based staff members and volunteers, who have involved us in the stimulating preparatory stage for the ambitious exhibition they are sponsoring, "Linus Pauling and the Twentieth Century." Making its debut in San Francisco in September of 1998, this multimedia exhibit is scheduled to travel to various cities around the world—a highly appropriate tribute to this world traveler and world-peace advocate.

Rudy Marinacci, for the graphic design of the book's cover.

Joanne Shwed of Backspace Ink, Pacifica, California, for her multifaceted, computer-knowledgeable work as book designer, copyeditor, and production editor.

Margaret Frazier for last-stage editorial assistance.

Photographer *Dan Escobar* of San Francisco, for permitting us to use his photograph for the book cover. It originally appeared in a 1991 article on Linus Pauling in *California* magazine.

Steven Stone, Esq., son of Pauling's main vitamin C mentor, biochemist Irwin Stone. Steve introduced us personally to the principals of a dynamic new publishing house conveniently close to home: Rising Star Press.

And last, but scarcely least:

The founders of *Rising Star Press* in Los Altos, California: *Carl A. Goldman* and *Michole Nicholson.* Both have worked closely and amicably with us all along the way.

Permissions

National Academy of Sciences, Washington, D.C.: for "Thomas Addis 1881-1949," in *Biographical Memoirs,* Vol. 63 (1994).

National Science Teachers Association, *The Science Teacher,* Arlington, Virginia: for "The Social Responsibilities of Scientists and Science," Vol. 33, no. 5 (May 1966).

Norwegian Nobel Committee, Oslo, Norway: for "Science and Peace," the 1962 Nobel Peace Prize lecture, 1964. Copyright © The Nobel Foundation, Stockholm, 1963.

Nuclear Age Peace Foundation, Santa Barbara, California: for "Reflections on the Persian Gulf 'War,'" in the organization's newsletter (1991).

W. W. Norton, New York: for *Red Scare: Memories of the American Inquisition—An Oral History,* by Griffin Fariello (1995).

Physicians for Global Survival, Canada: for "The Path to World Peace," in *The Prevention of Nuclear War* (1983).

Notes on Sources

Given by page number on which the selection initially appears. Linus Pauling is the author of all texts cited here, though in several instances he was coauthor. A slash mark (/) between years given indicates that Pauling's talk was given in the first year but published in the second.

PRELUDE: A SCIENTIST'S WORLD

19   Addendum to Chapter 1, "The End of War," in *No More War!* Dodd, Mead & Co., New York. Originally published in 1958; reprinted in 1964. A new 25th Anniversary Edition was reprinted with addenda in 1983.

PART I: EDUCATION AND SCIENCE IN A DEMOCRACY

26   "Senior Class Oration," a speech given at the graduation ceremony, Oregon Agricultural College, June 22, 1922. From original typescript at Pauling Papers / OSU.

29   "Science and Democracy," a talk given at the Tau Beta Pi Banquet held at the Athenaeum, California Institute of Technology, November 26, 1940. Previously unpublished; taken from the original typescript and handwritten notes at Pauling Papers / OSU.

31   "Union Now," a lecture given in Pasadena, California, July 22, 1940. Original typescript at Pauling Papers / OSU.

34   "Science in the Modern World," a sermon-lecture given at the First Unitarian Church of Los Angeles, California, on August 12, 1951. It was later printed and distributed by the church as a small publication.

41   "The Significance of Chemistry to Man in the Modern World," in *Engineering and Science*, January 1951. Vol. 14, no. 4, 10-12, 14.

44   See note above.

45   "Technology and Democracy," a talk given on May 6, 1955 at the
            University of Puerto Rico; manuscript and typescript at Pauling
            Papers / OSU.

PART II: WAR, PEACE, AND DISSENT

52   Excerpt beginning, "Until 1945, I doubted that the world—" from
            A Lifelong Quest for Peace, p. 64.

53   "Atomic Energy and World Government," 1945; typescript at Pauling
            Papers / OSU.

56   "Will the United States Accept Its Greatest Responsibility?", a
            typescript dated April 24, 1947, with handwritten marginal notes; at
            Pauling Papers / OSU.

58   "Thomas Addis 1881-1949," by Kevin V. Lemley and Linus Pauling.
            Biographical Memoirs, Volume 63. The National Academy Press,
            Washington, D.C., 1994.

64   Ninth Report of the Senate Investigation Committee on Education,
            State of California, 1950/1951.

67   Red Scare: Memories of the American Inquisition: An Oral History by
            Griffin Fariello. W. W. Norton, New York, 1995.

69   "A Disgraceful Act," The Nation, Vol. 178, no. 18 (1 May 1954).

71   "Advice to Students," published in the Caltech monthly, Engineering
            and Science, April 1954/1955.

73   "The Social Responsibilities of Scientists and Science," Vol. 33, no. 5
            (May 1966). Reprinted with permission from NSTA Publications,
            Sept. 1990, from The Science Teacher, National Science Teachers
            Association, 1840 Wilson Blvd., Arlington, VA 22201-3000.

78   Extract beginning "Ten percent of the American people—" from
            "Every Test Kills," Liberation, An Independent Monthly, February
            1958.

78   Edited from several transcribed interviews by Robert Richter for the
            Nova program shown on PBS-TV, "Linus Pauling—Crusading
            Scientist," Richter Productions, New York, 1977.

80   "An Appeal by Scientists to Governments and People of the World,"
            was reprinted in a number of places, including No More War! (1958).
            It began as "An Appeal by American Scientists." Pauling often
            discussed in detail its underlying motivation, as in his Nobel Peace
            Lecture.

82   "Hearing Before the Subcommittee to Investigate the Administration
            of the Internal Security Act and Other Internal Security Laws of the

Committee of the Judiciary." United States Senate, 86th Congress,
Second Session, June 21, 1960 (Washington, D.C.: U.S. Government
Printing Office, 1960).

INTERLUDE: A PARTNERSHIP IN LIFE . . . AND PEACE WORK—AVA HELEN AND LINUS PAULING

The main sources for this composite first-person account by Linus Pauling of his wife's influence on his humanitarian ideas and political activism are:

"The Path to World Peace," in *The Prevention of Nuclear War* (proceedings of a symposium held at the University of British Columbia, March 5-6, 1983), privately printed by Physicians for Social Responsibility.

Portraits of Passion: Aging, Defying the Myth, with interviews by Marshall B. Stearn, Park West Publishing Co., Sausalito, California (1991).

A Lifelong Quest for Peace: A Dialogue Between Linus Pauling and Daisaku Ikeda. Translated and edited by Richard L. Gage. Jones & Bartlett, Sudbury, Mass., 1992.

"An Episode That Changed My Life," an article by Linus Pauling that was unpublished until a portion of it appeared in *Linus Pauling in His Own Words: Selections from His Writings, Speeches, and Interviews.* Simon & Schuster, New York (1995).

Several typed general statements that Pauling would send out from LPI to young people asking for guidance.

Transcriptions of conversations with Robert Richter during the preparation of the Nova documentary, "Linus Pauling—Crusading Scientist" (1977).

The primary source for Ava Helen Pauling's personal remarks are the Robert Richter talks (above). Her talk on "The Second X-Chromosome" is in manuscript form at Pauling Papers / OSU.

Linus Pauling's personal statements about his wife's death are taken from unsent handwritten letters to his children and "notes to self"—all at Pauling Papers / OSU.

PART III: IN THE NUCLEAR AGE

101   The quotation beginning, "The discovery of methods of controlled release—" is from "One World—or None at All," 1947 talk at meeting of Progressive Citizens of America, a typescript at Pauling Papers / OSU.

103   "Atomic Energy and World Government," a talk given at the
        Hollywood-Roosevelt Hotel to members of the Hollywood
        Independent Citizens' Committee of the Arts, Sciences, and
        Professions (ICCASP) on November 30, 1945. From typescript at
        Pauling Papers / OSU.

106   "The Ultimate Decision," printed as a small pamphlet (undated) by the
        Southern California Peace Council, and also in Louisiana State
        University's *Southwest Report*, May 1950 (Vol. 2, no. 8:14-17).

109   "The World Problem and the Hydrogen Bomb," *New Outlook* 7, no. 5
        (1954).

112   Edited from transcribed interview with Linus Pauling conducted by
        Robert Richter in 1977 for the Nova program, "Linus Pauling—
        Crusading Scientist," produced by Richter Productions and shown
        widely on PBS channels around the nation.

116   "Every Test Kills," published in *Liberation, An Independent Monthly*,
        February 1958.

121   Chapter 9 of *No More War!*: "The Need for International
        Agreements," Dodd, Mead & Co., New York, 1958.

125   The Oslo Conference statement, May 1961, was privately printed.

129   "Why I Am Opposed to Fallout Shelters," published in *Liberation, An
        Independent Monthly*, November 1961.

136   "Science and the Future of Humanity," in *Graduate Comment*, Wayne
        State University, October 1963. Volume VII, No. 1. Publication of a
        talk given there earlier in the year.

141   Addendum to Chapter 5, "Radiation and Disease," in *No More War!*,
        updated 25th Anniversary Edition published in 1983 by Dodd, Mead
        & Co., New York; original publication date 1958. (Apollo edition
        1962.)

PART IV: PEACE THROUGH HUMANISM

149   Chapter 9 of *No More War!*: "The Need for International
        Agreements," Dodd, Mead & Co., New York, 1958.

151   "A Proposal: Research for Peace," Chapter 10 of *No More War!*,
        Dodd, Mead & Co., New York, 1958.

153   "Research for Peace," a lecture given at Mt. Hollywood
        Congregational Church, Los Angeles, 20 March 1959. From
        typescript at Pauling Papers / OSU.

157   The profile of Albert Schweitzer, written in 1965, was published in
        both Spanish and German translations, but it was not printed in its

original English form until now. This is an excerpt from the complete text, courtesy of coauthor John F. Catchpool, M.D., Sausalito, Calif.

164   The book *Existentialism and the Modern Predicament* by F. H. Heinemann (1953; Harper paperback edition 1958) was among the many books in Pauling's office at the Linus Pauling Institute in Palo Alto. Pauling's handwritten notes within it were first noticed by his secretary Dorothy Munro, who showed it to editor Barbara Marinacci in 1994. It is now at Pauling Papers / OSU.

166   "Humanism and Peace," Linus Pauling's address to the American Humanist Association at Cleveland, Ohio, on March 17, 1961, responding to his election as Humanist of the Year for 1961. Published in *The Humanist*, March-April 1961.

169   Extract beginning, "It is, we think, dangerous to have organizations—" from the Paulings' report on the Oxford Conference, published in *The Minority of One*, May 1963.

169   *A Lifelong Quest for Peace:* A Dialogue Between Linus Pauling and Daisaku Ikeda. Translated and edited by Richard L. Gage. Jones & Bartlett, Sudbury, Mass., 1992.

170   "Linus Pauling on Science and Peace" (the 1962 Nobel Peace Prize lecture), with an introduction by Gunnar Jahn. Center for the Study of Democratic Institutions; the Fund for the Republic. New York, 1964. The lecture, given in December 1963, was printed in 1964 in several different publications.

172   The 1962 Nobel Peace Prize lecture, 1963. See above.

174   See note above.

PART V: THE SCIENTIST IN SOCIETY

182   Extract beginning, "As scientists, we have not had any special training—" is from speech on "The Position of the Scientists" given at *Pacem in Terris* II convocation in Geneva in May 1967. Pauling's talk was published in several places, including *Bulletin of the Atomic Scientists*, Vol. 23, no. 8 (October 1967).

183   "Notes from Around the World," in Caltech's monthly magazine, *Engineering and Science*, Vol. 18: 15-17 (April 1955).

185   "World Morality and World Peace," in *The Emerging World (Jawaharlal Nehru Memorial Volume)*, Asian Publishing House, New York, 1964.

188   Also excerpted from the source given above.

190   Paragraph beginning, "I have never advocated unilateral
             disarmament—" comes from "The Role of Unilateral Action," *Yale
             Political, A Journal of Divergent Views on National Issues,* Vol. 3,
             no. 3.

191   Paragraph beginning, "I dislike imperialism—" from *Science and
             World Peace* (Azad Memorial Lectures, Part II). Indian Council for
             Cultural Relations, New Delhi, India, 1967.

192   Introduction to *The Futile Crusade: Anti-Communism as American
             Credo,* by Sidney Lens. Quadrangle Books, Chicago (1964).

194   "The Nature of the Problem," speech given at the *Pacem in Terris (I)*—
             Peace on Earth conference held in New York City, in February 1965.
             Printed in several places, including "The Proceedings of an
             International Convocation on the Requirements of Peace, Sponsored
             by the Center for the Study of Democratic Institutions," edited by
             Edward Reed. Pocket Books, New York, 1965.

199   "The Social Responsibilities of Scientists and Science," in *The
             Science Teacher,* Vol. 33, no. 5 (May 1966).

202   *Science and World Peace* (Azad Memorial Lectures), Indian Council
             for Cultural Relations, New Delhi, India, 1967.

209   *Foreign Policies and Disarmament* (the Fourth M. Ct. M.
             Chidambaram Chettyar Memorial Lecture, February 1967), Hoe &
             Co., Madras, India, 1967.

214   Pauling's handwritten notes for May 6, 1970 talk to "SLAG," U.S.
             Geological Survey, Ames Research Center, Mountain View, Calif.
             The manuscript is at Pauling Papers / OSU.

217   "The Possibilities for Social Progress," in the *British Journal of Social
             Psychiatry,* Vol. 4, no. 1, 1970. (Pauling's talk was given at the
             Second International Congress of Social Psychiatry, August 4, 1969.)

PART VI: FUTURE PROPHECIES

223   From the typescript for an address to be given at Albert Schweitzer's
             Centennial Birth Anniversary Commemoration Symposium on
             "Reverence for Life and the Way to World Peace," sponsored by the
             Albert Schweitzer Fellowship of Japan, Tokyo, September 25, 1975.
             Typescript at Pauling Papers / OSU. (The published Pauling talk, "We
             Must Throw Off the Yoke of Militarism to Achieve Albert
             Schweitzer's Goal for the World," is rather different. One talk may
             have been given in Tokyo, and the other in Hiroshima. However,
             Pauling was known to depart from previously prepared talks,
             especially to the general public.)

226   From Pauling's prepared script for his appearance before the Senate Committee on Government Operations, Hearings on "Our Third Century: Directions," February 6, 1976. At Pauling Papers / OSU. Published by U.S. Government Printing Office, 1976, pp. 154-158.

233   "What Can We Expect for Chemistry in the Next 100 Years?", *Chemical and Engineering News*, American Chemical Society, Vol. 54, no. 17 (April 19, 1976).

234   "The Path to World Peace," in *The Prevention of Nuclear War* (proceedings of a symposium held at the University of British Columbia, March 5-6, 1983), privately printed by Physicians for Social Responsibility.

239   Addendum to Chapter 10 of 25th Anniversary Edition of *No More War!*, reprinted by Dodd, Mead & Co., New York, 1983.

241   "Chemistry and the World of Tomorrow," the Priestley Medal Address, was published in *Chemical and Engineering News*, April 16, 1984.

        Derek Davenport's article on the Priestley Medal address was published in *Journal of Chemical Education*, October 1998.

243   Coauthored by Linus Pauling and signed by the participants in the Dubrovnik Workshop on the Electronic Structure of Molecules, Cavtat, Yugoslavia, August 28-September 3, 1988.

246   "Prospects for Global Environmental Protection and World Peace As We Approach the 21st Century," speech at Soka University, Los Angeles, August 22-24, 1990. Printed by Soka University, 1992.

248   "Reflections on the Persian Gulf 'War,'" published by the Nuclear Age Peace Foundation, Santa Barbara, 1991.

253   Chapter 10 of *No More War!* "A Proposal: Research for Peace," Dodd, Mead & Co., New York, 1958.

258   *Science and World Peace* (Azad Memorial lectures, Part I), Indian Council for Cultural Relations, New Delhi, India, 1967.

POSTLUDE: MAKE YOUR VOICE AND VOTE COUNT!

265   "The Duties of a Graduate," a commencement address given on May 27, 1983, at Cook College, Rutgers University of the State of New Jersey. The typescript was duplicated as a publication.

Linus Pauling and Peace:
A Timeline

Focus is primarily on Linus Pauling's (LP) peace, political, and humanitarian activities and award during his lifetime. Also notes events and career honors that strengthened his professional reputation.

1901   February 28: Linus Carl Pauling born in Portland, Oregon

1917   October: Enters Oregon Agricultural College (OAC) in Corvallis

1922   Receives B.S. degree in chemical engineering. Has taught several undergraduate classes in chemistry; also studied oratory. In fall enters California Institute of Technology (Caltech) in Pasadena, CA, as graduate student. Learns new technique of X-ray crystallography for determining molecular structure of minerals.

1923   Marries Ava Helen Miller (AHP) in Salem, Oregon, in June. Four children: sons Linus Jr. (1925), Peter (1931), and Crellin (1937); and daughter Linda (1932).

1925   Awarded Ph.D. from Caltech in chemistry, with emphasis on mathematical physics.

1926-7   Guggenheim Fellowship enables LP to study in Europe, with intent to apply new quantum mechanics physics to structural chemistry. Autumn 1927: returns to Caltech as assistant professor of theoretical chemistry. (Becomes full professor in 1931.)

1932   Though Great Depression has deepened, Republican LP votes for Hoover in presidential campaign; Democrat Ava Helen supports Franklin D. Roosevelt.

1933   Elected as youngest member of prestigious National Academy of
            Sciences. . . . Receives first honorary degree (D.Sc.), the first of many,
            from his alma mater, Oregon State College (now University).

1934   Approving of how FDR's New Deal is relieving nation's
            socioeconomic distress, LP supports Democratic candidate for
            governor, Upton Sinclair, and his socialistic EPIC (End Poverty in
            California) program, but Republican candidate Merriam wins.

1936   LP backs FDR—first time he has voted for a Democrat in a
            presidential election. . . . Elected to membership in elite American
            Philosophical Society (later becomes VP).

1937   Caltech appoints Pauling as Chairman of the Division of Chemistry
            and Chemical Engineering, and Director of the Gates Laboratory.

1939-40   The Paulings, alarmed by Nazi Germany's victories over European
            democracies, join Union Now. LP urges American support of
            Britain's fight against Axis powers. Begins government research
            projects developing rocket fuels, explosives, medical needs.

1941-45   LP has nephritis, then usually fatal, but meat-free diet slowly repairs
            kidneys. Continues war-connected work, which accelerates with U.S.
            entry into WWII. Actively participates in National Defense Research
            Council (NDRC) and Office of Scientific Research and Development
            (OSRD) until war's end.

1942   Both Paulings protest U.S. government edict to confine in "relocation
            camps" over 100,000 Japanese Americans living on West Coast. AHP
            involved with American Civil Liberties Union (ACLU). (Two years
            later, neighborhood hate-mongers vandalize Pauling home and
            threaten their lives when Paulings employ a young Nisei awaiting
            induction into U.S. Army.)

1945   After U.S. drops two atomic bombs on Japan to end WWII, LP gives
            talks to public about atomic energy and its potential uses in future.
            Soon expresses view that since nuclear warfare is unacceptable,
            working for world peace has become essential. Encouraged by AHP,
            studies international relations, current politics, economics. Regards
            just-founded United Nations as best way to establish world
            government and enforce world law.

1946   LP asked to join "Einstein Committee" and help educate American
            public about world changes brought on by invention of nuclear
            weapons. Becomes active in Hollywood chapter of liberal
            Independent Citizens' Committee of the Arts, Sciences, and
            Professions (ICCASP).

1947   LP pledges to devote half his time toward achieving world peace, and
         to mention its importance in every public lecture he gives in future. As
         competition between U.S. and USSR deepens into Cold War, LP gets
         reputation as left-wing "Commie" sympathizer; FBI monitors his
         speeches, activities, and associations.

1948   Receives from Truman the Presidential Medal for Merit, highest war-
         service award to civilians. Given "for exceptionally meritorious
         conduct in the performance of outstanding services to the United
         States from October 1940 to June 1946."

1948   Joining Progressive Party, LP supports Henry Wallace's 3rd-party
         candidacy in presidential election, but to avoid splitting liberal vote
         AHP votes for Truman—who wins, surprisingly, against Republican
         Dewey.

1949   LP is president of the 50,000-member American Chemical Society,
         but office tenure is stormy because he tries to politicize ACS in a
         liberal direction. . . . LP speaks as U.S. delegate at an international
         peace conference in Mexico City, which turns out to be communist-
         affiliated.

1950   February: LP gives speech at Carnegie Hall critical of U.S. go-ahead
         for H-bomb. Several months later, the Korean War assures rapid
         development of new fission-fusion superbombs. . . . November: LP,
         subpoenaed by Calif. Senate Investigating Committee on Education,
         is questioned about his defense of university faculty members refusing
         to sign anticommunist loyalty oath. He declares he is not a communist
         but strongly supports citizens' rights to privacy in political beliefs.

1951-54 LP suspends much activism due to Caltech trustees' criticism of his
         public statements, attacks in the press, investigations of his political
         affiliations, and Passport Division's refusal to renew the Paulings'
         unlimited passport. The latter arouses protests from liberal politicians,
         journalists, even science colleagues. . . . In 1954 LP resumes strong
         antinuclear voice, giving talk about 3-stage superbomb exploded in
         Bikini: "The World Problem and the Hydrogen Bomb." . . . U.S. State
         Department overrides Passport Division when LP is awarded Nobel
         Prize in Chemistry for 1954, enabling Pauling to collect it.

1955   After Nobel ceremony in Stockholm at end of 1954, the Paulings
         travel to India and Japan. . . . July: LP signs two key antiwar
         documents: Russell-Einstein Manifesto and Mainau Declaration. (The
         former launches peace-seeking Pugwash Conferences.) . . .
         November: when asked to discuss passport problems, LP assures
         Senate Subcommittee on Constitutional Rights of Committee on the
         Judiciary that he has never been a Communist and isn't even a
         "theoretical Marxist."

1956   Paulings buy 165-acre ranch property along the California coast, south
            of Big Sur, with money from Nobel Prize in Chemistry. (Eight years
            later will use Nobel Peace Prize earnings to build a new home there.)

1957   An LP talk about dangers of radioactive fallout at Washington
            University, St. Louis, inspires him to create scientists' appeal to ban
            nuclear bomb tests. Signed by over 2,000 American scientists in
            several weeks, it is distributed worldwide; eventually brings in
            signatures from over 13,000 scientists in 50 nations. . . . LP receives
            Grotius Medal for Contributions to International Law. . . . Paulings
            make first visit to USSR.

1958   January: the Paulings turn over signed test-ban petitions to U.N.
            Secretary-General Dag Hammerskjöld. LP, who has alerted press to
            significance of the Appeal; will defend it in coming months. . . .
            February: debates weapons testing with physicist Edward Teller on
            PBS TV. . . . May: faces a panel of hostile reporters on "Meet the
            Press." . . . LP and 17 others (inc. Bertrand Russell and Norman
            Thomas) sue U.S. Defense Dept. and AEC in attempt to halt nuclear
            tests; plan similar lawsuits in Britain and USSR. Public health
            concerns force the 3 nuclear nations to begin negotiating ban on
            testing. . . . LP publishes *No More War!* . . . Under pressure at Caltech,
            LP resigns as chairman of chemistry division.

1959   July: the Paulings visit Albert Schweitzer at his clinic in West Africa.
            . . . August: attending 5th World Conference Against Atomic and
            Hydrogen Bombs in Hiroshima, LP helps to draft the Hiroshima
            Appeal.

1960   LP is hopeful when moratorium on nuclear testing proposed by USSR
            is accepted by U.S. and Britain, pending negotiations for test-ban
            treaty in Geneva. . . . Subpoenaed by Senate Subcommittee to
            Investigate Administration of Internal Security Act, LP refuses to turn
            over list of the scientists who helped circulate 1957 petition, says he
            wants to protect them from harassment. He risks imprisonment for
            contempt of Congress: people around U.S. are outraged. At 2nd
            appearance, after LP is interrogated on his support of "suspect" leftist
            organizations and movements, he is allowed to go home.

1961   Named Humanist of the Year by American Humanist Association, LP
            lectures members on "Humanism and Peace." . . . France begins a
            series of nuclear tests, causing the USSR to end moratorium, followed
            in 1962 by the U.S. . . . Paulings begin circulating "Appeal to Stop the
            Spread of Nuclear Weapons," eventually gathering 200,000
            signatures worldwide. They also call a conference in Oslo, where
            attending scientists sign document calling for end of nuclear testing
            and nonproliferation of nuclear weapons.

1962   Pauling protests President Kennedy's decision to resume atmospheric testing in April. The Paulings picket the White House, but attend banquet for Nobelists afterwards. . . . LP is awarded the Gandhi Peace Prize. . . . October: LP sharply criticizes JFK's handling of the Cuban Missile Crisis, which risked nuclear war.

1963   LP sues *National Review* for writing editorials that maliciously aim to destroy his good character, and enters other similar lawsuits. . . . Partial test-ban treaty signed among nuclear nations. When ban takes effect October 10, LP notified that he has been awarded (belatedly, for 1962) the Nobel Peace Prize for his efforts to stop atmospheric testing of nuclear weapons. . . . Dismayed by critical reaction to this honor at Caltech (and elsewhere), LP announces he will leave faculty and join staff at Center for the Study of Democratic Institutions, whose founder-director is Robert Hutchins.

1964   The Paulings move to Santa Barbara, where LP becomes Research Professor in Physical and Biological Sciences at CSDI; this "think-tank" sponsors conferences combining intellectuals from different professions who focus on world problems. . . . The Paulings attend the Australian Congress for International Cooperation and Disarmament in October.

1965   February: LP speaks at CSDI-sponsored Pacem in Terris Convocation in NYC, where he and others protest Vietnam War. . . . LP supports call by Martin Luther King Jr. for boycott and embargo on Alabama until 50% of eligible black voters are registered in state. . . . August 8: Nobel Peace Prize recipients appeal to world leaders for a cease-fire in Vietnam—among them, LP, M.L. King, Schweitzer. . . . LP given Order of Merit, Republic of Italy.

1966   LP receives Carl Neuberg Medal in NYC and gives talk on "Science and World Problems." . . . Named Supreme Peace Sponsor of World Fellowship of Religion.

1967   LP in India to give Azad and Chettyar Memorial Lectures. . . . May: attends Pacem in Terris II convocation in Geneva and gives speech, "Peace on Earth: the Position of the Scientists." . . . At Expo 97 in Montreal gives Noranda Lecture to public on "Science and the World of the Future." . . . In fall takes leave of absence from CSDI to rejoin academic community, becoming visiting professor at UC San Diego for two years.

1968   Receives Martin Luther King, Jr. Medical Achievement Award, for having identified the molecular cause of sickle-cell anemia. LP gives talk on "Scientific Discovery: Its Impact upon Man," at 1st Annual MLK Memorial Lecture.

1969   Professor Pauling criticized for vehement anti-Vietnam War statements and other radical activities. Unhappy with conservative politics in Calif. university system, LP accepts faculty post at Stanford. Paulings move to San Francisco area in June.

1970   LP accepts International Lenin Peace Prize for 1968-69 at the Soviet Embassy in Washington, DC, for "stronger peace between nations." . . . His *Vitamin C and the Common Cold* becomes bestseller; afterward LP will become best known to American public as prime promoter of vitamin C. By now he has proposed concept of "orthomolecular medicine" and devotes much of his research to nutritional biochemistry.

1973   Linus Pauling Institute of Science and Medicine (LPI) founded as nonprofit California corporation and then receives tax-exempt status from IRS. . . . In autumn the Paulings take first trip to People's Republic of China.

1974   LP becomes Professor Emeritus of Chemistry at Stanford University. From now on will have LPI as his research and professional base; also works there on peace-connected projects.

1975   September: President Gerald R. Ford gives LP the National Medal of Science and praises him for the "extraordinary scope and power of his imagination that led to contributions in structural chemistry, molecular biology, immunology, and molecular medicine." (Award was proposed twice before but turned down by the Nixon Administration.)

1976   In U.S. bicentennial year LP talks to Senate Operations Committee on "Our Third Century: Prospects." . . . April: gives future-looking Centennial Address of the American Chemical Society: "What Can We Expect for Chemistry in the Next 100 Years?" . . . AHP has surgery to remove malignant stomach tumor.

1977   June 1: "Linus Pauling Day" is proclaimed by Oregon governor Bob Straub. . . . NOVA series on PBS TV broadcasts Robert Richter's new documentary, *Linus Pauling—Crusading Scientist*. . . . Paulings go to Iceland, where he presides over conference on "The Environment and the Future of Man."

1978   In Moscow, LP receives Lomonosov Gold Medal, the Soviet Academy of Sciences' highest award. . . . Given Award of Merit by Decalogue Society of Lawyers.

1979   The U.S. National Academy of Sciences gives its first Medal in the Chemical Sciences to LP. . . . He receives Gold Medal of National Institute of Social Sciences.

1981   LP given 80th birthday party in San Francisco. . . . In August, AHP's
            stomach cancer returns after 5 years and is declared inoperable. . . .
            Oregon State University (OSU) sets up annual Ava Helen Pauling
            Lectureship for World Peace, and LP gives first lecture. . . . December
            7: AHP dies.

1982   LP receives Women Strike for Peace award. (AHP had been an officer
            in organization.) . . . Given Distinguished Achievement Award by
            American Aging Association.

1983   ACS announces that LP will receive its most prestigious award, the
            Priestley Medal, for his contributions to chemistry and for many
            services to the organization over the years.

1984   July: with other international antiwar activists (incl. 3 other Nobel
            Peace laureates), LP sails to Nicaragua aboard *Peace Ship* with
            emergency supplies for population deprived of basic needs by U.S.-
            arranged blockade against nation's socialist regime. . . . September:
            LP chairs LPI symposium on "Nutrition, Health, and Peace" in San
            Francisco, sponsored by Japanese shipbuilder Ryoichi Sasakawa.

1986   LP given Sesquicentennial Commemorative Award of the National
            Library of Medicine, "for service to mankind and honor to America."
            . . . The highly popular *How to Live Longer and Feel Better* published.
            Ordinary Americans consider LP a nutrition guru; write to him at LPI
            for advice about health. . . . Pauling decides to give his papers and
            memorabilia, including his medals, to Oregon State University.

1987   American Chemical Society gives LP its Award in Chemical
            Education. . . . Given Peace and Culture Award by Soka Gakkai
            International; Ben-Gurion Award by Ben-Gurion University of the
            Negev, Israel; Lifetime Achievement Award, Bertrand Russell
            Society (first recipient).

1989   National Science Foundation's Vannevar Bush Award is given to LP
            in Washington, DC "for pioneering with vision, boldness, and drive,
            the exploration and settlement of new frontiers in science, education,
            and social consciousness."

1991   January: LP purchases ad space in *New York Times* for public appeal
            ("STOP THE RUSH TO WAR!") against war with Iraq in the Persian
            Gulf after the invasion of Kuwait; calls for economic sanctions and
            direct negotiations with Saddam Hussein. . . . LP's 90th birthday is
            celebrated in San Francisco; 2 days later a symposium on the chemical
            bond, honoring LP, is given at Caltech. . . . Given special peace award
            by Nuclear Age Peace Foundation in Santa Barbara, which later
            publishes his talk on the Persian Gulf War.

1994   June: program honoring LP given during annual meeting of the Pacific
            Chapter of American Association for the Advancement of Science
            (AAAS) at San Francisco State University. LP attends in a wheelchair,
            frail with age, surgery, and chemotherapy treatments for cancer . . .
            August 19: Pauling dies at home at Deer Flat Ranch on Pacific Coast.

Awards given posthumously to Linus Pauling for his service to humanity:

1994   Benjamin Franklin Award for Distinguished Public Service,
            American Philosophical Society; Albert Schweitzer Peace Medal,
            Albert Schweitzer Peace Center (Germany); Ettore-Majorana-Erice
            Science for Peace prize, Ettore Majorana Center for Scientific Culture
            (Italy).

Index

LP = Linus Pauling; AHP = Ava Helen Pauling

A

Abolition of war, 32, 53, 75-76, 150, 163, 193, 176-7, 225, 242, 247. *See also* Disarmament; Peace movement
Academic and research freedom, 35-36, 38, 46-47, 63. *See also* Science, "pure" (research)
Activism, 13, 20, 39, 62, 213. *See also* Citizen's duties; Scientists' responsibilities in society
Addis, Thomas, 57-62
Alpha helix (LP discovery), 66
Alsop, Stewart, 139
Alvarez, Luis and Walter, 238
American Association for the Advancement of Science (AAAS), 116, 286
American Chemical Society (ACS), 39, 232, 241, 281, 284, 285
American Civil Liberties Union (ACLU), 91, 280
American Humanist Association, 163, 165, 282
American Philosophical Society, 280, 286
Anticommunism. *See* Communism, American fear of; McCarthyism
Anti-Semitism, 28-29, 60
"Appeal by Scientists to Governments and People of the World, The," (LP's, 1957-58), 73, 78-79, 91-2, 172, 282; quoted, 80. *See also* Nuclear test-ban petition
"Appeal to Stop the Spread of Nuclear Weapons" (LP/AHP), 92, 124, 282
Arms control. *See* Disarmament; Inspection systems; Negotiations: arms-limitation
Arms race, 12, 54, 82, 136, 149-50, 191-93, 234, 240, 244. *See also* Cold War; Militarism, cost of; Military-industrial establishment; Nuclear arms proliferation; Nuclear stockpiles; "Overkill"
Atomic bombs. *See* Hiroshima and Nagasaki; Nuclear weapons
Atomic energy. *See* Nuclear energy

Atomic Energy Commission (AEC), 69-70, 102, 108, 111, 112, 118-20, 128, 140, 141-143
Ava Helen and Linus Pauling Papers (at OSU). *See* Pauling Papers, Ava Helen and Linus
Ava Helen Pauling Lectureship for World Peace (at OSU), 85-86, 285
Azad Memorial Lectures (in India), 200-8, 217, 229, 257-60, 282. *See also* India; *Science and World Peace*

B

Balkan genocide, 14, 243
Bernal, J. D., 29
Bikini bomb, 73, 74, 108, 153, 172, 173. *See also* Thermonuclear bombs
Bill of Rights (U.S. Constitution), 23, 81, 82. *See also* Civil and human rights: in U.S.
Birth defects (caused by high-energy radiation), 113-4, 117-20, 133, 166. *See also* Mutations, genetic
Bombardments (compared among wars), 153, 250
Boyd-Orr, John (Lord), 38, 123
Britain. *See* British Commonwealth; Great Britain
British Commonwealth of Nations (in WWII), 31-33
Bulletin of the Atomic Scientists, 35, 102, 242-3
Bush, George, 248-252

C

California Institute of Technology (Caltech), 9, 12, 25, 29, 47, 50, 62, 77-78, 86, 87, 89, 113, 156, 270, 280, 281, 283; LP's conflicts at, 63-64, 177-8
California State Legislature's Investigating Committee on Education (subpoena of LP), 64-66, 281
California, University of, at San Diego (LP at), 212, 283, 284
Caltech. *See* California Institute of Technology

Cambodia, 215
Cancer (caused by high-energy radiation),
112-5, 117-20, 142-4, 151. *See also* Fallout,
radioactive
Cancer and Vitamin C (1979), 235
Capitalism, 13, 23, 191, 203, 224. *See also*
Economic and political systems; Free
enterprise; Military-industrial establishment;
Rich vs. Poor
Carbon-14, 112-3, 133, 142-4, 154, 163
Catastrophe, global, 243-5. *See also* Holocaust,
nuclear; World War III
Catchpool, John F. (Frank), 156
"Cavtat Declaration, The," 243-5
Center for the Study of Democratic Institutions
(CSDI; The Center), 9, 178, 183, 188, 190,
193, 198, 199, 212, 283
Chemical and biological weapons research and
warfare, 174, 175-6, 191, 252, 260-1
Chemistry, LP's contributions to, 7, 11, 62, 66
Chettyar Memorial Lecture (in India), 200,
209-12, 283
China, People's Republic of: admittance to
U.N., 124, 174, 184, 185; as communist
nation, 12, 51, 62, 106; diplomatic
recognition of, 13, 174, 184, 185; as nuclear
nation, 57; Paulings' visit to, 284
Citizens' duties, 26-28, 265-6. *See also*
Democracy; Scientists' responsibilities in
society; Voting
Civil and human rights; in U.S., 60, 180, 188,
213; in world, 13, 31, 148, 173, 176, 190,
196-7. *See also* Bill of Rights; Democracy;
Freedom; Humanism
Civil disobedience, 236. *See also* Nonviolent
protest; Revolution, human rights
Cobalt bomb, 35, 109, 110
Coexistence, U.S. and Soviet, 52, 77, 123, 139,
184,187. *See also* Soviet-American
cooperation
Cold War, 12, 40, 47, 50, 51, 55, 62, 135, 139,
184, 187, 190, 191, 201, 258, 281; end of, 55.
191, 245-6. *See also* Communism, American
fear of; Iron Curtain; McCarthyism; Soviet
Union
College Chemistry (1950), 58
College education, 24-28; 263-6. *See also*
Youth, LP's advice to
Commoner, Barry, 79
Communism: American fear of, 7-8, 50, 55; in
China, Cuba, Nicaragua, Soviet Union: *See*
entries under nations' names. *See also*
McCarthyism; "Peaceniks"
Communist Party: in U.S., 50, 63; in USSR, 23
Competition between capitalism and
communism. *See* Economic and political
systems, conflict between
Computers, 149, 188, 189
Condon, Edward, 79

Conference Against the Spread of Nuclear
Weapons (LP/AHP, 1961), 124-8, 282
Cooperation, importance of, 52, 54, 55, 97, 155,
245
Cousins, Norman, 153, 169
Cuba, 135; as communist nation, 12, 13; and
Missile Crisis, 135, 283

D
Declaration of Independence (U.S.), 212, 260
Defense industry. *See* Military-industrial
establishment
Democracy: education in, 23-47; evolution of,
29-30; participation in, 264-6; and science,
24-47; and technology, 35; in U.S., 29-30;
in world, 173. *See also* Revolution, political;
Voting
Democratic Party, 50, 279, 280. *See also* New
Deal
Deterrence (nuclear): as doctrine, 53, 136;
possible incidence of, 135
Deuterium, 122. *See also* Lithium deuteride
Dictatorship. *See* Totalitarianism
Diplomacy, international, 150, 151, 154-5, 225.
See also Negotiations; Treaties and
agreements; United Nations; World law
"Dirty bombs," 133, 154. *See also* Fallout,
radioactive
Disarmament, 70, 76, 82, 126, 132, 135,
174,190, 193, 239, 261. *See also* Abolition
of war; Nuclear test-ban treaties and
agreements; World law
Discoveries, scientific: practical applications,
see Technology and science; independent
nature of, *see* Science, "pure" (research)
Diseases: eradication of, 34, 196, 205; induced
by high-energy radiation, *see* Cancer;
Leukemia; Mutations, genetic; planned for
biological warfare, *see* Chemical and
biological weapons research and warfare.
See also Health issues (LP's interests);
Malnutrition; Orthomolecular medicine
Disparity in income, living standards. *See*
Militarism, cost of; Rich vs. Poor
Dissenters and agitators: as important to
democracy, 13; in 1960s, 213-4
DNA (deoxyribonucleic acid), 19, 66, 67, 99,
117, 195, 208. *See also* Mutations, genetic
Dodd, Thomas, 81
DuBridge, Lee, 178

E
Eastern Europe (Soviet bloc), 40, 62, 245, 246
Eaton, Cyrus, 168
Economic and political systems, conflict
between, 51-52, 55, 74, 187, 209, 233, 244.
See also Capitalism; Communism;
Totalitarianism

Education: important to democracy, 14, 23-47; in liberal arts, 25, 26, 45; in science, *see* Science education; about societal and nuclear problems, *see* Scientists' responsibility in society
Ehrlich, Paul, 234
Einstein, Albert, 14-15, 34, 36, 37, 47, 52, 73, 76, 90, 105, 107, 138, 157, 182; quoted, 230-1
Einstein Committee, 105, 112, 280
Eisenhower, Dwight, 79, 139, 162, 211, 242, 256
Elections. *See* Democracy; Revolution, political; Voting
Emergency Committee of Atomic Scientists. *See* Einstein Committee
Employment, 196-7, 226, 227, 230. *See also* Unemployment
Energy. *See* Fuels, fossil; Nuclear energy; Nuclear reactors
England. *See* Great Britain
Environmental concerns, 14, 201, 221, 222, 224, 225, 228, 234, 244-5, 265. *See also* Fallout, radioactive; Fuels, fossil; Pollution; Population problems
Espionage, 51, 55, 62, 103. *See also* Communism, American fear of; FBI; McCarthyism
Ethics and ethical principles. *See* Golden Rule; Morality and ethics; Suffering, minimization of
Expo 67 (Montreal, 1967), 212, 283

F

Fallout, radioactive, 7-8, 75, 80, 107, 108, 110, 111-20, 130-2, 140-1, 154; LP's studies of, 78-91, 107, 108, 133-7, 142. *See also* Nuclear test-ban petitions; Radiation, high-energy
Fallout shelters, 128-32
Fariello, Griffin, 67-8
FBI (Federal Bureau of Investigation), 63, 82, 102. *See also* Espionage
Federation of Atomic Scientists (FAS), 53, 54, 102. *See also* Bulletin of Atomic Scientists
Ford, Gerald R., 284
France, 32, 260; as nuclear nation, 132, 133-4
Franco, Francisco. *See* Spain
Franklin, Benjamin (quoted), 145
Free enterprise, 23, 202-3, 224. *See also* Capitalism
Freedom, 226, 244. *See also* Academic and research freedom; Bill of Rights; Civil and human rights; Democracy; Revolution, political
Fuels: fossil (oil and coal), 36, 54, 141, 228; nuclear (fission and fusion), *see* Nuclear reactors
Fusion, controlled, in power plants (nuclear reactors), 109, 122

Fusion-fission bombs. *See* Thermonuclear bombs

G

Gandhi, Arun, 86
Gandhi, Mohandas, 193. 214
Gandhi Peace Prize, 283
General Chemistry (1947), 39
Genetic mutations. *See* Birth defects; Mutations, genetic; Radiation, high-energy
Geneva, agreements and negotiations in, 125, 132, 135, 138, 151, 210
Genocide: in Nazi Germany, 28-29; in former Yugoslavia, 14, 243
Germany: Nazi, 23, 28, 31-33, 50, 51, 153; post-WWII, 121-2. *See also* West Germany
Gofman, John W., 141-4
"Golden Rule," the, 38, 185, 186-7
Gorbachev, Mikhail, 246
Great Britain: in India, 183, 184; as nuclear nation, 54, 114, 121, 124; in WWII, 30, 31. *See also* British Commonwealth of Nations
Great Depression (U.S. in 1930s), 50, 279, 280. *See also* New Deal
Gulf War, Persian, 14, 247-5, 285

H

Hager, Thomas *(Force of Nature)*, 14
Hammarskjöld, Dag, 79
Hanford (Wash.), 54, 141
Happiness, human, 46, 166, 167. *See also* Suffering, minimization of; Youth, LP's advice to
H-bomb. *See* Bikini bomb; Thermonuclear bombs
Health issues (LP's interest in), 14, 25, 48, 216-27, 263-4. *See also* Orthomolecular medicine
Hiroshima, LP & AHP in, 222, 282
Hiroshima and Nagasaki bombs (WWII), 51, 52, 69, 75, 90, 101-2, 105, 113, 116, 122, 140; compared with thermonuclear bombs, 106, 109, 137, 153, 172, 193, 197. *See also* Nuclear warfare
Hitler, Adolf. *See* Germany, Nazi
Ho Chi Minh, 212. *See also* Vietnam War
Hollywood, 63, 81
Holocaust, nuclear (depicted or projected), 9, 12, 16, 20, 34, 39, 82, 107, 110, 139-40, 189, 198, 235, 236-8, 265. *See also* World War III (anticipated)
Hoover, Herbert, 50, 279
How to Live Longer and Feel Better (1986), 185, 235, 285
House Un-American Activities Committee (HUAC), 62, 80, 82
Human germ plasm, damage to. *See* DNA; Mutations, genetic

Human intelligence and ingenuity, 19-20, 109, 149, 167, 195. *See also* Technology and science

Humanism, 127, 148. *See also* Civil and human rights; Humanitarianism

"Humanism and Peace" (1961), 165-8, 194, 282

Humanitarianism, 16, 147, 152. *See also* Humanism; Suffering, minimization of

Humankind: evolution of, 16, 165-8, 195; future evolution of, 167-8; propensity for warfare, 8, 30, 49, 168. *See also* Human intelligence and ingenuity

Hussein, Saddam. *See* Iraq; Gulf War, Persian

Hutchins, Robert M., 178, 283

Hutchinson, Joseph, 207, 229

Hydrogen bomb (H-bomb). *See* Thermonuclear bombs

I

I. F. Stone's Weekly, 53

Ikeda, Daisaku, 169, 245

Immorality: of nations, 153, 185-7; of war, 101, 127, 136, 149-50, 251-2. *See also* Nationalism

Independent Citizens' Committee for the Arts, Sciences, and Professions (ICCASP), 63, 280

India: economy of, 201, 202-4; as nuclear nation, 125, 257-61; Paulings in, 183-4; population problems, 201-2, 205-8. *See also* Nehru, Jawaharlal

Inspection and control systems, nuclear, 123, 237-8, 175

International law. *See* United Nations; World government; World law

International relations, 150, 151. *See also* Cold War; Nationalism; Negotiations; Nuclear treaties and agreements; United Nations; World law

Inventions. *See* Technology and science

Iraq, 250, 252. *See also* Gulf War

Iron Curtain, 147, 150, 170. *See also* Cold War; Eastern Europe; Soviet Union

Israel, 67, 125, 224, 249; as nuclear nation, 147, 150

J

Jackson, Andrew, 30

Jahn, Gunnar (Nobel Peace Committee; quoted), 170-1, 223

Japan: in WWII, 31, 50, 101, 104, 197. Paulings in, 222. *See also* Hiroshima and Nagasaki bombs

Japanese-Americans during World War II, 8, 280

Jefferson, Thomas (quoted), 29-30

John XXIII, Pope, 193-5, 196-7, 198

Johnson, Lyndon, 211, 214

Justice (as principle), 13, 49, 139, 152, 176. *See also* Bill of Rights; Civil and human rights; Morality and ethics; World law

K

Kennedy, John F., 79, 100,121, 129, 133-5, 193, 209, 283; proposal to U.N. General Assembly, 136-9

Khruschev, Nikita, 133, 135

King, Dr. Martin Luther, Jr., 180, 188, 209, 214

Kistiakowsky, George, 238-9, 240-1; quoted, 242-3

Korean War, 63, 81, 106, 224, 249, 281

Kuwait, 247-9, 251

L

Land-grant colleges (U.S.), 25. *See also* Oregon Agricultural College

Las Vegas, 111

Law. *See* Civil and human rights; Justice; World law

Lawrence Livermore Laboratory, 142, 143. *See also* Gofman, John W.; Teller, Edward

Lemley, Kevin V., 57

Lenin, V. F., 55, 214

Lenin Peace Prize, International, 214, 284

Lens, Sidney, 191

Leukemia, 113, 117-20, 143. *See also* Fallout, radioactive; Radiation, high-energy

Libby, Willard F., 118-20

Liberation magazine, 129

Lifelong Quest for Peace, A, 245

Life magazine, 129, 130, 171-2

Limited test-ban treaty. *See* Partial Test-Ban Treaty (1963)

Linus Pauling Institute (of Science and Medicine), 9, 156, 222, 268, 284

Lithium deuteride (in fusion bombs and reactors), 122, 153, 172

London Times, 138

Los Alamos (N.M.), 54, 68, 89,103, 242

Loyalty oaths: in Calif., 64-66; in U.S., 62-63

M

MacBride, Sean (quoted), 174

McCarthy, Joseph R., 62, 81, 91, 169. *See also* Cold War; Communism, American fear of; McCarthyism

McCarthyism (era characterized), 47, 62-70, 81, 82, 91. *See also* "Peaceniks"

McNamara, Robert, 139

Mainau Declaration, 72, 281

Malnutrition, 207, 216, 217, 265. *See also* Population problems; Starvation

Manhattan Project, 51, 105. *See also* Nuclear research history

Marxism, 50. *See also* Communism; Communist Party; Russian Revolution; Socialism

Mathematics: education in, 43-44; used in statistical studies, 44
"Maximum permissible dosage" (of high-energy radiation), 120, 141-4
Medal for Merit (Presidential or National; given to LP in 1948), 31, 281
Media, LP's relations with, 53, 115
Mental disorders (LP's interest in), 7, 78, 216-8
Militarism, costs of: in India, 204, 207, 229, 245; in U.S., 12, 37, 47, 53, 137, 140, 154, 238, 254, 256; in USSR, 137; in world, 148, 149, 201, 249, 196, 224, 230. *See also* Arms race; "Overkill"
Military-industrial establishment, 13, 138, 139, 176, 209, 213, 232. *See also* Atomic Energy Commission; Capitalism; Cold War; Nationalism
Mill, John Stuart, 163, 187, 226
Mills, C. Wright (quoted), 155
Minerals, 11, 19, 167, 235
Minimization of suffering. *See* Suffering, minimization of (LP's doctrine)
Missiles, nuclear, 123-4. *See also* Disarmament; Holocaust, nuclear; Nuclear weapons proliferation; nuclear stockpiles
Molecular biology, 7, 11,14, 62, 165, 242. *See also* DNA
Morality and ethics, 16, 149, 152, 165, 176, 185-7. *See also* Humanism; Immorality of nations; Nationalism; Philosophers and philosophy
Moratorium on nuclear testing (1958-1961), 100, 124-5, 132-4
Morse, Wayne, 67
Murrow, Edward R., 81
Mutations, genetic, 96, 113-4, 137, 150, 166, 197. *See also* Birth defects; DNA; Evolution, human; Fallout, radioactive; Radiation, high-energy

N

Nagasaki bomb. *See* Hiroshima and Nagasaki bombs
Nation, The, 53, 69
National Academy of Sciences, 57, 79, 111, 280, 284
National Committee for a Sane Nuclear Policy (SANE). *See* SANE; *see also* Cousins, Norman
National Defense Research Council (NDRC), 49, 280
National Institutes of Health (NIH), 49
Nationalism, dangers in, 30, 38, 53, 110, 123, 127, 151, 176-7. *See also* Immorality of nations; United Nations; World government; World law
National Medal of Science (given to LP in 1975), 284
National Review, 182
National Science Foundation, 39

Nature of the Chemical Bond, The (1939), 39, 67
Negotiations: arms-limitation, 82; peace, 110-11, 123. *See also* Geneva; Nuclear test ban treaties and agreements; United Nations
Nehru, Jawaharlal, 67, 68, 183-4, 185
Nevada Test Site, 111-2, 140-1
New Deal (FDR's), 50, 227, 280
New Scientist journal, 14
Newton, Isaac, 37, 182
New York Times, 68, 106, 133, 182-3, 248, 285
Nicaragua, 13, 220, 222, 285
Nixon, Richard M., 62, 185, 214, 215, 284
Nobel, Alfred, 163, 170, 171, 172, 173, 231
Nobel laureates, 71, 72, 79, 134, 163, 213
Nobel Peace Lecture (LP's), 172-7, 184, 185, 194, 260-1
Nobel Peace Prize: 156, 162, 174, 223, 231-2; LP's (1962/63), 9, 11, 85, 92, 115, 135, 144, 146, 170, 177-8, 181, 183, 283
Nobel Prize in Chemistry (LP's in 1954), 8, 11, 66, 68, 71-72, 73, 85, 92, 181, 281
Noel-Baker, Philip (quoted), 174
No More War! (1958; 1983), 15, 121, 149, 151, 194, 217, 235, 238, 252-7, 282
Nonproliferation. *See* Nuclear weapons proliferation
Nonviolent protest, 215, 251
Norway, 32, 33. *See also* Oslo
Nuclear accidents, 78, 122-3, 132, 141, 174
Nuclear Age Peace Foundation, 247, 252, 285
Nuclear energy (power), 33-34, 55, 56, 83, 101-2, 150, 228. *See also* Nuclear reactors; Nuclear research history; Nuclear weapons research
Nuclear explosions: compared with previous bombs, *see* TNT; explained, 103-4
Nuclear free-zones, 127
Nuclear Freeze movement, 222
Nuclear holocaust. *See* Holocaust, nuclear; World War III (anticipated)
Nuclear nations, 121, 124, 173, 257-61. *See also* Nuclear test-ban treaties and agreements, *and listings under* China; France; Great Britain; India; Israel; Pakistan; Soviet Union; U.S.
Nuclear reactors (plants): negative opinions of, 122, 141. *See also* Nuclear energy
Nuclear Regulatory Commission, 140
Nuclear research history, 36-37
Nuclear stockpiles, 80, 104, 121-3, 173, 174-5, 189, 192. *See also* Arms race; "Overkill"
Nuclear test-ban petition (LP's): American scientists', 91, 282; international, 9, 73, 92, 156, 282. *See also* "Appeal by Scientists to Governments and People of the World, The"
Nuclear test-ban treaties and agreements, 124-5, 132, 133, 152, 163. *See also* Moratorium on nuclear testing; Partial Test-Ban Treaty

Nuclear testing, 80, 101, 105-45; by nuclear nations (statistical), 114, 137. *See also* Fallout, radioactive; Nuclear test-ban petition; Nuclear test-ban treaties and agreements

Nuclear warfare: scenarios, 101-2, 280; threatened by U.S., 135, 139. *See also* Hiroshima and Nagasaki; Holocaust, nuclear; World War III

Nuclear weapons proliferation, 8, 124-8, 136-7, 138, 191. *See also* Oslo Conference on Nonproliferation (1961)

Nuclear weapons research, 12, 102, 175. *See also* Nuclear testing

Nutrition, human, 14, 221-2. *See also* Health issues; Malnutrition; Orthomolecular medicine

"Nutrition, Health, and Peace" (LPI 1984 conference), 285

O

Oak Ridge National Laboratory (Tenn.), 54, 120, 141

Office of Scientific Research and Development (OSRD), 280

Oppenheimer, J. Robert, 34, 35, 62, 68-70, 84, 104

Oregon Agricultural College (OAC), 24-28, 45, 48, 49, 86, 264, 279. *See also* Oregon State University

Oregon State University (OSU), 9, 15-16, 25, 85, 234, 268, 280, 285. *See also* Linus Pauling Institute; Pauling Papers, Ava Helen and Linus

Orthomolecular medicine, 14, 58, 213, 284. *See also* Nutrition, human; Vitamin C

Oslo, 9, 124, 172, 178, 223, 282

Oslo Conference on Nonproliferation (LP & AHP's, 1961), 124-5

"Overkill," 153, 172, 191, 192. *See also* Arms race; Nuclear stockpiles

Overpopulation. *See* Population problems; Starvation

Oxford Conference of Non-Aligned Peace Organizations, 168-9, 170

P

Pacem in Terris conference, 193-8, 283

Pakistan, as nuclear nation, 125, 257-261

Partial Nuclear Test-Ban Treaty (1963), 77, 135, 163, 170, 173, 184

Passport problems (LP's), 8, 47, 66-68, 281

Paul VI, Pope (quoted), 224-5

Pauling, Ava Helen Miller (LP's wife): background, 25, 84-89; illness and death of, 98-99, 222, 232, 234, 284, 285; influence on and assistance to LP, 15, 24, 53, 66, 73, 83, 85-95, 124, 171, 183, 234-5; quoted, 93, 94, 96-97

Pauling-Kamb, Linda (LP's daughter), 89, 171, 267, 279

PAULING, LINUS—characterized as: activist, agitator, 13, 20, 39, 47, 50, 62, 73, 108, 213; agnostic, 13, 148; courageous, 1, 12-13, 144-5; educator, 8, 12, 14, 24, 52; humanist, humanitarian, 13, 147-77; moralist, ethicist, 1, 16, 20, 148; patriotic, 24, 31, 49; peace advocate, 7, 25-26, 40, 53, 90-91; persecuted for activism, 63-68; in prophetic role, 16, 221-261; researcher on peace issues, 53, 90-91; science researcher, 111-2; social scientist, 12, 200-8; speaker, 8-9, 12, 13, 15, 25, 31, 33, 62, 90, 101-2, 105, 113; thinker, 20; writer, 13, 14, 15-16, 213

PAULING, LINUS—personal life: awarded honors, 11-12; childhood, 22, 24; children of, 15, 86-87, 98, 183, 279; death of, 9, 261; higher education, 24-25; illnesses, 9, 31, 57, 58, 280; lawsuits initiated by, 182-3; marriage, 34, 179 (see Pauling, Ava Helen); media attacks on, 7-8, 53, 115

PAULING, LINUS—prominent areas of public recognition. *See* California Institute of Technology; Center for the Study of Democratic Institutions; Linus Pauling Institute; Nobel Peace Prize; Nobel Prize in Chemistry; Orthomolecular medicine; Vitamin C

Pauling, Linus, Jr. (LP's eldest son), 7-9, 89, 267, 279

Pauling Institute. *See* Linus Pauling Institute (of Science and Medicine)

Pauling Papers, Ava Helen and Linus (at OSU), 15-16, 85-86, 93, 268

Pauling ranch on central Calif. coast (Deer Flat Ranch), 99, 164, 219, 234, 282, 286

Peace movement, 169. *See* Abolition of war; Disarmament; "Peaceniks"; Pugwash Conferences; World peace

"Peaceniks" (treatment of peace advocates as subversives), 7-8, 31, 47, 63, 91. *See also* McCarthyism

Peace research. *See* World Peace Research Organization

Petition, test-ban. *See* "Appeal by Scientists to Governments and People of the World"; Nuclear test-ban petition

Philosophers and philosophy, 163-4, 155, 185-7. *See also* Morality and ethics

Pitzer, Kenneth, 118, 120

Plutonium, 35, 104, 106, 122, 143-4, 153, 172, 260

Political systems. *See* Communism; Democracy; Economic and political systems; Socialism; Totalitarianism

Politics and politicians, 20, 139

Pollution, 207, 221, 229, 265. *See also* Environmental problems

Population problems, 14, 200, 205, 216-7, 221, 222, 224, 233-4, 228-9, 244, 245, 256-7, 265; in future, 14; in India, 200, 205-8; in U.S., 229-30, 256
Poverty. *See* Malnutrition; Population problems; Rich vs. poor
Priestley, Joseph, 71, 145, 241-2
Priestley Medal (ACS), 241, 285
Probability laws and voting in democracy, 43-44
Public opinion, importance of, 35, 144-5, 176
Pugwash Conferences (on Science and World Affairs), 77, 168, 175, 195, 239-40
"Pure" science. *See* Science, "pure" (research)

R

Radiation, high-energy: dangers of, 7-8, 11, 80, 139, 141-4; used in medicine, 11, 56, 141. *See also* Fallout, radioactive
Radiation sickness, 112, 117, 130. *See also* Radiation, high-energy: dangers of
RAND-Everett-Pugh studies of nuclear war and fallout, 131-2, 236
Reagan, Ronald, 63, 235, 238, 241, 250
Relativity, Theory of (Einstein's), 36, 47, 182
Religion: role in causing wars between groups, nations, 246-7
Research for peace. *See* World Peace Research Organization
Research, scientific. *See* Science, "pure" (research); Scientific method
Resources, natural. *See* Environmental concerns; Fuels, fossil; Minerals
"Reverence for Life" (Schweitzer's doctrine), 156, 161, 167
Revolution: nuclear, 151; in human rights, 188-90; political, 29-30, 176, 209, 260; scientific, 244. *See also* Democracy; Russian Revolution; "Triple Revolution, the"; Vietnam War
Rich vs. poor, 23, 188, 196, 202, 216, 221, 222, 224, 230, 265. *See also* Capitalism
Richter, Robert, 93, 261, 267, 284
Roosevelt, Franklin D. (FDR), 50, 279, 280. *See also* New Deal
Rotblat, Joseph, 76, 77. *See also* Pugwash Conferences
Royal Society of London, 67, 79
Russell, Bertrand, 73-77, 148-157, 179, 236, 282, 285
Russell-Einstein Manifesto (1955), 72-77, 148, 281; quoted, 74-76
Russia. *See* Soviet Union
Russian Revolution, 50, 55

S

SANE (National Committee for a Sane Nuclear Policy), 169
Scandinavian nations: foreign investments disallowed in, 203; socialism in, 191, 203

Schweitzer, Albert, 118, 156-63, 167; nuclear and peace concerns, 156-157, 162-3, 222-3, 225, 282, 283, 286; quoted, 223
Science (journal), 114
"Science and Peace" (LP's Nobel Peace Prize Lecture, 1963), 172-177
Science and technology. *See* Technology and science
Science education, 24, 40-43, 45-46. *See also* Scientists' responsibilities in society
Science, "pure" (research), 13, 34, 35-36, 46, 51, 121, 213
Scientific method, 37, 40, 43, 136, 181-2, 198, 225
Science of peace (LP's concept). *See* World Peace Research Organization
Scientists: "autocracy" of, 35; as early religious leaders, 195; international fellowship of, 38, 128, 195-6 ; in technology, 195; in weapons development, 188, 239, 252-4. *See also* Technology and science
Scientists' responsibilities in society (as pubic educators on science and nuclear issues and as activists), 16, 19, 26-28, 37, 39, 93, 136, 147, 193, 200
Self-interest and morality, 136, 155
Senate, U.S. (LP's testimonies): Constitutional Rights Subcommittee of Judiciary Committee (1955), 66, 281; Internal Affairs Subcommittee (1960), 80-83, 282; Committee on Government Operations, 226-232
Service to society. *See* Citizens' duties; Scientists' responsibilities in society
Siberia (as Soviet nuclear testing site), 133-4
Sickle-cell anemia, 78, 156, 283
Sinclair, Upton, 50, 280
Smoking, health dangers of, 143, 217
Snow, C. P., 199
Socialism, 28, 50, 61, 191, 203. *See also* Communism; Soviet Union
Social sciences and scientists, 43, 181, 198-9
Soka Gakkai International, 245, 268, 285
South Pacific, nuclear testing in, 108, 109, 111, 132, 134. *See also* Bikini bomb
Soviet Academy of Sciences award (1978), 284
Soviet-American cooperation, 50, 51, 55-57, 63, 91. *See also* Coexistence (U.S. and Soviet)
Soviet attacks on LP's scientific thinking (theory of resonance), 67
Soviet Union: nuclear arsenal of, 40, 51, as nuclear nation, 54, 103, 109, 192. *See also* Cold War; Gorbachev, Mikhail; Lenin, V. I.; Stalin, Josef; Russian Revolution
Spain, 61, 153
Stalin, Josef, 23, 31, 55, 61, 62, 184
Stanford University (LP at), 212-3, 284
Starvation, 196, 207, 210, 224, 228-9, 44. *See also* Population problems

State Department, U.S., 66-68, 107-8, 281. *See also* names of presidents and cabinet members
Statistics, use of, 43-44, 201-7, 217
Stockholm, 8, 172
Stockpiles, nuclear. *See* Arms race; Nuclear stockpiles; "Overkill"
Streit, Clarence, 31
Strontium-90, 108, 117, 154. *See also* Fallout, radioactive
Suffering, minimization of (LP's doctrine), 57, 163, 165-7, 185-6, 195-8, 226, 227
Superbombs (fission-fusion types). *See* Thermonuclear bombs
Sweden, 71, 260. *See also* Stockholm
Szilard, Leo, 56, 101, 105

T

Taiwan (Formosa), 184
Technology and science, 11, 16, 31, 34, 136; to benefit humanity, 26-28, 35, 37, 40, 46, 136; impact on world changes, 150, 225; in warfare, 30, 136, 253
Teller, Edward, 105, 115-6, 130-1, 214, 282
Terrorism, high-tech: 53, 122; by U.S., 251
Test-ban petition and treaties. *See* Nuclear test-ban petitions; Nuclear test-ban treaties and agreements
Thant, U, 138
Thermonuclear bombs, 34, 69, 70, 72-76, 105-11, 172, 281. *See also* Bikini bomb; Fallout, radioactive; Nuclear testing; Nuclear weapons research; Teller, Edward
Third World countries: supplied weapons by industrialized nations, 221, 259-60; economies of, *see* Rich vs. poor. *See also* India; Vietnam
TNT, compared with nuclear explosions, 36, 103-4, 106, 153, 173
Tokyo, 153, 222
Tolerance of diversity, 244. *See also* Golden Rule; Humanism; Religion; Suffering, minimization of
Totalitarianism, 1, 14, 23, 30, 31-33, 47, 176, 260. *See also* Germany, Nazi; Soviet Union; Spain
"Triple Revolution, The," 188-9
Truman, Harry S., 31, 39, 62, 105, 107, 281

U

Underground nuclear tests, 137-8
Unemployment, 50, 189, 223, 227
Unilateral actions by nations, 135, 140, 190
Union Now, 8, 31-33
Union of Soviet Socialist Republics (USSR). *See* Soviet Union
Unitarian Church, First (of Los Angeles; Paulings members of), 34, 95, 108, 148
United Nations (U.N.), 9, 13, 31, 33, 52, 70, 79, 124, 125, 136, 147, 176, 178, 244-5, 254, 280

United States (U.S.): isolationism in, 8, 33; moral responsibilities of, 56, 150, 252; political hypocrisy of, 14, 24. *See also* Capitalism; Cold War; Democracy; Soviet Union; World War I; World War II; World War III; names of presidents (and administrations)
University of California-San Diego (LP at), 212, 282
Uranium, 36, 104, 106, 12, 143, 172
Urey, Harold C., 104, 105, 107
USSR. *See* Soviet Union

V

Vannevar Bush Award (1989), 285
Vietnam, history of, 174, 210-1
Vietnam War, 14, 163, 174, 185, 194, 198, 208-12, 213, 214-222, 224, 249, 263, 283, 284
Voting, importance of, 19, 23, 43-44, 97, 176, 263-6

W

War. *See* Abolition of war; Gulf War; Holocaust, nuclear; Humankind, propensity for warfare; Nuclear warfare; Vietnam War; World Peace; World Wars I, II, III
Wars: small, dangers of, 126, 176; future, *see* Holocaust, nuclear; World War III
Weapons of war, 32, 34, 175-6. *See also* Chemical and biological weapons research and warfare; Nuclear weapons research; Nuclear warfare
West Germany, 139, 260
Women Strike for Peace, 91
Women's International League for Peace and Freedom, 91
World government, 29-30, 31, 238, 39, 54, 107. *See also* United Nations; World law
World law, 13, 31, 124, 132, 148, 173-7, 194. *See also* United Nations
World peace, efforts to achieve. *See* Abolition of war; Disarmament; Pacifism; Peace movement; "Peaceniks"
World Peace Research Organization (proposed by LP), 171, 178, 252-7
World War I, 12, 25, 37
World War II, 8, 12, 24, 28-29, 31-33, 37, 48, 49, 50, 51, 116, 153, 249, 253, 280; U.S. in, World War III (anticipated), 38, 52, 53-54, 56, 83, 116. *See also* Nuclear holocaust
World wars, comparisons of casualties in, 37, 116, 153

Y

Youth, LP's advice to, 26, 70-71, 88, 263-66
Yugoslavia, 212. *See also* Balkan genocide; "Cavtat Declaration"

About the Editors

BARBARA MARINACCI has written or coauthored seven books in her own name, including *O Wondrous Singer!—An Introduction to Walt Whitman, California's Spanish Place-Names, Commodity Speculation for Beginners,* and *Vineyards in the Sky.* Through the years, as a developmental editor, she has produced many other books as well, including ghostwritten ones. Trained also in nonprofit management, she has often been involved, as editor/writer and consultant in development and long-range planning, in the work of various nonprofit human-service organizations. For several years she served as executive director of a community counseling center in Los Angeles.

Years ago, as an editor at the publishing firm of Dodd, Mead in New York, Barbara Marinacci persuaded Linus Pauling to write *No More War!*—the highly influential book that not only details Pauling's concerns about nuclear weapons, testing, and warfare, but also expresses his ideas regarding the necessity and means of achieving world peace. Much more recently, she originated and edited the anthology *Linus Pauling in His Own Words: Selected Writings, Speeches, and Interviews.* The work was begun prior to Dr. Pauling's death. "But there just wasn't space enough for most of Pauling's words regarding peace, humanitarianism, and the scientist's essential role in society, along with his observations about and proposed solutions to serious world problems," she declares. "That's why I wanted to do this second book now—apart from the fact that it was Pauling's own first preference."

From 1992 to 1996 Barbara Marinacci was a consultant with the Linus Pauling Institute of Science and Medicine (LPI) in Palo Alto, California, where she edited the *LPI Newsletter* and worked on fundraising and other projects for this research facility focused on nutritional medicine and human health. In August of 1996, when LPI moved to the campus of Oregon State University, she remained at her home near San Jose, where she operates an editorial service called The Bookmill.

RAMESH KRISHNAMURTHY is the Project Director at Oregon State University Library Special Collections—home of the Ava Helen and Linus Pauling Papers, where he has been working with the large and growing archive since 1989. He also holds the position of research scientist at the International Institute for Human Evolutionary Studies. He is the editor of *The Pauling Symposium* (a collection of papers by notable scholars and historians on Linus Pauling published by Oregon State University Press, 1996); and coeditor of *The History of Atomic Energy Collection: A Catalogue of Holdings at Oregon State University*, published by James Cummins Booksellers. Possessing special expertise in both the installation and instruction of digital electronic systems for archival purposes, he often travels to other libraries and research facilities to serve as a consultant.

Krishnamurthy, who was born in India, has spent the last 10 years primarily in the United States. His educational background includes a B.S. in Biology, a B.Sc., in Chemistry, Botany, Zoology, an M.S. in Wildlife Biology, and an M.A. in Interdisciplinary Studies (Anthropology). He will soon earn a doctoral degree in Anthropology from the University of Oregon. While working with the Pauling Papers at OSU, he has also been active in several organizations that are involved in international peace, security, environmental issues, and human rights. As an independent radio producer for Oregon Public Broadcasting Radio, he has produced over a dozen programs related to national and international issues. He recently served as a member of the Board of Governors of the United Nations Association of the United States of America, and as a Counselor to the World Federalists Movement.

Rising Star Press
P.O. Box BB
Los Altos, CA 94023
Phone: 650/966-8920
Fax: 650/968-2658
e-mail: Rising.Star.Press@Worldnet.ATT.net